Against Politics

Is the state a necessity, a convenience, or neither? It enforces collective choices in which some override the preferences and dispose of the resources of others. Moreover, collective choice serves as its own source of authority, and preempts the space it wishes to occupy. The morality and efficacy of the result are perennial questions central to political philosophy.

In *Against Politics* Jasay takes a closely reasoned stand, based on modern rational-choice arguments, for rejecting much of mainstream thought about these matters. In the first part of the book, "Excuses," he assesses the standard justification of government based on consent, the power of constitutions to achieve limited government, and ideas for reforming politics. In the second part, "Emergent solutions," he explores the force of first principles to secure liberties and rights, and some of the potential of spontaneous conventions for generating ordered anarchy.

Written with clarity and simplicity, this powerful volume represents the central part of Jasay's recent work. Fully accessible to the general reader, it should stimulate the specialist reader to fresh thought.

Anthony de Jasay is also the author of *Choice, Contract, Consent* (1991), *Social Contract, Free Ride* (1989), and *The State* (1985).

Routledge studies in social and political thought

Against Politics

On government, anarchy, and order

Anthony de Jasay

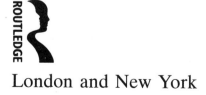

London and New York

First published 1997
by Routledge
11 New Fetter Lane, London EC4P 4EE

Simultaneously published in the USA and Canada
by Routledge
29 West 35th Street, New York, NY 10001

Phototypeset in Times by Intype London Ltd
Printed and bound in Great Britain by
T.J. International Ltd, Padstow, Cornwall

British Library Cataloguing in Publication Data
A catalogue record for this book is available from the British Library

Library of Congress Cataloging in Publication Data
De Jasay, Anthony.
    Against politics: on government, anarchy, and order / Anthony de Jasay.
    1. Libertarianism.   2. Anarchism.   3. Legitimacy of governments.
    4. State, The. I. Title.
JC585.D4 1997
320′.01′1–dc21   97–8448

ISBN 0–415–17067–2

In vain you tell me that Artificial
Government is good, but that I fall
out only with the Abuse. The Thing,
the Thing itself is the Abuse!

Burke

Anthony de Jasay
Photograph by Lucinda Douglas-Menzies

Contents

Introduction

Government both incites and executes collective decisions. They are reached by way of some decision mechanism designed to make one view, one interest, one order of preferences prevail over others, most of the time by the application of established rules, peacefully, without recourse to violence. What is loosely described as democracy is one such mechanism, though of course there is a wide range of others. Their differences, important as they may be, are dwarfed by the significance of their common feature, namely that in each, some decide for all. They decide, albeit usually by different rules, not only among the alternatives that are up for choice, but also over what "domain," over what kind of alternatives collective choice should be exercised, by what rules, and what shall be left over for individuals to decide separately for themselves. Constitutions and their amendments belong to the latter type of decision, but so does, less obviously but no less centrally, the proportion of material resources preempted by fiscal means for public rather than private purposes. The collective decision mechanism, in making public choices, implicitly determines the residual area where private choice remains effective.

The morality of requiring all to abide by the decisions of some as a matter of duty or, less ambitiously, as a matter of inclining before the threat of force, has always seemed problematical. If it had not, if the binding character of collective decisions had not had a morally dubious overtone, the great bulk of political philosophy from antiquity to our day would not have revolved around the legitimacy of politics and the justification of the state.

Broadly, three positions can be taken on the matter. The state is either a necessity, or a convenience; or it is an imposition shored up by the delusion that it is necessary or convenient.

Necessity, if it were proved, would of course sweep away the moral argument. If it is just not possible to live in society without subjecting some people to the will of others, morality cannot require that they should not be subjected; "ought" presupposes "can." Any remaining argument is shifted, so to speak, down the line to the manner of subjection and the conditions that elicit consent to it. Ideas of the social contract and of the self-limitation of government readily suggest themselves if one takes this position.

Convenience, rather than absolute necessity, as a justification for politics likewise implies some form of contractarian bargain and consent to government on condition that it is a limited one. The whole convenience argument rests on the idea that the benefits of binding collective decisions are real but not boundless, and the surrender of autonomy the rational individual will concede in return is not total and unconditional either, but a measured dose under a properly balanced bargain. From the notion of a profitable trade the justificatory argument imperceptibly moves on to the fiction of a successfully concluded bargain between two parties, man and government, whose terms the individual can control, and preserve intact after he has subjected himself to the agreed collective decision mechanism.

If much of this reasoning is baseless, and the state is simply an enforcing mechanism to enable a winning coalition to exploit the residual losing coalition without recourse to violence, the delusions of necessity and convenience are of course an aid to the efficiency of the process. So are the delusions of a social contract founding a limited government, which confers legitimacy and reduces the need for last-resort coercion.

Which of these characterizations of collective choice and its justification is more plausible and closer to experience, is liable to be judged by gut feeling, intuition and existential stance. The resulting judgment, moreover, is apt to be biased by the accumulated weight of apolitical culture going back to the Enlightenment (and indeed beyond it to more unlikely spiritual sources), in which governments have inculcated hope and faith in their own meliorist vocation – and did so in all sincerity.

There must be room, and need, for more probing and analysis of these matters by rational-choice methodology than they usually receive. Not that rational choice is a particularly persuasive assumption; nor that the theory based on it is particularly easy to apply to society and its politics in any but the loosest, most informal manner; but there is no other, for irrationality has no explanation and offers no purchase for theory. Above all, the rational-choice approach has the negative virtue of making little use of a vocabulary of political discourse in which most of the key words are twistable according to the needs of the argument and the purposes of the speaker, having as they do no narrow, precise meaning in ordinary language. In particular, the spate of doctrines that passes for liberalism in America, and that has lately crossed the Atlantic to replace its older namesake in Europe relies extensively for its content on soft, malleable terms such as "fairness," "reasonableness," "acceptability," "solidarity," and "equality of opportunity" that can signify almost anything while still preserving their positive emotional charge and wide appeal. These essentially twistable words are the pivots of a loose doctrine that, as one would expect, feels as comfortable as a pair of carpet slippers. The feeling of comfort is enhanced by the ruthless misuse of the concept of "rights" that people just have, or have "conferred" on them, which entail no costs, and that it is insensitive, brutish to question. In its positive mode, rational-choice discourse may be uncomfortable and bleak; in its normative mode, it can only say very little with any confidence (which I, for one, regard as one of its virtues, but critics of Paretian economics and methodological individualism certainly have some excuse to regard as a vice). However, unlike the discourse revolving around easily twistable words, reasoning from the assumption of rational choice at least imposes a modicum of discipline. In these essays, I have sought to obey this discipline, and though I have no doubt violated it here and there, the violation was inadvertent and I hope not fatal for the argument.

A book that calls itself "Against politics" and whose central aim is to make a logically rather than empirically derived case, owes it to the reader to say right at the outset what sort of points it is not seeking to make. In Edmund Burke's words that serve as the book's motto, it does not deal with the "abuse" of what he calls Artificial Government, good per se if only it were clean, held in check, really devoted to the common good, parsimonious, just, intelligent in setting policies and efficient in carrying them out. It does not reproach it for falling short in all these respects, for breaking promises and abusing power. The case is made against "the thing," not the abuse, for "the Thing, the Thing itself is the Abuse" – or so I claim. The target is government not misgovernment.

Little or no attention is therefore paid here to propensities for waste and incompetence, the institutional interests of bureaucracies, the mismatched motivation of voters and of politicians in electoral politics, or the perverse tendency, so ably explored by the public-choice literature of the last few decades, for politics to produce grossly suboptimal solutions. To the extent that they appear as the "abuse of the Thing," they divert suspicion from the "Thing itself," which might be good if it were not "Abused." The latter implication underlies the thrust of much contractarian thinking. If only the basic institutions of society, and in particular the constitutional contract, can be got right, there is hope for the rest. In an earlier writing, I likened the constitution to a chastity belt whose key is always within the wearer's reach. No basic institution chosen collectively can be, and remain, intrinsically better than collective choice, "the Thing itself."

What, then, is the vice that is inherent in "the Thing itself," rather than in how it is used or abused? The case made here is that the vice is primarily ethical, though the primary offense against ethics has repercussions in less lofty zones of life, notably upon the self-enforcing, self-healing, self-maintaining capacities of the spontaneous arrangements of society.

All nonunanimous politics – and unanimous politics would of course be redundant, and an oxymoron – is redistributive, not only in the narrow everyday sense that the taxes of some go to supplement the resources of others, but in the broad sense of a severing of the link between costs, material and moral, and the benefits they produce, and in the even broader and almost truistic sense that a collective choice mechanism causes one preference ordering to prevail over a different one that would prevail if no such mechanism were in place, though how the two orderings differ may be partly conjectural. Burdens, obligations, are imposed by collective choice, rather than assumed voluntarily for the sake of the benefits they procure to their bearers. The consequence is the creation of a gigantic potential for free riding, both in the avoidance of burdens that others can be made to bear, and in the preemptive use of costless benefits in competition with other free riders. Conventions of civility, mutual support, respect for promises, contracts and property, the maintenance of order, and the sanctioning of violations all tend to atrophy. The logic of free riding demands that the functions of these conventions be shifted into the domain of government action and the enforcement costs be lifted from the shoulders of the beneficiaries. This result seems to be inseparable from the convention's sheer availability of a mechanism for providing goods and services at public cost, and is a permanent spur to ever wider redistribution. The borderline case, where all tangible and intangible resources are commanded and disposed of by collective choice, is not reached as a practical matter, and could probably never be reached even in some phalanster-like communitarian state, but the ethics of the system would seem to drive it in that direction if it were not for a multitude of mundane, indeed humdrum, obstacles, leaks, and evasions.

Justifying politics arising from any binding collective choice mechanism tends to involve two types of argument that are often run in double harness. One, which may refer to necessity or convenience or both, seeks to show that as the state is the means for enforcing the behavior that permits an acceptable level of social cooperation, or at the very least is the means for consciously furthering the common good, rational individuals would willingly consent to its authority and the monopoly of (legal) coercion that backs it. This is the fundamentalist argument. The other is reformist: it holds that while the state is necessary or convenient, it inclines to certain vices, and its power is potentially a great danger to its subjects or its neighbors. But these vices are not irredeemable, and the risks can be hedged against. It is all a matter of wise design, separation of powers, the rule of law, and the fostering of a culture that values reasonable compromises. Though the great mass of the literature along these lines is naïve and self-congratulatory, not all of it is. Both the naïve and the sophisticated streams are influential in current political philosophy, and both should raise some concern because they seem to authorize a degree of complacency.

The essays in Part I are all critical in nature, examining fundamentalist and reformist theses, while in Part II an attempt is made at formulating alternative theoretical positions. All the essays were written over the 1986–96 decade, and appear here as originally presented at conferences, lectures, or in journals; with the exception of chapter 8, "Before resorting to politics," which is slightly revised and whose last section is omitted as having no direct bearing on the central thesis of this book.

Consent as the foundation of legitimate political authority has sometimes been explained as a product of civilizing influences and the peaceful settlement of earlier conflicts between rulers and ruled. More recently, owing in part to the discovery of the close relevance of game theory to political theory, the fundamentalist justification of the state has returned to its robust, Hobbesian origins. Crucial social interactions are now seen as prisoners' dilemmas, where it is strictly irrational to keep reciprocal promises if they are costly and involve nonsimultaneous performances. Because first performers realize that rational second performers will default, they will not perform either. Cooperation rests on agreements, yet agreements, as Hobbes has it, are "vain breath . . . without the sword." All rational individuals realize that they are condemned to poor noncooperative solutions if there is no "sword," no contract enforcer of unchallenged power. Hence the rational self-subjection by all in the social contract, which makes all other contracts possible. And if contracts are possible, everything that is mutually agreeable becomes possible. "Self-contradictory contractarianism" opens Part I of this volume, basically by asking: if contracts require an enforcer, how could there be a social contract creating an enforcer without *its* enforcement being assured by a meta-enforcer created by a meta-social contract, and so on in an infinite regress. Criticism of the logic of the contractarian theory of willing consent calls, in a next step, for looking at the possibilities of grass-roots enforcement of agreements without benefit of a monopoly enforcer; at conventions as spontaneous alternatives to government; and the order rational individuals, conforming to conventions, might sustain. An equally basic consideration against the contractarian justification of collective choice, at least in its rigorous neoHobbesian form, is that social interactions are essentially continuous relations. The incentive structure of a one-off game, such as the genuine prisoner's dilemma, is of doubtful relevance to promises, agreements, exchanges that are part of continuous relations. Some attention is paid to these possibilities and considerations in essays in Part II. The key to reformist justifications of binding collective choice is that the scope and manner of government action can be laid down in advance of the government's actual actions, and that the former can so constrain the latter as to ensure their benign character. The choice of rules is claimed to respond to one set of incentives, choices within the rules to another, hence the choice of good rules (constitutions) can correct the perversities that lead to ultimately harmful government actions. The essay "Is limited government possible?" takes issue with the assumptions of this line of reasoning.

As distinct from locking government into rules that permit only harmless or useful actions, another conventional defense affirms that it is possible to find indisputably rational grounds for political choices. "Frogs' legs, shared ends, and the rationality of politics" seeks to show that the realm of politics that can be held to be collectively rational is minute, while the rest of the domain actually occupied by politics, whatever else may speak for it, cannot be defended on grounds of rationality.

"Values and the social order" questions the role of holistic ends, such as equality, distributive justice, or "equal freedom" that cannot be achieved by an individual unless all others do, or are made to, achieve them as well. A social order that promotes such ends has serious defects in both functional and moral respects. The view that defects can be remedied by "piecemeal social engineering," and other common theses of social democracy put forward by Karl Popper, are challenged in "The twistable is not testable." The liberal programme, as formulated by Hayek, is examined for consistency and determinacy in the essay "Hayek: some missing pieces." His position on redistribution and public goods is found to be an open-ended invitation for politics to overrule the very individual choices he professes to defend.

Rule-based collective choice operating by preset mechanism implies that all, whether they agree or not, abide by the decision reached. This makes for pacific politics; it also causes it to proliferate, for collective decisions become, so to speak, "too easy" to impose. They are harder to reach, riskier to impose, hence rarer, when it is not votes that are counted, but forces that are weighted against one another. In "The rule of forces, the force of rules," the juxtaposition of substantive and procedural politics is used to develop some of the implications of James Buchanan's proposal for a liberal constitution.

The main burden of Part II is to show that certain social virtues, achievements, and functionally valuable institutions are, as Hume has suggested, prior to government, and their preservation is not contingent on political arrangements. Some foundation stones are thus laid for a theory of ordered anarchy, albeit without any attempt at elaborating a superstructure resting on them. Most of this work is performed in what is probably the book's most ambitious essay "Before resorting to politics," a reexamination of some of the first principles of social coexistence. It deals above all with liberty and property, their logic, and their survival conditions. A corollary argument challenges consequentialist habits of thought, and asserts that most politics is both ethically questionable and probably redundant as an instrument of social organization.

This train of reasoning is pursued in the essay on "Conventions: some thoughts on the economics of ordered anarchy." It shows how rational choices by state-of-nature individuals would normally lead to the emergence and local enforcement of two basic conventions, the respect for property and for reciprocal promises. "The glass is half-full" rebuts the argument that social cooperation even in small, let alone large, groups would be impossible without a central enforcer of commitments.

The final essay, "Liberties, rights, and the standing of groups," insists on the conceptual distinction between liberties and rights and the damage that can be done by confusing them. It defends a concept of liberty derived from feasibility and constrained by conventions and rights, and a concept of rights derived from reciprocal agreements. Communitarian and "multicultural" notions of group rights, which are conferred on some by imposing the corollary obligations on others, require a political realm for their exercise, in which the nexus between rights and obligations is obscured. They are either redundant because they usurp the work that ought to be left to individual liberties, or are inconsistent with other professed values of their advocates.

Part I

Excuses

1 Self-contradictory contractarianism*

Can it be rational to will the state? – or to will it away? Why societies need states, and if they do, what kind of state meets their need, remains an evergreen quandary that each generation has been pondering anew, often with some passion. That this should have been the case is perhaps odd, considering that societies and states live much like Siamese twins, or so we perceive them. Our current usage of the two words "society" and "state" is revealing: a society would not be fully fledged, complete, and deserving of the name if it lacked a state of its own. It is probably a sound conjecture that if we nevertheless keep questioning the nature and necessity of the link and keep producing justifications for it, it is because of the discomfort we feel in the face of two of its attributes that seem to clash. One is that this link forces us, sometimes with great severity, to do what we would not freely choose to do and to forbear from what we would choose. It is doing so, not at some finely drawn moral margin, but over a major part of our feasible choices. In particular, it takes the lion's share of individually earned and owned resources and uses them in ways that the individual in question would not have chosen, for otherwise there would be no call for choosing them collectively. The other is that all this seems, in some more or less obscure manner, legitimate: the state's force weighs on us with our consent, and we could not reasonably want to have it otherwise.

The clash, which seems tantamount to masochism in the individual and to a dilemma of coexistence in the group, has been reconciled time and time again by successive versions of social contract theory; yet the discomfort subsists, and explanations-cum-justifications of the state are renewed in ever more sophisticated and elegant forms, lately somewhat clarified by game and decision theory.

Three main reasons tend to be invoked for why the state of nature, in the sense of an attempt by large groups of people to interact to mutual advantage without recourse to a sovereign state, is not viable or is at least wastefully inefficient.

* This chapter was originally published in *For and Against the State* edited by J. T. Sanders and J. Narveson (1996) Lanham, MD: Rowman & Littlefield. Reprinted with permission.

The first is that whenever individual benefits from a common enterprise are not directly proportional to the individual contributions,[1] the assumption of burdens and the distribution of the resulting benefits is potentially conflictual. It is possible for some to get a better deal if others get a worse one. In such situations, the cost and incentive structure of social cooperation has the makings of a prisoner's dilemma: it is good if all contribute and benefit, but it is better for each to benefit more and contribute less, and best of all for each to contribute nothing. Rational men dispose accordingly. They do not contribute, do not fulfill their promises to contribute, and default on agreements providing for reciprocal contributions. There will thus be no systematic cooperation among them without the systematic and putatively impartial use of force, or its threat, to enforce reciprocal promises. Any entity that has the will and the authority backed by overwhelming force to perform this function is a state. (Needless to say, the argument does not imply that a state is, nor that it can in theory or in practice possibly be, limited to this function.)

Under the same heading, it is also said that if agreements could not be enforced, then there also could be no agreement on how to divide the fruits of cooperation and division of labor. Income distribution is a function of factor ownership; unless property rights in (nonhuman) factors of production are first agreed, the distribution of the surplus because of cooperation is subject to a bargaining problem, which may not be soluble. Before cooperation, the division of labor, and "the market" become possible, therefore, the state must define property rights, that is, decide who owns what.[2]

The second reason calling for the state is that if, in spite of the first reason, cooperation is nevertheless possible, then so is free riding on the back of it, and both burdens and benefits will be "unfairly" distributed unless the state prevents this.

The third reason that is frequently cited, though no rigorous argument supports it, is that even assuming systematic and universal cooperation, successful bargaining about the resulting surplus, and no free riding in the ordinary sense, a distribution of net benefits could still emerge that may not be just or, since the justice of distributions is in the eye of the beholder and cannot be ascertained in the same way as matters of fact can be, would not be felt just by a substantial part of society. This would put sustained cooperation in jeopardy. To save it, the state must – and only it can – bring about the redistribution that engenders the required degree of social cohesion.

Only the first of these reasons is really decisive. The case for the necessity of the state, derived from rational-choice theory alone, stands or falls with it. The others, and their numerous progeny that crop up in political agendas, are either derivatives of it or, if they have independent status (e.g., problems of fairness), are not intersubjectively valid. If the first reason for the state does not hold, it must generally at least be possible, though not assured, to realize mutual advantage and overcome social dilemmas (*n*-person games whose dominant equilibrium is Pareto-inferior, for example, the "war of all against all," or the "tragedy of the commons") by agreement. For the divergence between what is rational for any individual player and for all the players taken collectively springs from the irrationality of relying on mutually beneficial reciprocal promises if it is indeed the case that breaking the promise secures a better outcome ("payoff") for any party, whatever the other parties to an agreement may choose to do. Contracts, then, are never willingly honored. Now, if promises are kept and agreements do bind, any collectively rational outcome, that is, any interaction whose effect, including any negotiable externalities, is at least weakly Pareto-superior to its next-best alternative, can ultimately always be brought about by a contract whose execution is assured, that is, one which it is individually rational to conclude.

The only interactions that could not be contracted for and required the intervention of the state would be ones whose effects on the parties were Pareto-noncomparable, good for some but bad for others. Here, the state would be needed, not because contracts do not bind, but because if they do bind, the prospective losers would refuse to enter them. Imposing the Pareto-noncomparable solution just the same by the threat of force is to be deemed good, to be carried out and commended, if the bad of the losers is deemed smaller than the good of the gainers from the interaction. This is, of course, not a question of fact, but a value judgment calling for, and intended to justify, controversial political action. It may have merit, but it is not intersubjectively defensible.

If contracts do bind, however, it is never very obvious why any change that is Pareto-superior should not become the equilibrium solution of a cooperative game, why the costliness ("transactions cost") of such solutions should be an obstacle as long as they still yield a net benefit that is divisible, and why coercive arrangements requiring the maintenance of a state are expected to be, all in all, less costly and more efficient than voluntary ones. Whichever way we turn the various supports that have been provided for the body of theories that explain why it is rational to have the state, only the problem of keeping promises is crucial and indispensable.

> Thus bridges are built; harbours open'd; ramparts rais'd; canals form'd; fleets equip'd; and armies disciplined; every where, by the care of government, which, tho' composed of men subject to all human infirmities, becomes, by one of the finest and most subtle inventions imaginable, a composition, that is, in some measure, exempted from all these infirmities.[3]

In thus ending the famous passage of the Treatise where two neighbors agree to drain a meadow, Hume certainly does not seek to belittle the blessings of government, nor does he directly rule out the idea that its invention, even if in historical fact it was not, *could* have been inspired by the good its subjects expected to reap from their subjection to it and the harm they trusted it to protect them against. His "Of the Original Contract"[4] is not really concerned with what could or could not have been agreed, but rather with what was not – a flank attack to which contractarianism, with its "as if" reasoning, is arguably not vulnerable. More central and more deadly to the theory of the state as an instrument that rational men would have chosen is his account of what comes first, the possibility of binding agreements or the state as their enforcer.

This is the parting of the ways between Hobbes and Hume. The latter is categorical in asserting that the great enabling conditions of civilization are prior to the state, rather than being interdependent with it, let alone being brought about by it: "the stability of possession, its translation by consent, and the performance of promises ... are, therefore, antecedent to government."[5] Nothing in Hume suggests that political authority, however fine and subtle an invention it may be, is one that rational men would will and could not reject on pain of ceasing to be rational. On the contrary, he has no doubt that obedience to the government is the effect, and not the cause, of justice, where justice is defined as the due perform-ance of promises,[6] yet, if agreements bind prior to the state, how can the imperative need for it arise? – as distinct from the question of how states in history actually arose, and why they are obeyed once they have arisen.

For Hume, the evidence shows state power to be exogenous to society, springing "from quarrels, not among men of the same society, but among those of different societies,"[7] it originates "in usurpation or conquest,"[18] is obeyed by habit and domesticated by continuity. There is evidence to show neither that it is endogenous nor that it is an indispensable element of any viable society. If there were evidence, or if deductive proof were possible, social contract theory would long ago have become uncontro-versial, a stagnant backwater.

In fact, we have no firm clue to what good the state is a necessary condition of. If, for rational men, keeping onerous promises is dominated by breaking them, it could follow that some kind of protostatal authority is needed for a benign social order, but the premise of promise breaking is neither a conceptual truth residing in the nature of promises nor entailed in expected utility maximization or any other, perhaps less demanding, form of rationality. It is contingent on the facts of the case, and inferences from it may grossly fail to hold in the most prevalent and important social settings. It is an empirical fact that the state does stand ready to enforce onerous promises of a certain ("legal") kind; hence, the question of "anarchic" compliance does not arise, and if hypothetically it did, it could not be answered. It cannot sensibly be argued that the reason why the state enforces certain promises is that otherwise they would be broken, for we can only speculate about what would happen if there were no state (or, as in certain societies where it has recently collapsed, there were just the memory of one, preserved in broken-down institutions, lost virtues, and perverted social habits). We do see a historical regularity – one state to one society most of the time – but it would be abject functionalism to believe that this proves anything about the necessity or efficiency of the link between them. It is on the strength of this historical conjunction that many inductive claims about the state as a defining feature of civilization have been advanced. They are worth what induction is worth. Failing a more compelling deductive ground, Hume's step of conceding legitimacy to the state on conventional grounds is conceding plenty.

Contractarian theory is vastly more ambitious, seeking as it does to find a ground for legitimacy that, if established, would be nearly unassailable, without having to concede anything to resigned acquiescence, unthinking convention, and force of habit. Its ground is that since a possible society endowed with a state can be shown, on commonly agreed criteria of rationality, to be preferable to all other possible ones that lack a state, it is as if the society-cum-state had been chosen by unanimous rational agreement. If this argument stands up, it is of course immaterial that it has not in fact been chosen, but by courtesy of exogenous events has helpfully arisen in time, without having to be chosen in the first place.

To sustain such an audacious argument is to go out on a long limb. Attempts to see whether it will break have not, I think, been well fitted to the purpose. Such attempts have tended to find that it will bear, variously, a liberal, a Lockean, or a minimal state. These findings presuppose the possibility of agreement and then find a plausible set of terms on which to agree. To presuppose the possibility, however, is to suppose the hardest logical test already withstood. Testing the limb one more time, without this tacit presupposition, is the main object of the present chapter.

Curiously enough, at the base of contractarian theory we find no such presupposition. On the contrary, it is the very impossibility of agreement that creates the need for agreement – a paradox whose putative resolution along the road bears watching. The base is formed by Hobbes's two cardinal propositions. The first asserts that though it is better for all to have peace, it is better still for each to invade the property of the other with the result that all will be at war – a recognizable prisoner's dilemma situation, where the individually rational choice leads to a collectively irrational outcome. The second proposition is that mutually contingent promises are irrelevant and might as well not be made: "covenants... are vain breath." Without the second proposition, the first would lose its effect, for prisoners' dilemmas could always be evaded by mutually agreeable binding agreements.

Since all are aware of the force of the second proposition, and since the outcome, peace, which it renders inaccessible, is at least weakly preferred by each (i.e., "collectively rational") to the accessible equilibrium outcome, war, it is individually rational for all to reach for what appears to be an obvious instrument obviously within reach that will render accessible the peace that is collectively rational.

This instrument, the sovereign state, may be specified in the Hobbesian or the Lockean manner; the former deals with the necessary and the possible, the latter with the desirable and the commendable. These differences need not concern us at our level of inquiry. Whichever specification is adopted, enough features remain in common for the instrument to qualify as a state – to put it briefly, the common consent to found one if it does not yet exist, and to accept it as legitimate if it does.

This argument is going too well and too fast for its own lasting good and could do with a mild challenge and a brief halt before proceeding. For it may be questioned whether, in the Hobbesian paradigm and its diverse formulations, it is really individual rationality that opposes the collective one and must be overridden or rather its lack or its submersion under the weakness of will and the strength of the passions. The latter, in particular, is a widely favored reading of Hobbes.[9] Like many of the other classics, Hobbes's theory contains inconsistent elements. His reasoning exposing the "Foole," in particular, thoroughly undercuts the whole case he makes for wanting and accepting a sovereign. Since the Foole is demonstrably irrational or at least a fool, and since it is demonstrably best for each, individually, to respect "covenants without the sword," rational men can freely covenant with one another to keep the peace or jointly to adopt any other cooperative strategy they see fit; they have no use for the Leviathan unless it is to protect them from irrational ones and fools; but wouldn't that be cracking nuts with a steam hammer? I shall leave this question to one side for now.

Other inconsistencies, though of lesser import, are more obscure. Jean Hampton painstakingly explores most of them.[10] One, the role Hobbes sometimes assigns to the passions, however, can bear some further observation. It seems to me a mistake to equate the Hobbesian "passions" of fractiousness, eminence, and glory seeking with irrationality and to oppose them to the other, presumably rational, Hobbesian project of preemptively invading another's property as the best strategy for self-preservation. Glory, eminence, and self-preservation are alike in that they all function as final, noninstrumental ends. (If they could be shown not to be final, we could always put in their place the even more final ends with respect to which they were supposedly functioning instrumentally and carry on from there.) Final ends are all "passions" in the sense of being noninstrumental. They are neither rational nor irrational. If reason had any grip on them, they would be seen not to be final; they would be unmasked as instrumental. Reason, "the slave of the passions," can only guide practice with reference to the ultimate objectives the practice is intended to attain. It operates in the form of a hypothetical imperative: *if* this is your "passion," *then* do such-and-such. It does not dictate action with reference to itself; it must ultimately refer to something that is a datum for, and beyond, reason. It thus dictates the course of action that best leads to the satisfaction of such "passions" as govern people's ordering of available alternatives. Reason does not dictate what "passions" it is rational to have.[11] Both glory seeking and self-preservation can be perfectly consistent with the choice of "warre," – or not, as the empirical case may be. "Warre" would be irrational, not if it were motivated by glory seeking or some other passion, but if it failed to assuage the passion in question.

If rationality can, however, dictate either "warre" or peace or perhaps a mixed strategy between them, depending on which "passions" it is a slave of, the state becomes, not a universally rational instrument, but a rational instrument with respect only to certain passions and an irrational or a redundant one with respect to others. It would all depend on what passions people do in fact have; contractarianism would not be a consequence of rational choice in general, but of particular contingent facts that may or may not obtain.

What happens to the theory if all act rationally, but some are moved by radically different "passions" from others? Alternatively, what happens if some act rationally given their ruling passions, while others are inconsistent, have disorderly preferences and no ruling passions, and are unpredictable? Would it be rational for one subset of society to want a social contract and create a state, not to serve their own "passions" in isolation, but as a strategic response to the anticipated actions of others motivated by other passions or to the risks of wrongly anticipating the actions of those whose motivation is disorderly and unpredictable? The question has not, to my knowledge, been raised in the contractarian literature. The answer is not obvious and looks many layered; but there is a presumption that creating a state would compound the problem the fully rational subset faced in the state of nature, for suppose that given the sort of "passions" they have, their equilibrium strategy was peace, provided the complement also chose peace, but they did not know what passions, if any, governed the latter's choice. A state controlled by the fully rational subset could ensure that the others did not choose "warre," but a state falling under the control of the others may well allow them to choose "warre" or to introduce an altogether new, unforeseen strategy set where the best available strategy for the fully rational is to submit to gross exploitation by the others or simply to their sheer, pointless, and stupid inconsistencies.

Be that as it may, the contractarian case is not made of such heterogeneous material. It deals with a society where everyone is similarly rational and where the preferences of some are not shaped by passions vastly different from those of others. Assuming such a society as part of the theory's initial conditions is both a measure of its ambition and a source of its paradoxical nature.

The archetype as well as the common fount of every dilemma that appears to oppose individual to collective rationality is a master dilemma: the dilemma of contract, whose unique equilibrium solution is nonexecution of the contract, or "no contract." Obvious enough in itself, it is both a prisoner's dilemma and an explanation of why all genuine, properly defined prisoners' dilemmas, which it is in every player's interest to transform into cooperative games, are condemned to remain what they are, namely, noncooperative games.

In the dilemma of contract, after an exchange of onerous promises, if the first party performs as promised, a rational second party will default on his promise, since he has already had the benefit of the first party's performance and no further benefit would accrue to him from his own performance. Since his promise was onerous, he would in fact lose by not breaking it; moreover, this is common knowledge, and the first party is aware that his performance would be unrequited; therefore, he will not perform in the first place. Since this is common knowledge, too, concluding a contract that both parties know they will both default on would be a pointless exercise.

This has troubling implications. In the commonsense view of the contract, one party's promise is given because the other's is given, and both expect the other to execute the contract. In fact, the will theory of the contract tells us that it is the declared intention of each party to perform as promised, relied on by the other party, that creates the binding contract. If the execution fails or is in dispute, a party to the contract may seek remedy by applying to some third party, who may be an adjudicator leaving enforcement of the judgment to the plaintiff, as in early Roman legal practice, or an adjudicator-cum-enforcer, a sort of mechanic who fixes what got broken, but it is not the latter who creates the contract; it is the parties who do.

Noncooperative game theory, however, shows that rational parties can have no intention to perform and would not do so even if in a pregame setting they had intended to, and any declaration to the contrary on their part is an irrelevance. Obviously, reliance by either party on the promise of the other is absent, but if there is an enforcing agent programmed to remedy default, it is the intentions that become irrelevant, and the declarations relevant, for if they have been made in suitable form, the enforcing agent will exact their execution or the reparation of the consequences of nonexecution. It is as if it was the existence of the agent, or rather the expectation that it will act as it is programmed, that transforms irrelevant gesticulations and pointless exchanges of words into binding contracts.

It is crucial to the understanding of the putative resolution of the dilemma of contract that while an enforcing agent can, under certain conditions, enable the parties to pass from *n*-person noncooperative to (conflictually) cooperative games by entering into binding commitments, the interaction between the agent and either party remains a two-person noncooperative game. Nothing proves the possibility of a binding contract between the parties and the enforcing agent; there is no meta-agent that could, and would, enforce this contract. If there were, the parties would need a binding metacontract with this meta-agent, to be enforced by a supermeta-agent, and so on forever. An enforcing agent as a tool of the principal parties would presuppose an infinite regress of enforcing agents, each superior to the last.

Either party chooses between two strategies, to perform or to default. Which looks to be the better choice depends, in this game, on the expected reaction of the enforcing agent. The enforcer can act against the defendant only if it is able, either alone or in combination with the plaintiff, to threaten the defendant with sufficient force to make the latter prefer compliance to defiance. In addition, the enforcer must also expect to do better for itself if it enforces than if it does not.

The usual, albeit tacit, assumption of the enforcing agent acting as a programmed automaton, making no strategic choices, has no foundation in rational choice. Making this assumption is to assume away the principal–agent problem. Principals might wish the agent to enforce their contracts (at any rate, plaintiffs would; that defendants would is less evident). But will it comply? The agent has a set of alternative strategies of its own, choosing to enforce only if and to the extent that it finds doing so payoff maximizing for itself. What it expects to be payoff maximizing for itself depends, in turn, on the power of the several principals and their expected payoffs from performing or defaulting, from complying with enforcement or resisting it, and their expected payoffs from making the enforcing agent perform its duties or letting it default. For good measure, it also depends on the mutual consistency or otherwise of the several expectations, which, of course, is generally the case in noncooperative games.

Locked into the first-order, master dilemma that denies them the instrument of the contract and hence the escape into cooperative interactions, state-of-nature societies would, according to received theory, at every turn get caught on the horns of derivative, second-order dilemmas whose individually rational equilibrium solutions were collectively irrational, Pareto-inefficient. There must be, to be sure, countless such interactive situations. In each, however, there are four types of possible outcomes or payoffs for each player, and each player ranks them in the same descending preference order: "free riding," "reciprocal cooperation," "noncooperation," and "sucker." For well-known reasons that we need not rehearse, the dominant strategy of each player is not to cooperate, unless the dilemma of contract is first overcome, binding mutual agreements become possible, and the game is transformed. Some standard

types of such dilemmas loom particularly large in the popular consciousness and in political theory.

The oldest is probably the dilemma of tort. Life and limb are vulnerable, and, as Hume charmingly put it, property has the inconvenience of
"looseness and easy transition from one person to another."[12] If the
players respect each other's bodily integrity and property, and each knows
that the others do, all are well off. If one trespasses while the others
respect, the trespasser is better off still, and the trespassed on is worst
off. If all take costly precautions against being trespassed on, however,
all are worse off than they might be if they all respected, but this is still
the best that each can do for himself, given that the others have the same
preferences as he and the same strategies are available to them.

The public-goods dilemma is the standard dilemma that has attracted
the most attention from economists and social theorists. Suppose a good
is to be provided by a public for itself in a manner that (wholly or partly)
dissociates the getting of it from the paying for it. This may be, perhaps,
because it is too costly to reserve the good for the payers and to exclude
access to it by nonpayers or because it is deemed preferable for policy
reasons to demand no payment or only little payment. It may then be
collectively rational but individually irrational to volunteer to pay. Since
this is true of every member of the given public, a public composed of
rational individuals only cannot voluntarily provide the good for itself.
(This result, if it holds, holds regardless of the characteristics of the good,
i.e., of whether it is a "public good" in the textbook sense, with particular
properties as regards "excludability" and "nonrivalness." It depends solely
on the assumption of full or partial independence of individual contribution from individual benefit.)

In the dilemma of teamwork, the members of the team choose between
working and shirking. If all work, all are well off, but as long as enough
others work, each member is better off shirking than working. Each
knows that if he nevertheless chooses to work, he will be exploited by
the shirkers. The equilibrium solution is that all shirk, and there is no
teamwork.[13]

If enough soldiers stand up behind a parapet and shoot at the
approaching enemy, a few get shot, most do not, and they can defend
the frontier. The national defense dilemma results from the fact that
standing up and risking being wounded promises, for each soldier, inferior
payoffs to ducking, whether the other soldiers choose to shoot or to duck.
It is good if the enemy is repulsed, better still for each if he ducks while
the others repulse it, worse if the enemy is not repulsed because too few
stand up and shoot at it, but worst of all if one gets shot in vainly trying
to repulse it. The dominant equilibrium, therefore, is that everybody
ducks and the enemy is not repulsed.

The good Samaritan, at some cost to himself, stops and helps the victim
he finds by the wayside. The bad Samaritan passes the victim by and

saves the cost of helping him. He reckons that if another Samaritan who passes by is a good one, the victim will be helped and all will be well. If the other Samaritan is also a bad one, neither will help the victim, because being the sucker who stops and helps while the other speeds by to his destination is the worst possible payoff. Since each Samaritan knows this of the others, none will want to be the only one who stops, and there will be no good Samaritan acts, only a Samaritan's dilemma. Any traveler who falls victim to misfortune will be left by the wayside, though it would be better for all if they were helped in case of need and could rely on binding contracts of mutual aid.

The escape from every one of these dilemmas is tacitly or explicitly contractual. It leads through the escape from the dilemma of contract, which, in turn, leads through contract enforcement by an agent other than the parties themselves. The agent itself cannot be bound by contract to the parties as its principals if it is true that binding contracts require an agent for enforcement, since the supposition of an enforcing meta-agent to make the agent fulfill its contract would have to rely on the notorious infinite regress. A suggested, and I believe unsuccessful, solution to this impasse is treated below. If the impasse is a genuine one, the interaction of the contracting parties and the agent is a noncooperative game, where each player acts in what he thinks will prove to be in his best interest if every other player acts in *his* best interest.

Severely simplified, the game would follow something like the following schema: There are n players – $n-1$ citizens, who are the contract parties, and one state that the citizens have created in the pregame to enforce their contracts. For brevity, the former will be called Principals; the latter, the Agent. In extended form, players make strategy choices at each node of the game tree, and go on to the next node accordingly. At the first node, Principals choose between transferring power to the Agent (handing over their arms to it, giving it access to their other resources) or retaining power. The expected payoffs depend on how many other Principals choose to transfer. If enough do, and the Agent is made strong, "retain" is weakly superior, for the Principals who retained power reap the same benefits from enforcement at future nodes of the game as the ones who transferred but can better resist enforcement against themselves. On the other hand, if not enough Principals transfer and the Agent lacks power, "transfer" is weakly superior, for this strategy at best succeeds in empowering the Agent and, hence, provides for future enforcement. If it does not, because too little is transferred, the Principals can at worst recover from the weak Agent what little they transferred. Under these assumptions, the first node would yield a mixed strategy by which some Principals would transfer power and others would retain it (or where all would transfer some proportion of their power), making the Agent strong enough but leaving all or some Principals with some means of resistance.[14] (How retention of power is achieved need not be specified, but there seems to be a range of possible practices, from the concealment of arms to tax evasion – or at least "tax planning.")

The Agent itself cannot be bound by contract to the parties who are its Principals if it is true that binding contracts require enforcement by an Agent not party to the contract. The Agent, if it were party to the contract, could not be relied on to enforce it against itself. As I argued earlier in this chapter,[15] the supposition of a binding contract between contract parties and an enforcer entails the supposition of an infinite regress of enforcers (basically the same truth is expressed in the old rhetorical, and vain, question of *quis custodiet ipsos custodes* – who is to oversee the overseers?).

As is to be expected, the same paradox recurs at the level of every derivative social dilemma, whether it is of the tort, public goods, team-work, defense, or Samaritan type. One illustrative instance is Leslie Green's trenchant statement of the paradox in terms of public goods.[16] Instead of dealing with the enforcement of contracts as a precondition of cooperation and vice versa, he deals with authority as a precondition of the capacity to produce public goods and vice versa. Authority, com-manding obedience that overrides self-interest, is a (higher order) public good. It must first be generated in anarchy. Anarchy either can or cannot generate public goods. If it can, what need is there for authority? If it cannot, how can authority ever be generated in the first place? Green goes on to argue, I believe plausibly, that what he calls first-order public goods are more likely, because they are less difficult, to be produced in anarchy than is the authority that is supposedly required to overcome the public-goods dilemma and ensure their production. There is, then, no contractual exit from the state of nature: if the state is to be created by contract, it cannot be created, since it is its own antecedent condition.

It is, alas, a mistake to dismiss the finding about the contract as a mistake. Jean Hampton judges it to be such and dismisses it by positing an "empowerment" convention that produces the same performances as would the social contract if it existed and could be enforced.[17] Under the convention, most people come to obey the ruler, making him their Agent. Some people (the Agent's agents) punish transgressors of the convention. If people benefit from the convention, it will not unravel. Since it is in the Agent's interest that it should not, he will wield his power in a manner beneficial to the people.[18] Once the people discover the agency relationship, "they will be able to play their proper role as principal."[19] This is a puzzling assertion: Hampton appears to resolve the principal–agent problem by assuming that it has been resolved – but it has not. For "playing their proper role as principal" is no doubt meant to convey that they fully control the agent, as if he had no objectives of his own or no discretion to pursue them; but if this is the case, what possible interest can he have in the survival of the convention that empowered him? If it is not the case, the principal–agent problem subsists. The agent, once empowered, must have some discretion in using his power, and the problem of enforcing the due performance of his side of the implicit bargain with the people is logically the same as it would be in the putative social contract. The people, by transferring their own power to him, have accepted the role of the "first performer," the ruler is left with the role of the second, and whether we call this game structure a contract or a convention does not change matters. If it is a convention, it is a conflictual one depending on enforcement in the same way as the contract.

Suppose, counterintuitively, that the best payoff of the ruler is some discretionary use of his power but that the second-best payoff, where he totally lacks discretion and acts as an automaton, an inanimate tool in the hands of his principal, is still positive. This is the interpretation most favorable to Hampton. The people as principal must both empower the ruler and ensure that he gets only his second-best payoff, which is no doubt the understanding at the base of the convention.

Enforcement of the ruler's performance in the game is supposedly provided for by a strategy option that the people somehow retain in a metagame or extra game,[20] that is, to depose him if he takes liberties that they did not mean to allow him. It is not clear how, in practice, such an option can be retained. Talk[21] of object-language and metalanguage à la Tarski or of umpiring a baseball game and fixing the rules of baseball or laws and rules of recognition à la Hart help not at all in explaining the quite different problem of how power is both transferred to the ruler and retained by the people for the purpose of taking it back from the ruler if he abuses it.

It is, we are assured, a mistake to believe that this is a paradox, for "in modern democracies" the people are the "overseer of their rulers' performances"[22] and can depose them. Let it be noted, in passing, that Hampton's people act individually in letting themselves be "subjugated," but "interdependently"[23] when they depose their subjugator, which rather begs the question of collective action instead of answering it. It is a fallacy of composition to believe that if a group as a whole has some capacity, parts of the group must have parts of the capacity. Be that as it may, however, what the people depose, if they do depose, is a government, to be instantly replaced by another. They do not depose the state and have in normal times no power to do so, nor do they dismantle it partially, nor can they materially change the discretionary powers, opportunities, and rewards that control of the state confers. Whether a change of government will really and lastingly constrain and transform, in a beneficial manner, the way the ruler – any ruler as agent – seeks to enlarge and use the discretion that constitutes the whole point of his wishing to rule is admittedly an empirical question. Neither the history of democracy nor that of other forms of rule abound in encouraging answers, but they are in any case secondary to the more fundamental problem of the rationality of reciprocal promises (whether they are explicit contracts or merely tacit understandings) to perform certain onerous actions nonsimultaneously – a problem of irrational or at least inopportune choice that Hampton denies.

Her convention is depicted as a pure coordination game that all would rather play than not, which it quite clearly is not. This may be the cause of the obscurities in her argument. Some conventions, as is well known, are pure in the sense that both universal violation and universal adhesion are Nash equilibria; violation does not dominate. If enough people adhere, it is best for each and for all to adhere. No one can increase his payoff (reduce his burden) at the expense of other parties to the convention by violating it. Language, the use of money, and the rule of the road are the paradigmatic examples. Some authors, notably David Lewis, reserve the very name "convention" for such games.[24] Other, nonpure coordination games[25] leave room for conflicts of interest. As long as enough people adhere to them, it is better for each to violate than to adhere. Respect for property, "share and share alike," "women and children first," or waiting in a queue are such conflictual conventions, and they unravel unless enforced by some sanction (though, happily, for many essential conflictual conventions the mildest kind of sanctions suffice). Now, in Hampton's empowerment convention there is a sizeable conflict, for the payoff from "obey" is at least weakly dominated by the payoff from "transgress" if others obey and *a fortiori* if they do not.[26] Since this is so, the strategy her people are supposed to choose at the immediately preceding node of the game, namely, "transfer your power to the ruler," is, to use the technical term, not subgame perfect, for "retain your power" would have given (better) access to the superior payoff yielded by "transgress." This convention, then, either cannot get off the ground or must unravel if it does. It is characteristically a social dilemma with the same structure as prisoners' dilemmas, where the collectively rational solution is individually irrational and cannot be attained. In this, it is no better than the social contract.

My argument must not proceed to its preordained terminus without first coming to terms with a particularly daring quasi-contractarian diversion whose success, paradoxically enough, would have rendered all contractarianism, and hence my critique of it, otiose. I am referring to David Gauthier's widely remarked attempt[27] to show that it is individually rational for people to act in a way demanded by collective rationality in social dilemmas. This way is the abandonment of "straightforward" in favor of "agreement-constrained" maximization, where the latter course yields the Pareto-superior, collectively rational solution for the set of constrained, but not for the straightforward, maximizers. If this is so, it is irrational to remain a straightforward maximizer and make do with the Pareto-inferior solution; hence, constrained maximization will be positively selected, crowding out straightforward maximization.

Since individual rationality suffices to bring about the collectively rational solution, there is no need for an instrument of agreed coercion to enforce it, nor for a further, higher instrument to enforce this instrument's enforcing function, and so on; nor would it make sense to impute to the subjects of a preexisting state a will to obey it as if in compliance with an "as if" social contract. Consequently, the state could not be legitimized as the necessary condition of equating the individually with the collectively rational. If Gauthier had succeeded, he would have provided one proof of the possibility of ordered anarchy. This is not to suggest, however, that his lack of success – if that is indeed how his enterprise must, or will come, to be seen – is a sign that other possible proofs are not likely ever to be found.

The prevailing view taken by game theorists tended to be that "constrained" maximization is irremediably inconsistent with rational action in games whose strategy sets and payoff structures correspond to the prisoner's dilemma. The knockdown argument is the bold one that the statement "Noncooperation is the sole and dominant equilibrium" must be accepted as analytic, implicit in the description of all such games. A cooperative strategy equilibrium, corresponding to constrained maximization, cannot possibly be read into this game description, though it can perhaps be derived by suitably altering the description and transforming the prisoner's dilemma into some other game by changing the available strategies, the payoffs, or both. The least radical variation, employed by many social theorists to explain cooperation in conflict, is to introduce iteration: if the game is one in an expected consecutive series of prisoners' dilemmas – where at least some of the same players will play in some consecutive games and where players do not know which, if any, game is the last one of the series in which they will play – and some other not too difficult conditions are satisfied, the payoff structure is transformed and cooperation is the best of two or more possible equilibria. Gauthier, however, explicitly rejects (*Morals by Agreement*, p. 169) recourse to this transformation, for he wishes his thesis to be perfectly general and not contingent on such particular social facts as iteration and so on. He manifestly wants to drive the coach and horses of a cooperative solution through the prisoner's dilemma, not replace it with a different and less harsh game, albeit one closer to everyday reality.

Why he thinks he can do this is best understood by first recapitulating the received theory that explains why it cannot be done. A rational player's promise that he will play nicely (cooperatively) is an irrelevance, since he will play nicely or not, regardless of his prior promise, depending solely on which of the two strategies offer the greatest expected payoff. His promise will be ignored by the other rational players, who will never expect him to play nicely, if they see that he must see that the pair of possible payoffs from non-nice play (i.e., best and third best) are both superior to those from nice play (i.e., second best and fourth best), no matter which of their two possible strategies they adopt, the nice or the non-nice one. Consequently, their own strategy choice will not be affected by his prior promise. He will know that this is so, and they will know that he knows. The non-nice strategy will dominate regardless of who promised what and regardless of the dominant strategy being poorly rewarded with the meager third-best payoff.

Obviously, if commitments to strategies could be made binding, each rational player could offer a pregame commitment to nice play in exchange for a like commitment by the others. A contract could be profitably executed, securing for all the highest copossible payoff, that is, the second best. Since the binding commitment canceled the noncooperative move from the set of two available moves, the game will have changed from prisoner's dilemma to, say, social contract.

The charm of Gauthier's alternative to this received theory is that it aims to produce the same cooperative result without creating a contract enforcer. The pity of it is that his way of producing it rests on implausible premises. His rational players, annoyed by their inability to make their promises to cooperate credible to others, will as the next-best thing adopt a cooperative disposition. Personalities are transparent or, what is less of a strain to accept, translucent.[28] Consequently, their dispositions show,[29] enabling others with a like disposition to rely on them; but relying on them does not include exploiting them by not cooperating in turn and leaving them the ungrateful role of sucker.

If Gauthier's players can achieve the mutual cooperation the orthodox theory of the single-play prisoner's dilemma shows to be impossible among fully rational beings, mutual dispositions must be able to achieve something that mutual promises cannot. They must be valuable to have. How does one come to have a disposition? Can one simply choose to have one that others will discern? And what does it mean to have one? Clearly, a disposition to act in a certain way is something deeper and more than a discernible frequency, a statistical probability to act in that way. The latter can perfectly well be the result of decisions taken on the merits of each case, if the cases happened frequently to call for acting in that way. A disposition is nothing if it is no more than a tendency to act on the merits of cases.

What, then, is a disposition, if it is anything? I can see only two interpretations; both are possible and could hold together at the same time, though the second cannot hold under instrumental rationality. By the first interpretation, a person can select ends by following a disposition that privileges certain ends over others. More pedantically, his preference ordering of a given set of feasible outcomes will systematically deviate from the preference ordering of the same set by another person, and the systematic deviation can, without risk of contradiction, be imputed to his disposition to favor certain outcomes more than the other person does. If he therefore ranks morally commendable outcomes more highly and "selfish" satisfactions or material riches less highly than do his neighbors, we may say that he has a distinctively moral disposition. This disposition, however, is already incorporated in his payoffs if payoffs are defined as they should be, namely, as maximands, that is, to be chosen according only to their magnitude.

It may then be that a person's "moral" disposition weighs so heavily on his evaluation of outcomes that, for him, the payoff from mutual cooperation is actually greater than that from free riding, first best rather than second best. To say that this is so, however, is to say that for this player the prisoner's dilemma does not exist; it has not been resolved, rather it has been replaced by another game with a different, more innocuous payoff ranking. To say instead (as Gauthier seems to suggest that we should) that payoffs are indeed maximands and incorporate all that we are disposed to value or deplore about them but that people with a cooperative disposition will feel constrained by the disposition from maximizing them (albeit with felicitous results if others feel likewise) is to say that these people first rank the payoffs according to their disposition and then are prevented by the same disposition from acting as the payoff ranking dictates. This would be double counting and an incoherent interpretation of "disposition." Gauthier has too fine a brain to mean this.

The second interpretation deals not with ends (payoff rankings), but with means to the ends, with the actions that gain the payoffs. The rational man will, of course, select the course of action that, on the balance of reasons, appears to lead to the best payoff. Neither cooperation nor noncooperation must be privileged as a matter of disposition. One or the other must be chosen on the merits of the case. Indeed, to have a disposition at all, in the sense of systematically favoring one type of action over and above what the balance of reasons tells us, is to be making a systematic mistake. Deliberately to adopt such a disposition is to seek to be systematically mistaken. As Julian Nida-Rümelin more cautiously puts it, "it is an essential attribute of a rational person to be relatively free from dispositional determinants."[30]

It is bona fide theory to postulate that, as man does not live by bread alone, preference orderings are influenced by moral tastes, dispositions for and feelings of rectitude, honor, pride, shame, or sympathy and also that the prevalence of preferences formed under these influences will, at the end of the day, produce social outcomes that are superior not only in terms of these ennobled preferences, but even in terms of some narrowly material measure, say "wealth," as well as in terms of "selfish" individual interest (whatever that is taken to mean). It is also bona fide theory to explain the world by affirming that people systematically act more cooperatively than they should if they were aiming at the maximum fulfillment of their preferences (however, the latter may be influenced by cooperative or other dispositions) and also that this, too, will lead to superior social outcomes, but it is an inconsistency to uphold both the latter theory and the instrumental conception of rationality that underlies the only positive theory of choice we have. Game theory and social contract theory, as well as a lot else, are built on it. If it were discarded (and Gauthier would probably be among the last to want to discard it), perhaps in favor of categorical imperatives, in order to circumvent the problematic or even paradoxical nature of such institutions as the contract or the state, the paradoxes might be left by the wayside, but this would not make the respective theories less problematical; it would abolish them by ruling out the problem they are intended to illuminate.

What happens to the dilemma of contract if the necessity of enforcement by a third party, extraneous to the contract, is not assumed? Why should enforcement have to depend on the will of an enforcer, rather than on the opposing wills and interests of the parties themselves? Because a third-party enforcer is disinterested and impartial – so goes the conventional answer. It is perhaps too quickly taken for granted, however, that it is possible for a supreme enforcer to be disinterested and impartial in the manner in which the conventional view sees these qualities and that these qualities, assuming that they could be had, really represent some kind of necessary condition for contracts to be enforceable. The assumptions seem to me unwaranted. Instead of making them, it is surely better to renew the analysis of the dilemma of contract without them. By rights, it should reveal to what extent, if at all, they are needed.

Recall, first, Hobbes's very proper and logically impeccable insistence, remarkable in an alleged contractarian, that while men contract with each other to found the city, and their contract is enforced by the sovereign, the sovereign is bound by no contract to them and none could be enforced against it. As he puts it in *De Cive*, citizens submit to such bodies as "companies of merchants, and many other convents ... on such terms as it is lawful for any of them to contend in judgment against the body," but they submit in all things to the city; there are no terms to the submission, and it "is by no means allowable to a citizen [to contend] against the city."[31] The enforcer is not enforced by another enforcer.

The sequel, albeit implicit, is clear and almost writes itself. The transfer of legal power to the sovereign remains "vain breath" unless accompanied by the transfer of material power – arms or a lien over income and wealth. This is, so to speak, a pregame move that opens a noncooperative game (i.e., one without binding contract) between the sovereign and the subjects. There is an underlying intent to exchange – the sovereign is to use the power and consume the resources given up by its subjects to overcome their social dilemmas that would otherwise render their coexistence inefficient at best, intolerable at worst – but this exchange is not itself a contract. Its terms are poorly defined, not binding, and subject to at least partial nonperformance by one side or the other. No side has an advance commitment to, and nor will it do, anything that it is not in its interest to do, either because it is beneficial not to act or because it is enjoined by a threat of the use of force by the other side. Force can be resisted by force, successfully or not.

These alternatives can be translated into net payoffs, and they dictate the choice of mutually consistent equilibrium strategies by the two sides. If the cost of rebellion is high, if the expected ("risk-adjusted") value of its success is not very much higher, and if the very possibility of collective action against the sovereign is problematical (at least in normal peacetime conditions), then two plausible conjectures suggest themselves. The equilibrium strategy of the sovereign will be to use its discretionary power to satisfy its preferences, perhaps by exploiting all its subjects in the service of some holistic end, perhaps by exploiting some of them to benefit others. The equilibrium strategy of the subjects will be, not to resist, but to obey, adjust, and profit from the opportunities for parasitic conduct that coalition forming with the sovereign[32] at the expense of the rest of society may offer.

While a contract-bound contract enforcer, constrained to play a cooperative game, could be a rational social goal if it were not a logical contradiction – and I apologize for suggesting, albeit as a manner of speaking, that it could be rational to pursue an impossible goal – it takes courage to affirm that rational people could unanimously wish to have a sovereign contract enforcer bound by no contract. Such courage is either one of innocence or of the despair that the lack of any other alternative would inspire. The lack of alternatives has all too often been prejudged, typically by the very argument that we are contesting on the ground that it is either self-contradictory (contract can remedy the impossibility of contract) or circular (cooperation requires contract which requires cooperation). It is to this type of argument that we owe the proposition that the state is "prior to the market," because cooperation, including, of course, exchange, presupposes a legal infrastructure. If true, this would establish the impossibility of ordered anarchy. If untrue, ordered anarchy is perhaps possible. The question whether it is ultimately boils down to the issue of the enforcement of mutual promises without a final specialized enforcer. It is to this rock-bottom question that I now propose to turn.

The key is to find the characteristic elements of a noncooperative game where the strategy sets include the exchange of nonsimultaneous performances and where default by the second performer is not dominant. I will take it that a variety of actions – actual and potential, persuasive and punitive, ranging from self-help to mutual aid, and bought or hired help, and including information to be used in the selection of contract partners – can be taken by a potential plaintiff to induce performance and to reduce the probability of default. These actions (and forbearances) have resource and opportunity costs, and I will assume that the probability of default is inversely proportional to the total of such costs that the plaintiff incurs or is expected to incur. In similar fashion, actions to resist enforcement are available to the prospective defendant, and the effectiveness of resistance, hence the probability of default, is directly proportional to the cost that the defendant is expected to incur. The strategies of the parties are independent of any advance promise or commitment made in the past. Each side will do only what its interest, expressed by the expected payoff, dictates. In such a game, for contract to be an equilibrium the payoff from performing must be at least weakly superior to the payoff from defaulting. Several sufficient conditions can be imagined for this to be the case. One is that the expected cost of default is raised high enough by enforcement or its threat; a sufficient condition for this to happen is that the marginal cost of enforcement incurred by the first performer (the plaintiff in the event of default) is seen by both parties as no greater than the expected marginal benefit from specific performance or its equivalent in remedy.

At first glance, this looks a hopeless case, for once a first performer has performed, the (gross) payoff from not reciprocating is equal to the value of the contract, so that it pays the defendant to hang on to this gross payoff and resist enforcement by incurring resistance cost up to the contract value, that is, resist as long as his net payoff from defaulting is not negative. Likewise, it pays the plaintiff to incur enforcement cost up to the contract value, short of which his net payoff from enforcing is not negative. Both enforcement and resistance cost have the same upper bound within the same contract. Up to the upper bound, it looks as though it always pays to match enforcement with resistance, while beyond that it looks as though it never pays to enforce, and this must be common knowledge among the parties. Unless a unit of resources spent on enforcement is more effective than one spent on resisting it or unless the value of the contract is greater to the plaintiff than to the defendant, enforcement and resistance must cancel each other out. The threat of enforcement, then, must lack credibility, and the game reverts to the dilemma of contract. Its equilibrium is "no contract."

The gross and net payoffs change drastically, however, when calculated over a set of more than one contract, and they change in favor of performance rather than default by the second performer, for in such a set, the gross payoff that the second performer can gain by defaulting is at best the same as in a single contract, namely, the value of that contract. This best case, however, applies only to the last contract in the set. If the contract is not the last, the second performer loses some or all of the expected benefits from future contracts that he might have enjoyed if he had not defaulted on the present one, for other parties will either not deal with a known defaulter or will do so only on worse terms. This reduces the upper bound of the resistance cost that he will be willing to pay in order to succeed in defaulting and withstand enforcement. The enforcement cost that the first performer is willing to pay, however, now has an upper bound heightened by the effect that he expects successful enforcement in the present contract to have on the payoffs from future contracts. Reduced future enforcement cost is likely to be one source of this benefit. Only if the present contract is the last in the set will the enforcement cost that it is worth incurring not exceed the value of the contract. The long and short of it is that the opposing interests, evenly matched in the single contract, are tilted in the multicontract case: the resources it pays to spend on enforcement are increased, and those it is worth spending on resistance to it are reduced. This ceases to be true only for the last contract – a concept that is in urgent need of a close inspection.

It is easy to see, and well known from game theory, that if the last contract cannot be profitably enforced, and therefore will not be concluded, by jobbing backward, the parties will see that the last-but-one contract automatically becomes the last one and will not be concluded, and so forth, right back to the first contract, which will not be concluded either, so that the whole set unravels. This, if it were the case, would put paid to the prospects of ordered anarchy.

Reflection will show that there is in the relevant sense never, or hardly ever, a "last contract." In formal game theory, one postulates a probability of some event occurring or not occurring again in a consecutive series of events. A repeated game may be defined in terms of some probability that it will end before the nth repetition. Since each repetition brings n closer, the probability that the next game will be the last one keeps rising (along the lines of Laplace's "rule of succession"), and the strategy appropriate for the last game becomes progressively more attractive; a mixed strategy between performance and default may replace the cooperative strategy equilibrium that is best in an indefinitely repeated series of contracts. A rising probability that the last contract is near must act rather like a belief that the end of the world is nigh and there is no thereafter. If there is no reason to suppose that the world will ever end, however, or the likely end looks too far away for one more step toward it to matter, the parties would mislead themselves if they formulated a crucial determinant of their best conduct in such terms that the imminence of the "last contract" would be looking more probable with each successive contract, bringing a "take all you can while the going is good" strategy optimum ever closer.

If, instead, the parties reason in terms of a probability of the next game (i.e., the next contract) being the last one, and they do not take the probability in question either for high or (what comes to the same thing in the end) for rising, mutual performance is an indefinitely repeated equilibrium if it is an equilibrium in the present.

The next step in refuting the alleged threat to enforcement held out by the prospect of the "last contract" is to consider when a contract is really the last. In a contract where A is the first performer and B the second, if it pays A to incur enforcement cost in excess of the value of the present contract in view of the higher net payoff (lower enforcement cost) that the excess will secure in the next contract, incurring the excess may still pay even if there is no next contract with B, as long as there is a next contract with C or D. For symmetrical reasons, it may not pay B to default and incur resistance costs up to the value of the contract, even if it is his last contract with A, as long as he aspires to conclude another one with E or F. The tilt in favor of enforcement and/or to the detriment of resistance continues to and beyond the last contract between two parties, provided that one party expects to be contracting again with a third party and there is a significant probability of the best strategy of this third party being influenced by the strategies adopted in the earlier contract by the first two parties.

Stepping ashore from the cruise ship, the passing visitor to the exotic port is cheated, sold fake artifacts, and served an overpriced meal by a surly waiter. He leaves without tipping, having no more potent means for getting his own back. Whether he would have left a tip even if he had been better treated is a large question. In any event, he will lend no money to the natives and they will not sell him goods on credit, for everybody's contract with him is a "last contract;" he will not come back again, and if he ever did, he would not be able to tell who he had dealt with the first time round; he knows it, everybody knows that he knows, and if he does not, he should. If he acts as if he did not, however, and enters into "last contracts" where the other party has little interest to deal squarely, it is because it does not matter all that much to the transient tourist whether the deal is square or because he has no clue and no easy means of finding out, while the other party has little to lose if he did find out. Thus we derive the Transient Tourist Theorem: a last contract has a transient tourist as one of the parties, and neither party has much at stake. Unless both these conditions hold, it is unlikely that a contract should be the last within the game-theoretical meaning of the word.

Where parties can expect to deal again or can expect to deal with someone who has dealt or may yet deal with the other party or who is related to him by ties of blood, friendship, solidarity, or expected reciprocity or who has access to the same network of information and hears the same local gossip or trade talk – in short, where the parties live in a real society – a contract between them is most unlikely to work according to the pure logic of the abstract last contract. The latter may figure importantly in Hayek's "great society" with its "extended order" and in the "large group" of anonymous members who act in isolation, unnoticed by others, though it is not clear how, in that case, they can find anyone who will deal with them. It can rarely hold good among people who have names, live in particular places, make a living in particular occupations, have a past, and hope to have some kind of future.

Anyone who has a name, lives in a place, does something for a living – that is, anyone tied into the fabric of a society – would think twice before treating mutual promises as the single-play prisoner's dilemma says he must. He would have to look very carefully at all his affairs and tie up all his loose ends before defaulting on a contract, as if it were the last one he will ever enter. Feeling tempted, he would have to consider Hobbes's famous and unHobbesian answer to the rather Hobbesian Foole, who thinks that reason may dictate breach of promise and default.

> He therefore that breaketh his Covenant, and consequently declareth that he thinks he may with reason do so, cannot be received into any society, that unite themselves for Peace and Defense, but by the errour of them that receive him; nor when he is received, be retayned in it, without seeing the danger of their errour.[33]

Though it is but the merest sketch, the schema of the expected payoffs from performance and default and of the tilt of repetition that favor enforcement over resistance to it point to the direction where a full-bodied theory of ordered anarchy is most likely to be found. The sketch seems to me sufficient for predicting that the weight-bearing main arch of the theory would prove to be a complex convention, having perhaps unexpected self-enforcing properties about the keeping of mutual promises.

If there were a primary convention that mutual promises are contracts binding the promisors to performance, it would obviously be a conflictual one. As long as enough others adhered to it, it would seem best for each to violate it whenever he thought, with Hobbes's Foole, that the balance of reasons spoke in favor of his breaking a particular promise. Like all such conventions, the one about honoring contracts would therefore be fragile, unstable, and in need of stiffening by an adequate sanction. Whatever vocabulary it uses, it is at bottom always by this unmet need for sanctions that standard political theory explains the passage from convention to law enforced by a sovereign and justifies the replacement of anarchy by the state. We have paid what may seem more than enough attention in this essay to the logical and other difficulties involved in this passage, why it cannot be a contractually agreed one, and why it generates a principal–agent problem of limited government that is intrinsically insoluble, but if the primary convention about reciprocal promising were somehow to be coupled with a secondary convention about enforcing promises, the primary one would gain stability if the secondary one held stable. The two together would function as a single, complex convention that enforced itself as if it were a pure, nonconflictual one that it was in everyone's interest not to violate.

This complex convention, then, must be one that reason never, or hardly ever, dictates to violate. Such would be the case and everything would fall into its proper place without too much further ado if most people saw reasons as mutually compatible Kantian categorical imperatives. Perhaps they ought to, but we have no plausible theory predicting that in fact they will, *ex nihilo*, without good prior cause in education or experience: morality may well not impose itself. Happily, however, a lesser requirement will do nearly as well to start with. The primary convention will be stable if instrumental reasons seldom, if ever, dictate its violation, that is, if the Hobbesian hypothetical imperative, "If performing brings you a better payoff than defaulting, then perform; if it does not, do not," generally counsels adhering to the convention.

In a set of contracts with nonsimultaneous performances that are interrelated, however loosely, by having some of the same parties and being the object of some common information, the cumulative payoff sum accruing to performers is (at least weakly) superior to the sum accruing to defaulters. From this can be derived the predominance of the maximum of resources that it pays to devote to contract enforcement in the set over the maximum that it would pay to devote to resisting enforcement. This means, putting it summarily, that enforcement must potentially have the upper hand and hold out the more credible threat. Default, therefore, will tend to have the inferior payoff and the threat of resisting enforcement will be less credible.

The sum of the payoffs from performance being greater than that from default (or from a randomly mixed strategy) merely means that performing is collectively rational. This is tantalizing but beyond the reach of voluntary action, unless it is individually rational, too. It is rendered such by the rationality of enforcing any single contract if it is part of an interrelated set and is not the last one.

Collective rationality underlies the behavior norm of the primary convention, "Always perform what you promised in exchange for another's promise." Individual rationality motivates the secondary or satellite convention that takes care of the conflictual character of the primary one: "Always enforce performances due to you" (eventually, "including performances due to others as well, if that is a cost-effective way of enforcing performances due to you"). Accessorily, "Always punish default."

These norms are stated without reference to the cost of adhering to them, since the theory tells us that the costs generally will not exceed what it is worth incurring. I am not dealing separately with adjudication, treating its cost as included in enforcement cost. Although the two functions are separate, or at least separable, the analysis loses nothing by lumping them together, nor would I attempt to prejudge the source of adjudication. It is hard to judge toward what kind of institution the task of adjudication would gravitate within the framework of a convention of honoring and enforcing contracts. Panels of the parties' peers seem a not-unlikely solution, but *pace* Robert Nozick and his "dominant protective agency,"[34] I see no intrinsic reasons why either adjudication or enforcement would naturally end up in the hands of a single agency (or of a few specialized agencies, for that matter). Neither in efficiency nor in impartiality does scale seem to bring increasing returns and monopoly to possess a comparative advantage.

The secondary, satellite convention protects the superior payoff sum justifying the primary one and allows the collectively rational solution, that is, binding contracts, to be realized.

It is important to grasp the sense in which this complex convention is self-enforcing. A typical conflictual convention, for example, "wait in the queue" or "no littering," is stabilized by a satellite convention whose norm is to sanction queue jumpers and litterers, but if sanctioning is costly it is not clear that it is in anybody's interest to assume the task at his own expense. It is thus not clear that the satellite, enforcing convention is itself self-enforcing. Many such are probably not, and if they nevertheless survive, they do so by depending on binding contracts that reallocate benefits and costs. They may also depend on yet another convention, such as "do your civic duty," sanction queue jumpers and litterers regardless of whether it pays you to do so and without having agreed to do it against due compensation. The contract-enforcing satellite convention, on the other hand, is self-enforcing because it is, most of the time, in the individual contractor's interest to devote such resources (whether his own or borrowed) to the enforcement of his own contract as are adequate to deter default. The primary convention, prevailing over a set of contracts, ensures that adequate resources will in fact be generated and can be made available in case of need. These interdependent functions are all built into the complex convention.

There is no guarantee – there never is – that this theoretical construct would withstand the tests of reality if the occasion for such tests could possibly arise, as no doubt it cannot. Its rival, however, the theory of the state as a necessary condition of contract enforcement and of the solution of social dilemmas, suffers from this disability to a perhaps even greater extent, for how do we test the necessity of the state if we cannot remove it and, *ceteris paribus*, see what happens? For what it proves, we may recall the prevalence of a respect for reciprocal, protocontractual commitments in primitive societies and for contracts in extraterritorial trade and in international relations devoid of a sovereign enforcer. These are telling us that the construct of conventional enforcement could find a place in a possible world and has at least some outward resemblance to experience.

Having said all this, most of what is needed for recognizing our own much-neglected, belittled, and underused capacity for circumventing (not solving) social dilemmas by binding agreements has been said. Collectively rational arrangements can be reached, if reaching them is worth the trouble, without benefit of states and the constitutions meant to bend them to our service. The whole social order has self-enforcing properties that, like muscles, develop with use or atrophy with disuse. They are imparted to it, in the last analysis, by the self-enforcing properties of the complex convention that upholds contracts. States are an imposition, sometimes useful, sometimes a millstone, always costly, never legitimate, and never a necessity for binding agreements. If they were, it is hard to see how a state could ever be created, as if by agreement, before it existed. Theories that dwell with apparent ease in logic traps of this type in arguing for its legitimacy can be redeemed, if at all, by their placatory qualities only as some lay opium for the people.

NOTES

1 The proportionality condition is ambiguous, and purists would say that it is meaningless, unless all contributions on the one hand and all benefits on the other are homogeneous. This will be the case, for example, if all contribute sums of money and all get back quantities of one and the same good in proportion to the money. If, however, contributions consist of labor, the good bad or indifferent, clever or clumsy work of the several contributors must first be converted to a common unit, and the conversion is problematical. The same is true of any other contribution or benefit in kind. In perfectly competitive markets, contributions can be compared and measured in terms of their marginal value productivity and benefits in terms of their price. Plainly, however, this solution is not available in every case, and proportionality can at best be a matter of commonsense judgment. The same ambiguity pervades problems of distributive justice where it is often desired to apply some equality postulate, but it is not always clear whether any two magnitudes are equal or not.

2 Unless the state is there to decide this, we are told, "access to goods services and life itself will be decided on the basis of 'might is right' – whoever is stronger and shrewder will win" (G. Calabresi and A. D. Melamed, "Prosperity Rules, Liability Rules, and Inalienability: 'One View of the Cathedral,'" *Harvard Law Review* 1972, reproduced in S. Levmore, *Foundations of Tort Law*, New York: Oxford University Press, 1994, p. 251. The view that property relations must be decided by the state and remain ill defined if they are not is a widely used tacit assumption in many branches of the social sciences, not least by the law-and-economics school. It is warranted by neither theory nor evidence.

   If it is true that people in the state of nature cannot make agreed bargains (because their agreements are unenforceable), then they cannot have division of labor, markets, property, and all the rest either, and the argument in the paragraph above is redundant. Its addition to the basic promise-fulfillment and agreement-enforceability argument is double counting. The text by Calabresi and Melamed, unlike many other law-and-economics texts, does not make this mistake. What it asserts is that agreements in the state of nature are possible, but since their terms would be decided by strength and shrewdness, they would be unfair. This, of course, is a matter of opinion and cannot usefully be discussed, except perhaps in very roundabout ways, starting way back from first principles.

3 David Hume, *A Treatise of Human Nature*, 1740, 2nd edn, Oxford: Clarendon, 1978, p. 539.

4 In David Hume, *Essays Moral, Political, and Literary*, 1748, Indianapolis: Liberty Classics, 1985.

5 Hume, *A Treatise of Human Nature*, p. 541.

6 Ibid., p. 543.

7 Ibid., p. 540.

8 Hume, "Of the Original Contract," in *Essays Moral, Political, and Literary*, p. 471.

9 Cf. Leo Strauss, *The political Philosophy of Hobbes*, Chicago: University of Chicago Press, 1952.

10 Jean Hampton, *Hobbes and the Social Contract Tradition*, Cambridge: Cambridge University Press, 1986, ch. 2.

11 For a valuable juxtaposition of the hypothetical and the categorical imperative and the idea of a noninstrumental rationality, see Robert Sugden, "Rational Choice: A Survey of Contributions from Economics and Philosophy," *Economic Journal* 101 (1991): 7536. Cf. also M. Hollis and R. Sugden, "Rationality in Action," *Mind* 102 (1993).

12 Hume, *A Treatise of Human Nature*, p. 489.

13 What is one to make of the story of the gang of Chinese workmen straining on a rope as they pull a barge upstream on the Yangtze River? An overseer walks alongside the team, cruelly whipping now one, now another, when they do not pull hard enough. One of the barge's passengers is an American lady much preoccupied by human rights, who protests at the treatment the workmen are subjected to. She is told that it is they who employ the overseer and pay him to whip them so that the boat should get pulled to the place where they will be paid.

   Is this a story of the contractarian state? One pertinent observation suggests itself: the overseer is no stronger than any one of the workers, let alone any subgroup within the team. He has a whip, but they have a rope end, which can hurt almost as much. In addition, even a coalition of the overseer and a subgroup of workers could not profitably subjugate and exploit the rest of the team, because the whole team's strength is required to move the barge at all, hence, no redistribution of effort and no parasitism is feasible. None of these favorable conditions seems to obtain when the team is the whole society and the overseer is the state. One fundamental reason is that the teamwork of pulling the boat has a binary result: the boat either gets pulled to her destination or there is no payoff at all. By contrast, the social product is continuously variable: though some may shirk, something still gets produced as long as others work. There are gains to be had for a coalition of some against the rest, both in the allocation of burdens and in the distribution of benefits.

14 This, one might surmise, is a rational choice-type foundation for the Lockean ideal government and for the right of rebellion, both of which are difficult to understand if only the government is armed.

15 See pp. 19–21, above.

16 Leslie Green, *The Authority of the State*, Oxford: Clarendon, 1990, pp. 147–9.

17 Hampton, *Hobbes and the Social Contract Tradition*, pp. 268–84.

18 Ibid., p. 275.

19 Ibid., p. 276.

21 Ibid.

22 Ibid., p. 284.

23 Ibid., p. 283.

24 David Lewis, *Convention: A Philosophical Study*, Cambridge, Mass.: Harvard University Press, 1969.

25 Edna Ullman-Margalit, *The Emergence of Norms*, Oxford: Clarendon, 1977.

26 If "transgress" were not preferred to "obey," would there be any point in empowering a ruler to enforce obedience to norms? – though it might be useful when making a fresh start to appoint a prophet or a judge to suggest what norms we should all willingly choose to obey. In existing societies these choices have mostly been made long ago.

27 See David Gauthier, *Morals by Agreement*, Oxford: Clarendon, 1986. Gauthier's attempt is a double one: to show why voluntary cooperation in apparent prisoner's dilemma situations is rational and how rational people would agree to share the resulting cooperative surplus. For the present purpose, I shall ignore the second of these two elements.

28 There is a parallel, though not a meeting, between Gauthier's assumption of a disposition being discernible and the harnessing of "signal detection theory," the reading of minds from visible or audible signs, to advance a hypothesis of rational cooperation in single-play prisoners' dilemmas (R. A. Heiner and Dieter Schmidtchen, "Rational Selfish Cooperation in One-Shot Prisoner's Dilemma Situations," unpublished, 1994, and Heiner and Schmidtchen, "Rational Cooperation in One-Shot Prisoners' Dilemma Situations," unpublished, 1994. Cf. Robert Frank, *Passions within Reason: Prisoners' Dilemmas and the Strategic Role of Emotions*, New York: W. W. Norton, 1988). The hypothesis states that if one player forecasts that another will play cooperatively, the latter is more likely to do so. The relation is statistical and does not specify the direction of causation. Does the cooperative intention generate the forecast, or the forecast the intention?

Suppose player A expects player B to cooperate, and he is right for either reason. A can always earn a better payoff by defecting than by cooperating. To make cooperation nevertheless the payoff-maximizing move, A must assume that B's intention, or indeed his decision, to cooperate was dependent on B's correct forecast that A was going to cooperate; B would not have decided to cooperate today if he, A, were thereupon to decide to defect tomorrow.

This solution of the prisoner's dilemma follows the strange assumptions of Newcomb's paradox (as James Buchanan has pointed out in a personal communication). Significantly, one of the two players (player B) in Newcomb's paradox is God, who knows today what the other player will do tomorrow. The interaction of the players involves questions of foreknowledge versus free will. Pursuing them would take us far from game and contract theory in general and Gauthier's in particular. Molina of Salamanca proposed a solution, the *scientia media*, that depends on God's foreknowledge of man's will to accept his grace. Man, then, is in some sense free to cause God to withhold his grace, for God has foreknowledge of man's lack of will to accept it.

29 Gauthier, *Morals by Agreement*, p. 173.

30 Julian Nida-Rümelin, "Practical Reason, Collective Rationality and Contractarianism," in David Gauthier and Robert Sugden, eds, *Rationality, Justice, and the Social Contract*, Hemel Hempstead, Herts.: Wheatsheaf, 1993, p. 56.

31 Thomas Hobbes, *De Cive, or the Citizen*, 1642; Westport, Conn.: Greenwood Press, 1982, p. 68.

32 "Coalition-forming with the sovereign" is old-fashioned language imposed by the Hobbesian context. "An alliance of articulate, organized and self-serving groups in control of the state's agenda" calls the rose by another, more modern name.

33 Thomas Hobbes, *Leviathan*, 1651; Harmondsworth, Middlesex: Penguin Classics, 1985, p. 205.

34 Robert Nozick, *Anarchy, State, and Utopia*, Oxford: Blackwell, 1974, pp. 110–15.

2 Is limited government possible?*

Man is born free, and everywhere he is in chains. How did this change take place? I do not know.

INTRODUCTION

The famous opening passage in Rousseau's *Social Contract* is implicitly asking both why man is governed, and whether his subjection to government is legitimate. Social contract theory has since developed a fairly coherent answer. Its premise is that there are benefits – of which civil order is the arch-example – which men can enjoy without making a contribution to their production. Since under these circumstances no one has an incentive to contribute, no benefit could be produced unless the necessary contributions were extracted by the threat of superior force. However, if all would rather contribute and benefit – for example, maintain order by obeying the rules and pay to help make everybody else obey them – than not contribute and have disorder, then submission by all to the threat of force is morally equivalent to unforced, free choice. No matter how and why it took place in actual fact, submission is legitimate because it would have been rational to arrange it by voluntary contract.

The binary alternative – government or no government – raises neat questions and allows simple answers. It presents the normative and the descriptive aspect in apparent harmony: government ought to exist, and it does. The continuous alternative – not *whether* government, but *how much?* – defies that simple logic of unanimous preference. It involves at least three difficulties:

1 Some members of society may prefer more government than others. Hence it is impossible to state the "collectively" preferred alternative without weighing various persons contradictory preferences against one another. If this is deemed an inadmissible manner of making a descriptive statement of fact, one cannot even say how much government society wants.
2 Arguments, validly derived from various commonly agreed values, can be found in favor of both more and less government. It is impossible to settle the normative issue – how much government ought society to have? – without ruling out conflicting values or, at least, without trading

* This chapter first appeared in G. Radnitzky and H. Bouillon (eds) *Government, Servant or Master*, Amsterdam: Editions Rodopi bv, 1989. Reprinted with permission.

off pro and con arguments against each other *in some way that must depend on somebody's judgment*. Thus, no answer to the question of how much government can be free of charges of arbitrariness.

3 Worst of all, there may simply be no practical means by which society can adjust the actual size of government to what it "really" prefers or what it "ought" to have (assuming that one or both of these stipulations can be given an acceptable meaning). In the light of secular experience, it is very much an open question whether the size of government is really the product of an ascertainable "social preference," existing independently of the government whose size it ought to determine. For all we know government may be cause rather than effect.

It may indeed be the case that, to paraphrase Rousseau, man is born with a desire for minimal government and everywhere he keeps creating maximal ones.

WHO CHOOSES FOR WHOM?

An isolated individual is by definition sovereign over his choices among all feasible alternatives. They involve him alone, and no one else gains or loses by what he decides. In social life, he can still remain sovereign over choices involving him and others, as long as their interactions, generating mutual advantage, take the form of voluntary exchanges. If a society based only on pure exchange existed, it could have no politics: authority and subordination would be redundant.

The irreducible essence of political society is that certain alternatives are chosen for many individuals together; an individual may or may not participate in the making of these choices, but in any case he is not sovereign over them. This may be so as a matter of historical fact (such is the point of departure of positive theories of groups, of the state and of public law), or because man in society must be commanded and coerced in the spheres where reliance on voluntary exchanges alone would bring about inferior outcomes (such is the approach of normative theories of public goods). Thus, compulsory military service can be regarded either as the (ontological) result of legislation and its enforcement, or as the (teleological) countermeasure against the perverse incentives surrounding national defense, which makes voluntary service irrational and would leave the nation defenseless.

Decisions over which the individual is not sovereign are "collective" in the sense that they are made *for* him and others similarly placed in his group or society. They may also be collective in the much more complex and contestable sense that they are made "collectively" *by* the set of persons concerned. The first sense is always applicable to collective decisions, the first and the second together only in particular political systems. According to this criterion, we can distinguish two versions of the social contract and two kinds of political system.

THE OLD SOCIAL CONTRACT

The first (and historically older) kind operates as if there were an implicit contract between two holistic entities, "government" and "people." The former may be embodied in a tribal chief, a council of elders, a monarch, or, more informally, in an oligarchy such as ruled over Renaissance Venice, Whig England, or the Soviet Union. Government is a person or a body, sovereign over and distinct from the society to be governed.

The contract between government and people, whether inspired by custom, precedent, divine right, pragmatic calculation, or utopian ideology, provides for some frontier, or at least for guidelines to draw it, between matters decided by the government and matters left to private choice, with an intermediate area over which corporative orders, associations, and nonsovereign authorities exercise limited decision rights.

The frontier between government and society, wherever it is drawn, is stable if their implicit contract is enforceable or if it is self-enforcing. It might be best to look at these notions in the context of examples.

Post-Carolingian government for three or four centuries rested, if at times uneasily, on a tacit contract between king and feudal orders. Each tried, from time to time and with fluctuating success, to enlarge its decision rights at the other's expense. The king sought to push forward the limits of royal sovereignty; the prelates of the church, the great land-holding families and the towns, in kaleidoscopic alliances, were pushing back, protecting, and when feasible widening their "liberties" and privileges. Pushing too hard, on too broad a front, was a breach of the social contract. Such breach was far from riskless, for respect of the status quo, however imperfectly defined by precedent and by canon and feudal law, was in theory enforceable, and in practice sometimes successfully enforced by the offended party, since the use of force had not yet become a government monopoly. Force was widely distributed across feudal society, permitting self-help in defense of socio-contractual rights. Coalitions could be formed and reformed according to shifting needs and the interests to be defended. Variable patterns of alliances provided the makings of balance-of-power politics within society. Since, in the presence of nearly equal forces on both sides, aggression seldom promises a higher payoff than keeping the peace, while resistance to aggression often appears to hold out a lesser expected loss than surrender, more or less successful maintenance of the balance of power discouraged breaches of the peace and fostered respect of the contractual status quo. A fairly even distribution of force, combined with ease in making and unmaking balancing alliances, acted as a deterrent to substantial breaches of contract. The situation, despite some skirmishing and local conflict, amounted to a kind of informal constitutionalism, with the limits of government remaining stable as long as the distribution of power between the parties was broadly unchanged. The ideological support for this type of equilibrium was provided by the Thomist interpretation of natural right, and the doctrine of the right of resistance in defense of it.

Limited government has also proved possible under certain nonfeudal, absolutist regimes. Here, government clearly held the "monopoly of the use of force" and the "people" were largely disarmed. Nevertheless, for various good reasons, potentially absolute monarchies did not always "collectivize" all decisions, but willingly conceded private choice rights over important areas of life. The House of Austria did this during much of its reign, primarily because (apart from its periods of religious intolerance) it could adequately serve its dynastic interests in relatively easy-going ways. It was most of the time a "lazy tyranny," a government limited by its limited ambition and a taste for moderation.

A different kind of absolutism placed limits on government when the monarch, though ambitious, tried to reach his objectives by way of a "revolution from above" to activate and harness a civil society grown sluggish, stagnant, and inefficient under a system of unproductive incentives. Frederick the Great, and later Hardenberg and Stein, drew recognizable frontiers between private and collective decision spheres, trying to combine in an incipient *Rechtsstaat* self-restraint and activism at the same time. Analogous revolutions from above were attempted, less successfully, by Louis XV and also by Turgot and Necker in France, Joseph II in Austria-Hungary, Catherine the Great, Alexander II and then again, coming within a hair's breadth of success, by Stolypin in Russia. Stretching the concept of self-restraining absolutism, one might say that since the Second World War, Russia has gone back to limited government, albeit with its limits pushed as far forward as they will go: behind these frontiers, ordinary Russians have had irreducible rights to relapse into passivity, to choose how little they will work and how often they will escape into blind drunkenness, without being subjected to sanctions and economic costs as a consequence. The recent (late 1980s) agitation for reform from above, then, to the extent that it is more than just ineffective noise, is about pulling the limits of government back – wherever this can be done without endangering the ruling oligarchy – so as to induce society to move forward. It is, as it were, a proposal to revise the social contract between Party and Society, in the hope that individuals will use the enlarged private decision sphere for the initiatives and efforts the Soviet regime so badly needs to realize its ambitions.

In each of these examples of absolutism, whether lazy and obscurantist or ambitious and enlightened, the social contract is self-enforcing. Neither party to the contract can realistically expect to improve its chances by worsening those of the other side and pushing the frontiers of its own decision sphere over into the other's territory.

THE QUEST FOR UNANIMITY

Paradoxically, the effectiveness and stability of the frontier between the private and the public area is more problematical the nearer we get to the opposite polar case, where collective decisions are, in some conventionally agreed sense, taken *by* those concerned and the "sovereignty of the people" is uncontested. Here, the social contract is not between two parties who have partly conflicting interests to settle. It is, instead, everybody's contract with everybody else – or, as holists might say, it is society's contract with itself, if the notion of a contract with oneself were not self-contradictory. Leviathan is created by everybody's *unanimous* will and not by a bargain between two *opposing* interests. He is, as his original image was so clearly intended to convey,[1] the composite total will of all who are condemned to live together in society.

Though the idea of popular sovereignty goes back at least to Republican Rome if not further, its modern career begins with Marsilius of Padua and is inseparable from the tensions between church and state. It gets further impetus from both neoscholasticism and the Reformation, and finally reaches its logically complete form with Hobbes. (It is another, and bitter, paradox that it should be a work meant to justify absolute monarchy, and an author fleeing from the Puritan and parliamentarian revolution, whose legacy provided the ideological ground supporting "mutual coercion mutually agreed on" and "government of the people by the people.")

In embryonic form, popular sovereignty emerges in the parliamentary supremacy of eighteenth-century England, in Jefferson's America and, fleetingly, in the France of 1792. Its full realization, of course, is modern Western democracy. In the spirit of this social contract (or more precisely, quasi-contract), government is not a separate entity, and as Rousseau has pointed out (Rousseau, 1960, p. 164), cannot be a contracting party. It is an instrument of society, with no distinct will and interests; it is, instead, a reflection of the will and interests of the sovereign people.

The contract, such as it is, is difficult to interpret. It seems to involve everybody's promise to everybody else not to resist "their own" collective decisions. Its enforceability depends on an overwhelming concentration ("monopoly") of power to deter disobedience. What, however, shall pass for collective decisions? Between the status quo X and some other feasible state of affairs Y, when are we to say that one of the two has been collectively chosen and, under the contract, all must conform and obey it? Plainly, the unanimous preference of all concerned would suffice. If everybody wanted X, it would be absurd to declare that they have in fact chosen Y. But then no contract would be necessary; nobody needs a contractual obligation to make him agree with himself. Equally plainly, it cannot be their collective decision to have X if none of them wants it at least as much as he does Y; X could, in that case, only be chosen *for* them but not *by* them, and the social contract does not oblige them to accept such an imposed choice. In these two borderline cases of unanimity, the contract is fatuous or irrelevant or both.

It is relevant and has operational significance only if some want one alternative, others another. The social contract matters only because it permits nonunanimous decisions to become binding for all. Its effects must be that in the face of any pair of feasible alternatives X and Y, with divided preferences over them, all should be committed to accept one of the two and give up the other. How the pairs where an X wins are to be identified, and told apart from the pairs where a Y wins, is a postcontract problem. It is a matter of the "social choice rule" or "constitution."

The great difficulty impairing the credibility of the social contract is that it implies unanimous commitment by all to obeying one decision rule, the "constitution," before any such rule could in fact be adopted. For it takes a collective decision to settle upon a decision rule. Yet a prior rule may be needed to allow *this* decision to be collectively taken. Only unanimous decisions do not entail implicit or explicit acceptance of a decision·rule. But there is no a priori reason why unanimous selection of such a rule should be possible; we certainly cannot proceed by simply assuming that it is. How, then, can a collective decision be nevertheless reached, *before* there is a rule for reaching it? Yet the social contract is meaningless unless it is an agreement to respect an unknown rule, yet to be agreed upon.

This is a tall order. The contractarian ideology seeks to deal with it by arguing that not only the social contract, but the postcontract constitution, too, is unanimously agreed, because constitutional rules can be found that no one can have reasonable grounds for rejecting. The search for such rules must be confined to a set, all members of which are Pareto-optimal. This means that each rule must distribute "efficiently" the benefits available from collective decisions, so that there is no possible amendment of the rule which would augment the expected value of such benefits for someone without reducing it for someone else. If, within this Pareto-optimal set of possible rules, a certain rule would distribute the benefits mainly to one part of society, neglecting the rest, the latter would have reasonable grounds to object. On the other hand, if there are rules within the efficient set which are likely to cause "fair" distributions, or at least have no systematic distributive bias, they could be unanimously accepted as the best constitutional bargain anybody can secure, without anybody else having to accept a bias against himself.

CAN IMPARTIAL RULES BE "COMPLETE"?

There seem to be two ways of fulfilling this condition. Either individuals must be impartial and have no interests and preferences of the kind which collective choices reached by one decision rule are likely to serve better than those reached by another. Or the rule itself must be impartial, designed to produce impartial decisions which do not serve one interest more than another. Under the first condition, a "player" accepts any rule of the game because, unaware of having any comparative advantage or disadvantage in skills or endowments over the other player, he ignores whether the rule would favor his side or the opposite side. Under the second condition, acceptance is due not to *ignorance* or uncertainty, but to the player's positive *knowledge* that the rule in question does not favor one side.

The impartiality of individuals is obtained if (a) they are indifferent to how they will fare and simply have no particular interests (like zombies), or (b) they ignore them (Rawls's "original position"), or (c) they expect their interests to vary randomly over future periods, hence are unable to predict which rule would prove more favorable (Buchanan's "veil of uncertainty").

There may be great, troubled or tragic moments in a community's history where such states of mind prevail. Perhaps Germany's defeat in 1945 was such a moment. Only too obviously, however, they do not last; people do get wise to their particular situations and to the interests they do not share with everybody else. It is, moreover, possible for an impartial and indifferent state of mind behind the "veil of uncertainty" to prevail if constitutional rules are innocuous, in the sense that they are either vapid pieties asking to be shrugged off, or impinge only upon alternatives about which our future interests and preferences may genuinely go either way, but which do not materially affect our permanent interests. However – and here we come to the nub of the matter – a wealthy person, or one confident in his abilities, is likely to think that although he can have no certain knowledge of his or his children's future situation, they are apt to be better served by a constitution (for instance, one with suffrage tied to high property and educational qualifications, and with its amendment requiring, say, a nine-tenths majority) which makes egalitarian policies difficult to adopt. Such a person would, by the same token, have every reason to expect that equal universal suffrage and bare majority rule will operate to his relative disadvantage. Obviously, the converse is true of people who fear that their endowments, talents, and luck will not suffice to lift them above the median position in society.

If it is unrealistic to suppose that many, let alone all, persons can feel impartial with regard to decision rules, it is illusory to hold that there can be decision rules that are impartial while also being complete. A "complete" rule must be capable of producing a collective choice between any two feasible states of affairs, one of which is the status quo. At least some of these alternative states of affairs must involve changes in the distribution of advantage, well-being or whatever else individuals value. Under a complete rule, society is always able to opt for the distributional status quo or a specific change (or at least a measure designed to bring about a specific change) in it. Even a rule under which society always rejected any deliberate change – perhaps because a constitutional clause forbade any measure that would interfere with property and privilege – could be a technically complete rule, for in the face of any two distributional alternatives, it could always select one, the status quo. Patently, however, it would not be widely regarded as impartial in the above sense, for many people would consider it as conservatively biased. It would arguably tend to cause certain collectively provided benefits, such as the protection of property and the enforcement of contracts, to accrue mainly to those who have property, even if it could be proved that ultimately this worked to the advantage of everyone, including those who have no property.

A rule confined to yield only such decisions as have *no* distributional implications – though on reflection, there are few or perhaps no such rules – could no doubt be considered impartial. However, by definition it would be incomplete, leaving society without an agreed manner of resolving latent or overt conflicts of interest not "programmed" in advance by a preexisting system of property rights. The allocation of the tax burden, needed to produce public goods, is an obvious example. No particular allocation of that burden is inherent in any system of property rights (or, as some would say, any taxation is a violation of such a system). A rule that did not lay down how to decide about taxes would not be complete, while one that did could not be impartial.

SPLIT-LEVEL CONTRACTARIANISM

Modern contractarian thinking masks the extremely demanding character of its unanimity requirement by isolating two classes of social choice from one another: choices of states of affairs which remain out of reach unless one interest or preference is enabled to override another, and choices of the rules under which the former kind of choices must be made. The first class is by definition conflictual, while the second supposedly need not entail disagreement, does not leave any victors and vanquished, and permits unanimity. Hayek, for one, repeatedly insists on distinctions between *nomos* and *thesis*, law and legislation, general rules for allowing a spontaneous order or *kosmos* to emerge and particular decisions for running a social organization or *taxis*. In Buchanan's formulation, there is to be a distinction between choosing rules, and making choices within rules. His contention that these lie on two different levels, and that on the upper level unanimity is possible, depends on the upper level being "impartial" in the sense discussed above.

In Hayek's schema, the upper level is reserved for "rules of just conduct" which can, and ought to, be kept separate from "particular decisions." Rules of just conduct purportedly do not impinge on "particular private ends" (Hayek, 1978, p. 93). It is a harmless and riskless proposition that the application of a rule of just conduct can equitably resolve questions of justice, and will be unanimously accepted by all who want a just rule. It does not help us find the rule that is just, nor does it ensure that the men who compose society and must unanimously agree on the rules, will in fact do so. Moreover, a rule of just conduct, if it is found and agreed upon, will guide social choices among certain, mostly uncontroversial, alternatives but not among all. A rule that is only one of just conduct will not alone enable society to proceed to nonunanimous choices among all relevant alternatives; to be complete, it needs to be backed up by another rule whose criterion is not justice, but decisiveness.

Any complete decision rule has some bias that is predictable to some degree. Altering the rule has some systematic effect on the probability of the kind of choice its observance will produce. Democracy favors the preferences that are shared by many, plutocracy is helpful to ownership, aristocracy promotes "elitist" and distant social objectives, simple majority rule favors change, qualified majority or veto rules protect the status quo, and so forth. Consequently, the choice of a given decision rule is logically equivalent to the choice of a probability distribution of the alternatives that may be chosen within that rule.[2] Split-level decision theory, with upper-level decisions being uncontroversial and consecrated by unanimity, seeks to deny this logical equivalence.

Since social choice is inherently conflictual and a social choice rule probabilistically determines the social choices that its observance generates, it is inherently conflictual, too. A choice rule depending on consent can only be understood as if it were the solution of a bargaining problem; a solution which, if it is reached at all, can lie anywhere within the range of mutual advantage, at one end of which one party, class, group or interest gets most of the advantage from having a decision rule at all, at the other end another. There is in general no unique solution; different constitutions may be acquiesced to, depending on how the implicit post-contract bargaining fell out. However, since different rules tend to have different results, it would be inconsistent for society to want to keep the rule after it has ceased to want its results.

It is for this reason, if for no other, that a consent-based constitution must, in order to survive the passage of time and the ebb and flow of interest groups and their ideologies, incorporate some provision for its own amendment.

A constitution that under its own clauses and provisions cannot be amended must bend. Otherwise it will not be what fashionable political discourse calls "a living constitution." The twentieth-century evolution of the US Constitution at the hands of a Supreme Court that was "moving with the times" when it was not moving ahead of them, clearly shows that changing interpretation can achieve much, even without formal amendment. How the "spirit of the times" moves is plainly not independent of the very constitution whose evolution it brings forth. One can see in this feedback the makings of a hypothesis of "constitutional dynamics," under which given conservative, progressive, etc., choice rules help produce some change in the social balance of power, which, in turn, imposes some change in the choice rule, and so on, in a sequence which may be cyclical or cumulative.

A MINIMAL ARGUMENT FOR MINIMAL GOVERNMENT

Before moving on, I should like to spell out, as explicitly as I can, that the frame of reference in which I argue from the acceptance of collective choice rules to the limits of collective choice does not rely on and indeed excludes any built-in antagonism between state and society. Political thought often blames this antagonism for the loss of individual liberties, and there is something to be said for this manner of posing the problem. At our present level of abstraction, however, the state is a pure instrument of society; government does not seek to expropriate private rights; there are no corrupt and lazy bureaucrats, nor wicked politicians raising false expectations with their demagogy. Here, there is every reason for the public to be governed as much or as little as it wants to be; there are no trivial excuses for getting big government when society proclaims loudly that it desires a small one. It is in this pure form, free from ad hoc "malfunctions" and "distortions," that I propose to test the force of the paradox of limited government, praised everywhere but practiced nowhere.

Why, after all, is small government praised? – and why should any limit to collective choice be better than any other? The answer is usually built on some reference to freedom, and allows rhetoric to supersede close reasoning. It is all too easy to condemn "excessive" government intervention. Nobody is for "too much" state power; and being an apple pie-and-motherhood type of value, freedom is something we all approve. Yet there are freedom-derived arguments, meant to support one type of government, which can turn out to support the opposite type. The problem is too vast to be gone into here. But it should serve as a warning that Lyndon Johnson and Willy Brandt led governments aiming to increase freedom.

Looking for the ideal balance between the public and the private area would be a foolish ambition. For our present purpose it suffices to find at least one valid argument for small government (without denying that there may be valid ones against it, too) to establish the point that the question of collective self-limitation is not frivolous or irrelevant. On its strength we can claim that it matters a great deal whether it is at all possible to restrict the scope of collective choices and if so, how? – or if not, why?

The least demanding argument seems to me that the smaller is the domain where choices among alternatives are made collectively, the smaller will be the probability that any individual's preference gets over-ruled. For in the domain of private choices where he is sovereign, an individual need never override his *own* preference, though (on some definitions of free will) he is able to do so. Yet in collective choice *others* can do it to *him*. In private consumption, he spends his budget on the goods he chooses. In collective consumption, some of his budget is absorbed by taxes and will be spent on goods he may or may not have chosen. In terms of the decision rules typical of democracy, this means that only in collective choice does the individual ever risk finding himself in the minority. Under other types of decision rules, much the same is true to various degrees except when the rule is one of "anti-social choice" under which the given individual either has veto rights (no decision can be taken against his will) or is a dictator (all decisions are his).

A more conjectural argument can be built on imperfect foresight. Decisions affecting the future are meant to produce desirable conse-quences. Sadly, however, sometimes they turn out to be quite undesirable. When a social state of affairs, instead of being collectively decided, is left to emerge from a large number of individual decisions, the effects of the latter tend to be normally distributed: a few prove disastrous, a few are superbly good, and most are middling. The likelihood of the resulting state of affairs being totally disastrous or wholly superb is negligible. When, however, one collective choice is responsible for a state of affairs, no normal distribution can be relied upon. A single wrong decision that "seemed a good idea at the time" suffices to cause disaster. In loss of life and moral and material destruction, the collectivization of land in the Soviet Union and the Chinese Great Leap Forward were catastrophes as great as a world war. On a less apocalyptic scale, having an industrial policy under Peron has durably ruined Argentina and keeps ruining many other countries that seriously pursue one. Social engineering in Cambodia, Tanzania, Ethiopia, and, it would seem, in Rumania, is equal, in the horrible and degrading nastiness of its effects, to a mortal epidemic or a cruel war. Self-inflicted social catastrophes are, in their tragic foolishness, even sadder than disasters inflicted by nature, history and geography. This is an argument for limiting the capacity of government to produce change; an argument which, if it does not appeal to everyone, should at least appeal to the mistrustful, the cautious, and the worldly-wise.

An indirect but telling sign of the difficulty of durably restraining collective choice is the bizarre fact that alone among the great political currents, liberalism has no ideology.[3] Hayek, who considers that limiting the state is both desirable and possible, explains what is to be meant by the limitation of collectively agreed coercion as follows:

> The strict limitation of governmental powers to the enforcement of general rules of just conduct required by liberal principles refers only to the *coercive powers* of government. Government may render in addition, by the use of *the means placed at its disposal*, many services which involve no coercion except for the raising of the means by taxation
>
> (Hayek, 1978, p. 144, my italics)

The "means placed at its disposal" are not provided by the Holy Spirit. However, the coercion involved in procuring them seems to Hayek to be almost a side issue, incidental to the noncoercive provision of collective needs:

> The basic principle of the liberal tradition, that all the coercive action of government must be limited to the enforcement of general rules of just conduct, does not preclude government from rendering many other services for which, *except for raising the necessary finance*, it need not rely on coercion.
>
> ... I am the last person to deny that increased wealth and the increased density of population have enlarged the number of *collective needs* which *government can and should* satisfy. Such government services are entirely compatible with liberal principles so long as ... the wants satisfied are *collective wants* of the community *as a whole* and not merely collective wants of particular groups
>
> (Hayek, 1978, p. 111, my italics)

Taxation as a proportion of national income is a rough measure of the domains of collective versus individual sovereignty over material resources. It sounds almost like deadpan black humor to state that "except for raising the means," government need not rely on coercion to render services. Surely, once it has raised the means, it has applied all the coercion it can possibly need; if we treat such coercion as an exception, what is left of the rule? – and what could a liberal ever object to? There is an infinity of services to be rendered; they all satisfy some need. How much should be provided? We are in an ideological void in which minimal state, maximal state, and anything in between are equally admissible. However, the real sting of Hayek's statement of what is compatible with liberalism is in its tail, where he stipulates that the wants to be satisfied must be those of the community "as a whole."

HAYEK'S GENERAL WILL

This is not the first time that political thought has tried to separate the wants of the community "as a whole" from those of "particular groups" – the attempt to do so is far from typically liberal. Rousseau has, of course, done it by postulating the General Will, which is distinct from "particular general wills." He trapped himself so effectively that to get loose, he identified the General Will with what the majority decides *when it is not mistaken* about what it really wants.[4] Hegel and Marx reasoned in much the same way about the real purposes of history and the real interests of class. Hayek maneuvers himself into the same kind of circular argument by seeking to set apart general from particular collective wants. Collective wants could, of course, be classified as such, and ordered into some hierarchy, by the (value) judgments of a given person, such as Hayek, or I, or (best of all) the reader. The hierarchy could be called a "social welfare function" as formulated by that person. Decisions to maximize the function would effectively be his decisions (on behalf of the community) and not the community's decisions (on behalf of itself). This may work admirably for all we know, but is not the case we (or liberals in general) are discussing. Our problem is the case where the hierarchy of "collective wants" is some composite expression, summed in some agreed manner, of the interests and preferences manifested by the members of the community. The most widely agreed manner of expressing them is one-man-one-vote majority rule, though others are possible. Whichever it is, it is precisely this agreed manner of individual preference aggregation into a collective ordering that is supposed to be laid down in the collective decision rule.

When, therefore, Hayek calls for satisfying the collective wants of the community but not those of particular groups within it, does he have a means of identifying some "real" hierarchy of wants which is independent from what the community itself, via the agreed decision rule, expresses? Which "social welfare function" is he solving? If it is one written by himself or those of a like mind, the result is preordained, but the only practical way of realizing it is to vest collective decision rights in Hayek and those of us who feel like he does. If, however, it is "society's own" expression of its wants that is to stand for the social welfare to be maximized – which is implied in the liberal idea that people know best what they want – it will be the operation of the collective decision rule they have accepted, and nothing else, that can determine what is meant by a want of the community "as a whole."

Thus, to pursue Hayek's argument, if society wants to protect small bootmakers from factory competition,[5] and reaches the decision to do so by the agreed constitutional process, to say that bootmaker protection is *not* satisfying a collective want of society as a whole is equivalent to saying, with Rousseau, that the decision-makers of society (the majority, or whatever part is authorized to decide for all) was "ill informed" about the General Will. One might just as well judge, with the legendary professor of German commenting on the sentiment expressed in a Goethe poem: "*da irrt sich der Dichter*" ("in this the poet is mistaken").[6] But if society does not know what it really wants and Goethe is in error about his own sentiments, what is to stop anybody from claiming that he knows how to put right such mistakes? – and how can liberals object to paternalism, dictatorship or, more topically, to the "leading role" to be permanently reserved to a certain party?

In calling into question a certain decision, we are really calling into question the rule which was duly followed in reaching it. It is conceivable that a different rule would have produced a different decision, more in keeping with what some of us would welcome, and small bootmakers would not be protected. The proper object of argument, then, is to see whether a different decision rule, which would make certain kinds of decisions more difficult or perhaps impossible to reach, might have been agreed and upheld.

THE CONSTITUTIONAL LIMITATION OF SOCIAL CHOICE

Provided that it is obeyed, there is a type of constitutional rule that is foolproof in ensuring that certain collective decisions will *not* be reached. Such a constitution explicitly bans the choices of certain states of affairs, for example those that involve violations of the freedom of worship, assembly and speech, or the right to dispose of lawfully acquired property. Such a constitution is nevertheless technically "complete," for it enables collective choices to be made between the status quo and any other state of affairs. However, when certain states of affairs are meant to be discriminated against, the rule will direct society *always to select the status quo* instead. It is in this sense that certain rights could be said to be "inviolable" under a constitution. In the standard language of social choice theory, the rule would effectively permit collective choices only within a "restricted domain," leaving inviolable the areas outside it.

A roundabout and less foolproof manner of restricting the collective domain is to aggregate individual preferences, or more precisely the votes supposed to express them, in such a way as to give greater weight to those voters who would want to preserve the status quo in the area in question. If the rich want to keep, and the poor to change, the status quo in the distribution of wealth, a super-majority requirement, or a property qualification giving more votes to each rich person, will probably have similar effects as an explicit domain restriction in matters of property and taxation.

Little ingenuity is needed to devise a constitution which, by direct or roundabout means, tends to restrict the domain of collective choice to some definable sphere and by the same token limits the scope, functions, and power of government, making it "smaller" than it would be if the domain were unrestricted. On the long road to absolute parliamentary sovereignty in England, there were many periods when all policy was technically a royal prerogative and the King in council supposedly decided over war and peace, trade and navigation, yet the politically active part of the landed and the commercial "interest" could decisively control the money at the government's disposal, thereby setting limits to the scope of its actions. There is a plethora of constitutional devices for "rigging" rules and procedures in such a way as to clip the wings of the state. Reserving more decision rights to those who pay more tax is no doubt one of the most direct and uninhibited. However, the problem of securing limited government and individual sovereignty is not how to invent domain-restricting constitutional devices. It is to find the conditions, if there are any, under which such devices would be likely to be adopted, respected, and left intact for long enough to do any good.

Admit for a moment that society has inherited such a domain-restricting constitution from a past where views and wishes, interests and preferences were different; call it Rule A. What stops today's society from ignoring it and proceeding to collective decisions under some less restrictive constitution – call it Rule B? Force is an instrument controlled and directed by society; it cannot protect Rule A from violations if the balance of forces in society desires them. There is, under popular sovereignty, never an answer to the question: *quis custodiet ipsos custodes*? (Only when a force *outside* society comes into play can a constitution be *guaranteed*, in the manner of the armed force of the Soviet Union guaranteeing socialism in the countries under its tutelage, against the will of their respective peoples who would visibly prefer to live by a more congenial constitution.) Hayek, for one, does not consider the lack of force an inherent defect of constitutions: "To limit power does *not* require that there be another power to limit it" (Hayek, 1978, p. 93). Power, he explains, is derived from opinion. To make sure that opinion sets the *right* sort of limits, leading to the kind of government liberals can approve, he wants to entrust its formulation to a representative body, a second or third chamber, above coalitions of particular interests. No reason is advanced why the opinion enunciated by this body would be accepted as binding by a society, or any substantial part of it, in a situation where it wanted to use the "power" of collective decision-making for breaking down the very limits "opinion" has erected against it.

Unfortunately, the construction under which society's opinion keeps society's power from doing what society wants suffers from a failing common to much normative constitutional theory. The search for an institution or a rule – or a body to interpret it – that is representative yet stands above interests, decisive yet benign, conflictual yet unanimous, square yet round, is perhaps not a total waste of time, for it may have educational value. But those who would guide us cannot possibly find the object they are searching for, and it seems to me wrong of them to pass off the *searching* as if it were the *finding*. Needless to say that if there *is*, in fact, a dominant opinion in society in favor of Rule A, such that it overrides preferences and interests which lean towards Rule B, the problem of how to preserve Rule A and how to limit government *is*, in fact, solved. However, the existence of such a dominant opinion is not self-evident, it is not an empirically supported likelihood, and it certainly cannot simply be assumed and relied upon.

Failing the dissociation of "opinion" from interests – what Marxists are pleased to call false consciousness, but which is neither less nor more likely to exist for being "false" – the preservation of Rule A, or its replacement by Rule B allowing more active, and perhaps unlimited, government, is ultimately a function of the comparative preference rankings of the two sets of actual collective decisions expected to be yielded by each. As we found earlier, however, one set (or probability distribution of sets) is seldom ranked unambiguously higher than another, since political society is a tissue of partly conflicting interests, some of which are better served by one rule, others by another. Even for a single individual, neither set may dominate the other: while Rule A is kinder to taxpayers, Rule B should result in better public education, and if an individual is both a taxpayer and has school-age children, his preference is not immediately obvious. This is a *fortiori* true of multiperson groups and multigroup societies, within which a given collective decision involves gains for some and losses for others. For such communities, agreement on Rule A is one solution to their underlying bargaining problem, agreement on Rule B is another, but neither bargain is uniformly better for all parties. Can one, nevertheless, say that under certain conditions one solution "dominates" the other in the sense that one constitution will survive or will supersede the other?

Let us continue to suppose that today's society has inherited the domain-restricting Rule A; we will suppose, in particular, that under it society can never decide to take one person's (or one class of persons) property and give it to another. A complete rule has some provision for its own amendment. For Rule A, let it be a very restrictive one, just short of the unanimity requirement (unanimity would be a redundant requirement, contradictory to the essence of "social choice" – which must allow at least one contrary preference to be overriden). Thus, Rule A can be amended, and transformed into Rule B, if *not more than one* person opposes the amendment. Consequently, *any two* persons can decisively protect Rule A. Peter and Paul, the two richest, would presumably be the last two to give up opposing the amendment. A coalition of all the others remains "indecisive" in the face of their stand. But the coalition can turn itself into a "decisive" one, and gain Peter's property, if they can bribe Paul to join them. It pays them to pass from an indecisive coalition of all against n, to a decisive coalition of all against $n-1$, for although the payoff is diminished (less property gets shared out among more allies), it is at least sure to be obtained. There is a possible bargain to ensure the passage: under it, Paul keeps his property and shares Peter's property with the other members of the coalition, so that all members are better off and only Peter is worse off from the amendment. Thus, *under Rule A*, there is a decisive coalition both entitled to change over to Rule B, and having an advantage in doing so. When both these conditions hold, we will say that B dominates A.

(If Paul were mistrustful and far-seeing, he should never join the coalition against Peter, for once the constitution is changed and the requirements for decisiveness are relaxed, he could expect to be one of its first victims, against whom a decisive coalition would be formed. Forgoing the immediate gain and sticking by Peter to defend the old constitution would probably be his best policy. Nevertheless, history suggests that, motivated perhaps by envy and fear of the economic power of the richest, the merely rich are normally quite willing to join political alliances against the very rich. It is only in truly revolutionary situations, and then not always, that all property owners unite against the menace of the propertyless.) There seems to be enough basis here for a three-part thesis:

1 Any constitution, whether written or implicit in custom, can be amended de jure or de facto by a coalition large enough to be decisive for the amendment. (For "amended" we may read reinterpreted or circumvented; for "large enough" we may read influential, cohesive, or vocal enough, depending on the facts of the case.)
2 Each constitution can be associated with a probable set of collective decisions that become accessible under it. Constitutions providing for limited government allow access to smaller probability-weighted decision sets than those that do not restrict possible government action.
3 If all in a potential coalition that would be decisive under Constitution A, including decisiveness for changing it, weakly prefer the decision set accessible under Constitution B, A is dominated and unstable, and B is dominant over A. (B may in turn be dominated by C, and be unstable.)

MAXIMIZING FOR A MINIMAL DECISIVE COALITION

If this formal thesis has relevance for understanding how social decision rules evolve, it may help in identifying the particular constitutional solutions that are on a priori grounds likely to be dominant, or dominated.

A characteristic relation between two constitutions A and B is one where the probability distribution of decisions generated by the operation of A is a subset of that under B. Some states of affairs easily accessible under B will then be unlikely or difficult to reach, or even be totally inaccessible, under A. Since a decisive coalition need never choose a state of affairs whose expected value to it is negative, it would not be rational for it to value *positively* the *inaccessibility* of states of affairs. Consequently, the rule under which a certain set of alternatives is available to it, has prima facie as great or greater expected value to a *given* decisive coalition, than the rule under which some of the alternative states of affairs are unavailable. Rule B would thus dominate Rule A if the decisive coalition were the same in each.

If the rule change involves a change in the decisive coalition, too, a bargaining problem arises, for some of the additional alternatives that become accessible and have a positive expected value to the new decisive coalition in B may be disliked by the old decisive coalition in A. A bargain, compensating some of the latter out of the gains accruing to the new decisive coalition from the change over to Rule B, may or may not take place. (It may fail by miscalculation, or on the contrary, by virtue of superior calculation by some of the parties who refuse the present compensation for fear of more distant losses.) However, mutual advantage is available to make the bargain at least possible. There is thus at least a presumption that the less restrictive Rule B dominates the more restrictive Rule A.

In democracy, collective decisions are made by adding up the algebraic sum of unweighted votes. All who are allowed to participate in the decision have equal influence on it, no matter who they are and how intensely they like or dislike an alternative. Assuming that for reasons that are outside the present argument, these democratic features must in any case be accepted, one constitution will tend to dominate all others. It is one where the accessible and probability-weighted *decision set is maximized* and the *decisive coalition* able to impose its choice on everybody is *minimized*. Since a vote for the status quo weighs the same in the algebraic sum as one against it, the smallest set of votes that is still decisive is, of course, half of the votes cast plus one. In other words, in democracy the dominant constitution is one where a *bare majority* rules over an *unrestricted domain*. In Arrovian social choice theory, these characteristics are the consequence of axioms, selected with a view to being ethically satisfactory. It may be, however, that much the same consequence can be predicted, independently from ethical acceptability, by assuming that all have equal influence over collective choices and behavior is nonaltruistically utility-maximizing.

It is self-evident that as long as a decisive coalition is not at its minimum, *gains are available by reducing it*, since each reduction enlarges the losing set and decreases the number of gainers among whom the good taken from the losers is shared. It is only when the decisive coalition is reduced to a bare majority that no further gain can result from changing its size. It is likewise self-evident that gains are available to the decisive coalition by any widening of the domain of collective choice. Domain restriction is either fatuous (if it stops the decisive coalition from doing what it does not want to do anyway) or frustrating (if it stops it from doing what it wants to do).

These are, then, the basic arguments in support of the ominous prediction that when opinion is dependent on preference and interest, the end of the line of constitutional development is unlimited popular sovereignty, bare majority rule, and the erosion of obstacles that could prevent collective choice from overriding private choice.

The corresponding framework of public law may be fully respected and the organs of the state may be unreservedly subjected to it. There may even be a judiciary which, by a variant of the Indian rope trick, is independent of the power of the state and can somehow enforce the constitutionality of government actions. Technically, a *Rechtsstaat* can exist.[7] Nevertheless, government would not be limited in the accepted sense of the word. Without any violation of the constitution, lawful collective decisions, to satisfy what Hayek, in all good faith, approvingly calls "collective wants," could continually expand its role.

The satisfaction of collective wants has well-established special properties that make for continuous expansion. The principal such property is that while publicly provided goods and services have a total cost that is met from general taxation or public borrowing, their marginal cost to any individual consumer is zero or is subjectively seen as zero. Hence the net benefit he expects to derive from increased public provision of the goods he may want to consume is, subjectively and *ex ante*, always positive. (It is zero or negative only from goods he does not want at all or is already consuming to the point of total saturation.) These individually positive appraisals of the value of increased provision of some of the infinitely many goods and services that governments can produce get aggregated into collective preferences for *more* of this, that, or the other, without symmetrical collective preferences arising for less of something else.

It is an error to think that the phenomenon discussed above depends, as log-rolling does, on collusion among the champions of different public goods, each helping the other to get the "right" collective decision, as a condition of being helped when it is his turn to ask for the sort of public expenditure he wants. Even without collusion, the fact that publicly provided goods appear to be costless at the margin to the individual voter, makes it easier (more probable) to reach collective decisions that *provide*, than ones that *deny*. This seems to me a far more powerful and general factor for the growth of government than collusive log-rolling. In addition, the quasi-costlessness of publicly provided goods implies that their consumption can only be controlled by rationing, since it is not controlled by price. However, there are goods, such as free public education, public health care, welfare, and unemployment benefits, that cannot legitimately be rationed because they must be supplied to all comers who can demand them under a legislated *entitlement*. Using more of a good under an entitlement (staying on at school, or at university, getting optional surgery, remaining unemployed rather than choosing some inferior job) is costless or at least is cheaper than the marginal cost of the good. Expenditure under entitlements, therefore, tends to grow more or less uncontrollably, without any specific collective decision being taken to make it grow.

"PRIVATE FORTRESSES"

These tendencies to a limitless public sector and a limitless role for the state arise out of an incentive structure which is inseparable from the unlimited sovereignty of lawfully reached collective decisions. Where force is a centralized monopoly, controlled by the operation of a constitution, the latter is unchecked. It is liable to evolve towards its theoretically most rewarding, "dominant" form with unrestricted domain and bare majority rule. It is in this form that the ability to choose collectively has *the greatest expected value to each member* of a potential decisive coalition.

In reminding us that the capitalist organization of society reduces the risk run by dissenting individuals, Schumpeter spoke of "the private fortresses of bourgeois business," (Schumpeter, 1977, p. 151) which could protect minorities by offering them a livelihood that does not depend on public favor. It seems true enough that as long as such fortresses stand, the ability of a decisive coalition to bring about any feasible result it wants can be obstructed by their walls. There have been social organizations in history with many such private fortresses, great and small; not only great family-controlled capitalist empires, but yeoman farms and businesses just strong enough to assure the owners' independence. American society from the Philadelphia Convention to the First World War abounded in "private forts" of all sizes and shapes, each a minor obstacle to the sovereignty of the people, and it is tempting to infer that American government over this period was limited ultimately for this reason, and not because of the Lockean inspiration of the Constitution. Arguably, the latter was a symptom of the richly polycentric power structure and not its cause. The defeat of the Confederacy in the Civil War; the growing dependence of industry on public policies in the matters of tariffs, taxes, credit, and, towards the end of the period, regulation and anti-trust; the waves of populism; and the parallel though irregular progress of the Constitution towards unrestricted domain and majority rule; these developments formed a chicken-and-egg sequence, where the weakening of dispersed powers contributed to the breaking down of the limits of government, and vice versa. There is no room in such an essay as this for delving into the details of this process, nor for finding earlier parallels in European history. All we can note is that although it took its time in doing it, history on either side of the Atlantic seldom failed to get close to the theoretical end result, bare majority rule and practically unrestricted domain, a result which in a framework of abstract reasoning would come about instantaneously.

It is to history taking its time that we owe thanks for the brilliant but passing nineteenth-century interlude in Western civilization, with limited government and assured-looking private sovereignty of everybody's own decisions over crucial domains of economic and social life. If our more collective twentieth century is in some respects "better," less arduous, more clement and relaxed, it is in no small measure because it is living off the accumulation of moral and material reserves mostly squirreled away during that earlier private interlude.

ESCAPING THE RATIONAL CALCULUS

My argument was designed to lead to a certain conclusion, and it did: limited government with popular sovereignty is precarious, historically in retreat and, under certain abstract ahistorical assumptions, self-contradictory. One escape route, voluntary surrender of popular sovereignty to some small elite, a feudal lay or clerical hierarchy, an absolute monarch or a dictator, is ethically questionable and also imprudent: each of these alternative sovereigns would be capable of conducting limited government, but in fact none of them might end up doing so, and there is no assurance that we could make them.

However, the preservation of popular sovereignty inevitably means that constitutions as rules for collective choice are not received from the Holy Spirit exogenously, but are agreed amongst ourselves endogenously. Once it is understood that (at least tendentially, in terms of probabilities) given rules are disposed to produce given consequences, the hopeful contractarian distinctions between choices, rules for choosing, and rules for choosing rules, disappear. The distinctions are meant to make it rational for people to agree on constitutions unanimously, without much regard to relative gains and losses that might ensue from their operation. If rules can be related in some straight or probabilistic way to the choices they engender, their value is derivative, instrumental, and the same calculus of cost and benefit, net advantage, or expected utility must apply right through the chain. Goods, the rules for distributing them and the meta-rules for choosing these rules, form a single hierarchy whose ordering depends solely on our preferences and interests in the final goods at stake. In a pure utility-maximizing paradigm, nothing else can possibly explain constitutional choice.

It is then impossible to maintain that the coalition that is decisive under a certain rule will refrain from maximizing the advantages the rule offers, and will deliberately let its interests be frustrated by not fully exploiting it, and if need be changing it into a different rule.

We keep hankering for nobler, milder, and blander outcomes. But logic offers only the bleak perspective at the end of the road of constitutional development, the practical omnipotence of collective choice that selects its own rules.

At this stage if not before, it should be clear what makes this conclusion compelling and what would make it invalid. Either preference and interest are supreme, or they are not. To limit government, there must be something among the determinants of collective choice that overrides preference and interest, yet does not contradict the condition underlying any social contract, namely that collective choice is never independent of what significant numbers of individuals wish it to be[8]

Whatever this overriding determinant may be, it must be capable of constraining utility-maximizing conduct. It must thus confine the scope of the consequential calculus individuals wish to perform, in a way that will *create a restricted domain* in collective choice. Moreover, these constraints must not be perceived by the individuals concerned as the interdictions of an adversary, resented and if possible overcome – much as "bourgeois law," stopping collective choice from touching private property, was supposed to be resented and ultimately overcome in the mythology of the class struggle; they must form an integral part of individual motivations.

An old maxim of statecraft had it that *"un curé vaut douze gendarmes"* – one parish priest can make a dozen gendarmes superfluous. To be strictly true, the maxim should lay down that what the priest does for the present generation – in educating the young and in influencing the social climate – allows us to have a dozen fewer gendarmes a generation later. His effect is as much on people's respect for rules as on the evolution of the rules themselves, which may require fewer gendarmes to enforce. Men raised, whether by priests or others, to acquiesce in certain alternatives and to reject others almost by reflex action, without trying to excogitate the consequences, may simply refrain from opting for feasible public policies that would promote their interests, if such policies would violate "natural right."

We may say that such conduct is governed by standards that are *not derivable* from interests nor, of course, from preferences in any meaningful sense of that term. (There is a tautological sense in which "preferred" means "chosen," for whatever reason; under it, choice inspired by respect for a moral norm would still be choice dictated by preference. This sense of "preference" is, of course, redundant and useless.) An individual, some of whose choices are dictated by *standards*, has a built-in bias that can overrule his utility calculus. He opts for certain states of affairs not because of what their consequences will do for him, but simply for what they are.[9] We could, to follow the fashion, also say that his preferences are governed by a meta-preference, and so on from layer to meta-layer, meta-layer to meta-meta-layer, but nothing would be gained by piling ever longer words upon short.

The real question is not whether standards can overrule preference or, as Hayek has put it, whether opinions can limit state power. Evidently, they can if they are of the right kind and strong enough. To say so does not answer any problem, and is of no help in considering how such standards can take hold in a culture, and how they get eroded.

Abstract theory, which I think alone allows us to reduce the question of limited government to its essentials, has little or nothing left to contribute to the answer. How people get to feel the way they do is beyond political philosophy and economics. History and social anthropology may have to take over at this point, for the emergence of religions and taboos, and their resistance to the processes of secular enlightenment, is for such branches of knowledge to explain.

For what it is worth, I will, by way of postscript, nevertheless hazard my personal conviction that enduring limited government is only possible in conjunction with unreasoning acceptance, by significant parts of society, of certain metaphysical propositions. Perhaps only luck can ensure that they should be the "right" kind. However, dangerous and double-edged as they can be, religion, taboo and superstition have indispensable roles to play in curbing the calculations of reason, and in resisting the relentless advance of collective choice propelled by individual interest. Reason, if it is supreme, will never propose nor durably accept limits to its own scope. It will want to use the power of collective choice whenever it finds, or believes to have found, a chance for it to bring about some improvement in the "sum of wellbeing." Reason has, by its very nature, enough confidence in itself not to renounce, humbly and in advance, the use of its power to do good.

What do I mean by the "right kind of metaphysical propositions"? In his *Theory of Economic History*, my erstwhile teacher Sir John Hicks, borrowing from an ancient Arab chronicler, recounts how the people of Medina, menaced by a failure of the millet crop and fearing that speculators would corner the stock, went to the Prophet Mohammed and asked him to fix the price of millet. The Prophet is said to have protested indignantly that he could not fix prices, "only Allah can do that!"

This kind of reflex rejection, unjustifiable by reasoning, of the seductive possibility that the state can and legitimately may influence matters of production and distribution in "collectively chosen" ways, is the ultimate assurance we can have for limited government. Perhaps there are other, less bigoted ones. Be that as it may, the net result of confidently following the apparent dictates of reason in politics over the last hundred years or more, has been inglorious enough to teach us caution before we condemn old interdictions for their obscurantism.

NOTES

1 The title page of the original "Head" edition of Hobbes's most famous work shows the head and the torso of Leviathan composed of innumerable little human figures.

2 A constitution, then, is a lottery whose prizes are social choices favoring some over others. Depending on the prizes and their chances, some people will prefer one lottery ticket, others another. There is an analogy here with some principles of risky choices. We may choose between various prizes; or between lottery tickets offering chances of winning these prizes; or between lottery tickets offering chances of winning these tickets; and so on indefinitely. The higher one goes along the chain of lotteries, the further removed are the actual prizes, and the more difficult it may be to work out the correct choice, i.e., the choice consistent with the value of the final prixes. Mistakes of calculation may creep in. But this does not entitle anyone to affirm that it is rational to choose tickets on some basis *other than* the basis of reference to the values of the final prizes and the probabilities of winning them. Contractarianism is, so to speak, the belief in such an "other basis."

3 As the context no doubt allows the reader to realize, the reference is not to "liberalism" as understood in American politics.

4 "The General Will is always right, but the judgment guiding it is not always well informed. It must be *made to see as things as they are*, sometimes *as they ought to be*" (Rousseau, 1960, p. 204).

5 Cf. chapter "Economic Freedom and Representative Government," in Hayek (1978).

6 The legend has its origin in Eckermann telling posterity that contrary to his own erroneous lines, Fredericke was *not* Goethe's greatest love.

7 By way of a digression, we may reflect upon a perhaps frivolous question: if, by a gigantic effort of self-abnegation, the Soviet state brought itself to respect its own laws both when it suited the ruling oligarchy *and* when it did not, would it be a *Rechtsstaat*? Is the universality of the rule of law a sufficient condition for that condition, or must the law have some particular content?

8 This condition will be recognized as a loose restatement of Arrow's nondictatorship axiom (Arrow, 1963).

9 When it is the constitution itself that, in Arrow's words has "a built-in bias toward one alternative or another," it violates the condition that collective choice must be independent of the *nature* of the alternatives offered for choice, and depend only on how the individual voters *value* them. This condition is a consequence of the Arrow axioms, and is at the heart of the "impossibility" of social choice. (Cf. the compelling argument to this effect by Sen, 1985, pp. 1768–70). The condition enunciated in the text does not require that the constitution should have a "built-in bias" – a self-limiting bias would not be durable anyway. It requires, instead, that the voters themselves should be "biased," refusing to take certain "preferred" alternatives.

REFERENCES

Arrow K. J. (1963) 2nd edn, *Social Choice and Individual Values*, New Haven, CT: Yale University Press.

Hayek, F. A. (1978) *New Studies in Philosophy, Economics and The History of Ideas*, Chicago: University of Chicago Press.

Rousseau, J. J. (1960) "The Social Contract," in Sir E. Barker, (ed.) *Social Contract*, New York: Oxford University Press.

Schumpeter, J. (1977) *Capitalism, Socialism, Democracy,* London: George Allen and Unwin.

Sen, A. K. (1985) "Social Choice and Justice," *Journal of Economic Literature,* December, 1985.

3 Frogs' legs, shared ends, and the rationality of politics*

Politics asks "What is to be done?" and proposes a profusion of answers. Philosophy, when set to contend with politics, asks "when can one sensibly say that something, or for that matter anything, is to be done?"[1] That answers to this question are neither wholly formal, logical, and semantic, nor wholly empirical and technological, but both, and more than either, is, I think, plain enough. Isaiah Berlin's grand sweep through our *Geistesgeschichte* is a salutary reminder that this was not always plain to all; that political theory is a discipline in its own right; and that it feeds on both rationality and morality.[2] In a recent essay, Vincent Descombes argues that some currents of modern philosophy have concocted poor dishes from such rich ingredients.[3] Thin gruel does not take them far: "justificationist" philosophy (*Begründungsphilosophie*) reduces politics to a problem of individual morality,[4] while the "decisionist," who will not willingly concede either rationality or morality to his political ends, leaves *partis pris*, commitments to whim and sheer accident.[5] If political philosophy had real content, Descombes claims that it could prove to any rational person that, say, being a Nazi is the same kind of gross mistake as to hold that 2 + 2 = 5. But this it patently fails to prove.[6] However, these and other intricate arguments of his seem to support no identifiable proposition about what reason does, could do, or ought to do in politics.

ARS POLITICA

Much as one may sympathize with Descombes's critique of justificationism as redundant, existentialism as absurd, and much of modern political philosophy as talk in a talking shop, he seems to put forward no recognizable thesis about the rationality or otherwise of collective agendas in general. It is not clear how he would have us use reason to judge and rank-order political alternatives. His Aristotelian call for an "architectonic" *ars politica*, taking account of the "structure of human activities" that have their due place in the *cité*[7] is discouragingly obscure. We are

* This chapter was originally published in the *Journal of Libertarian Studies* 11, 2, summer 1995, pp. 122–31. Reprinted with permission.

asked to respect the intrinsic purposes and orderly interdependence of men's social functions – a call all would no doubt agree to heed. What, however, if we do heed it? Supposedly, we are then committed to treat literally everything as political in one aspect, and also as nonpolitical in another.[8] An example is needed to make this puzzle intelligible. It is not for politics to tell the doctor who is well and who is ill (nor how ill, needing how much medical attention), but it is for politics to say how many doctors there should be.[9] Yet, this cannot be right. Politics cannot with impunity decide the number of doctors (unless by "decide" we lamely mean "respond to medical needs") without also "deciding" the number of patients, and how ill they are. If doctors are to have enough patients and patients enough doctors, either both decisions must be collective (doctors and patients matched by the same *fiat* or the same political bargain), or both must be individual (the match between them emerging from the usual supply–demand adjustment processes). One of these solutions might be thought dictatorial, the other "anti-social,"[10] but at least both provide for balance and order. A hybrid of the two is internally inconsistent, generating disorder and deficit, and no "structure based" *ars politica* can make it fit the intrinsic purpose and content of human activities in the *cité* or anywhere else.

LA PLUS BELLE FILLE ...

Much of the old confusion we deplore in political theory, and much of the fresh confusion we spread when trying to get rid of what has been spread, springs from false notions of what rationality is and what it does. Rather like the proverbial loveliest girl who can only give what she has, rationality cannot be pushed to give the meta-rational. If it is pushed, it must disappoint the pusher. It is the miscasting of it in wrong roles, rather than rationality itself, that Oakeshott really blames in his classic indictment.[11] His main charge, however, is directed at cognitive presumption, at baseless and naive claims of knowledge, understanding and foresight, in short, at the temptation to overrate the "technology" of employing reason in politics.[12] Quite apart from the technological obstacle, which I shall leave on one side, however, there is a nonempirical conundrum, which, though equally well know, is often lost sight of.

At its lowest, rationality is an attribute of such thought and speech as conforms to the conventions of logic and grammar; thus, most people would call self-contradictory statements *non sequitur* deductions, and intransitive rank-orderings irrational. More ambitiously, rationality is also a condition of the validity of the hypothetical imperatives of the form "if you want the end E, you must do, possess, employ, sacrifice the set of means m." The specification of m is the task of practical inference. If m gets E, a necessary condition of rationality is satisfied; if m gets us E

more efficiently than any other available m', a sufficient condition is satisfied. But was it rational to want E to start with?

Note in passing that while some "value" is an attribute of some end, often the end is so strongly characterized by an associated value that the two words can be used interchangeably; sometimes we "pursue a value" no less than we "seek an end," when we employ some means. "An equal distribution" is an end; it carries the value of "equality."

By positing the rationality of ends or values (*Wertrationalität*) as well as of the means, or instrumental rationality (*Zweckrationalität*), Max Weber has lent authority to the bad habit of ascribing rationality to ends (or their values). That this form of "justificationism" or "foundationism" is impossible is, by now, a commonplace: for what enables us to say that E is rational is that we have at least one good reason to seek it; this reason functions as a further end E', with respect to which E is a ("rational") means; its rationality or otherwise is a function of its instrumental role in achieving the further end E'. If the latter is rational, it is because it achieves E''. Thus, we construct a regress E, E', E'', etc. Each member of it is justified as rational by backward induction from the last member that anchors the regress. The last member, of course, is by definition a final end that escapes backward induction; nothing is left over that would permit us to say that it is rational or not. The generalized attempt to say it presupposes an infinite regress.

Any finite regress of ends is *ended* by a final *end* or value, about which it is futile to ask to what else it leads, what comes after it, for what reason we pursue it. If the question were not futile, the end would not be final, non-instrumental. Since not every reason can have a further reason, the scope of rationality in choosing actions is strictly limited.

A set of practical inferences, forming a regress, has a very revealing common feature with a Gödelian formula for a logistic calculus: no matter how all-embracing is the set of sentences it represents, by Gödel's theorem it must always contain at least one "undecidable" sentence that cannot be proven within *that* system of logistic calculus. By making the system more all-embracing, we can prove the sentence only to find that the larger system now contains another undecidable sentence that cannot be proved within *that* system, and so on *ad infinitum*. No Gödelian system can out-Gödel itself.[13] The analogy between the final end and the undecidable sentence is not perfect, but it does not need to be to illuminate our point.

TO EACH, HIS OWN VALUES

The solution seems evident enough: the regress must be cut short somewhere. If prolonging it is futile, the sooner it is cut short, the better. Yet something is amiss with this attractive conclusion. Some ends are good cutoff points, but at others basic moral conventions insist that we prolong the regress.

If the end we want is frogs' legs, the rational means is to buy some, or perhaps to go to the restaurant where they do them properly. Whether it is rational to want frogs' legs at all is a silly question that provides silly answers: we want frogs' legs (E) because we like to eat them (E'), and we like to eat them because they taste good (E''). No harm is done by cutting off this chain of boring inferences early on, and little purpose would be served by proving that the taste for frogs' legs is a rational one. Ethically, there is nothing prima facie wrong with taste-relativism that puts tastes beyond dispute.

The same can hardly be said about value-relativism. "To each, his own value" can be defended, and it is the attacks that beg ethical questions, as long as the values concerned, and the ends which carry them, are *divisible*, so that an individual can have his without another individual being obliged to share it, too. However, some values are indivisible, or holistic, and cannot be attained by anyone unless they are attained by everyone, regardless of who wants them and who does not. If I value equality, and seek by political means a less unequal distribution of wealth, status or privilege in my community, everybody must enjoy, or endure, a more equal distribution if I am to enjoy equality. Unlike frogs' legs that can but need not be shared, equality *must* be shared, and those who are made to share it involuntarily are morally entitled to a better reason than that, for me, equality is a final value.

If so, it is now incumbent upon me to build a regress. I may find instrumental reasons: equality is the efficient or perhaps the sole means to stable property relations, social peace and harmony, and these in turn are indispensable means to the good life that all sane persons must want. Or else, I could try moral arguments: it is shameful that some should have so much and others so little, and even coercion is justified to put an end to such mutual degradation.

Instrumental reasons are true or false; moral ones right or wrong. However, only instrumental reasons can be proper inferences. Only they can, subject to the availability of empirical evidence in favor of the inference, be *intersubjectively* compelling, so that anyone confronted with the same evidence must in good faith accept them as the means to agreed ends.

So far, so good. What is rational must be intersubjectively so. Let us therefore set a necessary condition of rational politics: if someone advances an end that is political in the precise sense that its achievements is more than his private affair, because it generates unwanted externalities for others, we have a moral claim to a demonstration of its rationality. This can, of course, only be done by backward induction from another, more nearly final, agreed end. Failing that, claims of rationality must be abandoned in favor of other claims, perhaps those of morality. Backward induction requires a cutoff point from which to start moving backward. Can political philosophy specify cutoff points that cannot, in good faith, be rejected? And can the specification work as a reliable filter, purifying political agendas, leaving high and dry all the presumptuous goals that cannot be intersubjectively defended?

THE ARYAN UNIVERSITY

A Nazi rector is recruiting a third-rate faculty, he suppresses unbiased research, selects students by racial criteria, and devalues the academic standing of his university. Descombes argues that, since what a good rector (or a good soldier, a good doctor, a good father) must do is defined by the intrinsic purpose of the rectorial function, a Nazi rector is a contradiction in terms. The attempt to trick a Nazi, or for that matter (as he might have added), a socialist, into self-contradiction, the way Hilary Putnam suggests one could do, by making him explicate Nazism or socialism as instrumental ends, and provide *reasons* – reasons that are bound to lose themselves in incoherence and absurdity – *why* Jews should be persecuted or the "means of production" expropriated, must fail if the Nazi or socialist, after a few feeble steps along a poorly constructed regress of instrumental ends, cuts off the intellectual torture, and seeks refuge in a nonrational final end. He can flatly state that, for him, the purity and supremacy of the Aryan "race," or the end of exploitation, are final ends that it is neither necessary nor possible to derive from something else.

Descombes holds that what the Nazi or the socialist, with no proper place and no defined function in society, can claim, the Nazi rector (or general, doctor, paterfamilias, etc.), with his tasks embedded in the "structure" of the *cité*, cannot claim. He will get caught in the self-contradiction implicit in any attempt at being both a good rector and a good Nazi. But what exactly is this double attempt he is making? Why must it exclude tradeoffs, especially when it is the very "structure" of *his* ideal Nazi or socialist *cité* that calls for them? For it is no more incumbent upon a rector, whether Nazi or not, to treat the intrinsic purposes of academic rectorship as his single categorical imperative, than it is for the general to win the battle at any cost, or for the father to always put his children first. Why cannot the rector argue that educating and training dull Aryan or working-class boys and girls, rather than clever Jewish or bourgeois ones, and directing research into patriotic and socially salutary channels, may make for a lesser university, more modest advances in knowledge, but a better, "healthier," more just society? Is not this, in a minor key, the argument underlying the "positively discriminating" admissions policies of American universities today? I happen to find such positions repugnant, and believe that they soon prove to be slippery slopes, but I do not see how they can be intersubjectively rebutted.

THE REFUGE IN THE COMMON GOOD

Since only instrumental ends are open to the critical test of rationality by practical inference, the Nazi rector and his ilk, that is all who use politics as the efficient means for imposing their values on others, will, when pressed to justify their ambition, climb along the rising regress of ever more distant ends, until they reach what is, like patriotism for Dr Johnson's scoundrel, their ultimate refuge: the common good. It is tautologically the final end of politics; nothing else can or is needed to justify it. The content and drift of political philosophy depends to no small extent on whether it admits the concept of the common good, or rules it out as gobbledygook.

When trying to decide which it is to be, we are wrestling with what seems to me to be several distinct versions of what the concept might be intended to mean. I could identify at least three; none of these is rational or irrational. None, however, is totally impervious to the acid of analytical reasoning.

By the first concept, which could best be labeled mystical, the common good is not the good of all, nor anybody's in particular: it is genuinely nonderivative. It need neither be good *for*, nor desired *by*, any individual, past, present, or future. Its goodness, independent as it is from any-body's prudential interest, "subjective" preference, or right, is recognized directly, without reference to empirical evidence; it is found by cognitivist meta-ethics. The concept is liable to turn up in some religious or millen-arian guise. A strongly held common faith, a shared millenarian vision, may inspire a unique (but hardly a *complete*) view of the common good. Cognitive efforts to arrive at moral truths are quite unlikely to do so in a world where men differ and their interests conflict. Any unique view they may produce is liable to be incomplete, partial, pronouncing only on the few nonconflictual features of alternative states of affairs.

My second version is communitarian. It postulates a good state of affairs that is good *for*, in the interest of, or desired by, some community, without this postulate having to be substantiated by reference to its members. It is not subject to any unanimity or even majority test.[14] Instead, it is arrived at by treating the community as an indivisible holistic entity, as if it had a unitary personality, disposing of the means possessed by its members, having its proper will and interests, and engaging in practical reasoning to fit means to ends rationally. This "as if" manner of defining the common good is, in fact, always somebody's reading of the community's putative mind. The reading will rely on the reader's privi-leged insight into the community's history, culture, and the future it can at least partly shape by its own will. Needless to say, no two readings of this kind need coincide.

The third possible concept is aggregative, a sum composed of individual components, and called the *sum* of the good of some polity's members, *hence* the common good. Since individual members are in principle capable of saying, or otherwise revealing, what they consider good and better (both for themselves and, if they care, for others), they can provide some factual evidence to support the identification of a state of affairs as the common good. The evidence can ostensibly be made to go even further, and serve to establish rank-orderings of states of good, better, etc. for the polity, the *cité* "as a whole." Thus, the aggregative version has the singular distinction of claiming to describe, to find a fact. At least implicitly, it aspires to falsifiability.

However, for aggregation, the components must be both commensurate (so that anyone can tell whether my good is greater, as great as, or lesser than yours), and their differences must be cardinally measurable (so that anyone can tell *by how much* my good is greater than yours). There is no basis for supposing either to be the case. The technical literature has heavily labored the second of the two, although the first is both logically prior to it and morally far more fundamental. Yet unless both suppositions are made, that is unless comparisons are both interpersonal and cardinal, individuals' orderings cannot be added together to produce one complete common ("social") ordering. "Starting with Arrow's famous impossibility theorem, authors have formulated seemingly reasonable conditions that a preference aggregation procedure ought to satisfy, and then proved that the conditions are logically inconsistent."[15] No matter whether individuals order states of affairs by preference, prudential interest, or moral worth, the same comparability conditions apply throughout, and derivation of the common good by aggregations of individual orderings remains an impossible, or rather a nonsensical exercise. If a "social" ordering, putatively identifying the common good, is nonetheless produced, it is necessarily the product, not of arithmetic exploits, but of a set of value judgments concerning the relative weights deserved by individual orderings.

It is no use protesting that no such value judgments are in effect carried out, for whether they are explicit or implicit, they are entailed in the common ordering. Any political decision that, by invoking the common good, overrides the will and wishes of some to satisfy others, is the execution of a value judgment about individual wills and wishes. The more vulgar kinds of claims about the common good, of course, often masquerade as truth-claims. However, they cannot describe. They can only express preferences. They are unfalsifiable, forever bound to remain my say-so against your say-so.

Needless to say, value judgments as such are not disreputable. What is disreputable is to dress them up as findings of fact, for which evidence could in principle be found, or (as the classical utilitarians imagined) as the products of rational thought, deduced from self-evident propositions.[16] It is perfectly possible for me to share your value judgments, but it is never intersubjectively compelling for you to share mine, never a matter of straight practical inference, and never a bow to the rules of rationality. Only some partial orderings, capable of withstanding the Paretian test, get by without my say-so having to prevail over yours.

WHAT IS NOT TO BE DONE, NOR SAID

What is left for political philosophy "rationally" to say about what is to be done? Very little, it would seem. Means are suitable subjects for rational examination, once the ends are given. But *political* ends are either means in disguise, and presuppose other tacit ends looming beyond them, or they collapse into the common good; yet all versions of the common good we can easily identify raise the suspicion that nothing can be said about them that could survive intersubjectively.

A good deal, however, is left to be said about what is *not* to be done, and said, and why. Nine-tenths of practical politics is the making of nonunanimous decisions by some, which hurt others. Do we really want such decisions imposed as rational means to ends that are ultimately neither rational nor irrational, and must be posited by brazen assertion, mystical communion with the good, or occult value-comparisons between persons? Pareto-optimal outcomes offer a minimal morally legitimate space for a minimal state, and no more. Surely, it tells something about the ontology of politics that logic, morality, or both lend themselves so much better to condemning political action than to defending its legitimacy.

NOTES

1 On this loose definition, ethics, social choice theory, welfare economics, jurisprudence, and bits of game theory will all, at one time or another, turn out to be vital parts of political philosophy. I adopt the definition advisedly, to produce this broad result.
2 Isaiah Berlin, "La théorie politique existe-t-elle?" *Revue Française de Science Politique*, 11, 1961, reproduced in Isaiah Berlin, *Concepts and Categories*, London: The Hogarth Press, 1978.
3 Vincent Descombes, "Philosophie du jugement politique," *La Pensée Politique*, vol. 2, Paris, Gallimard le Seuil, 1995.
4 Ibid., p. 156.
5 Ibid., p. 138.
6 Ibid., p. 138.
7 Ibid., p. 154.
8 Ibid., pp. 152–4.
9 Ibid.
10 Note that neither solution need be wholly pure: their logic admits an alien element. In the "dictatorial" solution, the rich may buy themselves more medical care than is allocated by the dictator. In the "emergent" (market) solution, the charitable rich may buy (and the uncharitable made to buy) more medical attention for the poor than the latter could afford. These kinds of intrusions are impurities in an otherwise consistent system. That the number

and gravity of illnesses should be decided by doctors in one forum, the number of doctors in another, would be systemic inconsistency.

11 M. Oakeshott, *Rationalism in Politics*, London: Methuen & Co., 1962.

12 Karl Popper believed that the risk of doing so could be greatly reduced, and the technology itself developed and confirmed, by "piecemeal social engineering" (Popper, *The Open Society*, 1961 III.21, 1962, II). By piecemeal, he did *not* mean small scale (" ... we have put no limits to the scope of the piecemeal approach," 1961, p. 68). Piecemeal, for him, was not the opposite of large scale, but of utopian or holistic. Like the proof of the pudding, the test of holistic engineering was that " ... it turns out to be impossible" (ibid.). Piecemeal, then, is what is possible and works, and we shall know that our social engineering was piecemeal when we see that it has worked.

13 J. R. Lucas, *The Freedom of the Will*, Oxford: The Clarendon Press, 1970, pp. 524–6.

14 Strictly, of course, unlike unanimity, a "majority test" tests not what the community does or does not deem good. At best, it only tests what a majority within it deem good. Moreover, as has been known since Condorcet, majority tests are liable to generate self-contradictory, incoherent results when used to order more than two alternatives as good, better, best – which is hardly apt to enhance our respect for the test.

15 A. Hylland, "Subjective Interpersonal Comparison," in J. Elster and J. E. Roemer, eds, *Interpersonal Comparisons of Well-Being*, Cambridge: Cambridge University Press, 1991, p. 336.

16 The "diminishing marginal utility of income" was long treated as either self-evident, or requiring only minimal psychological assumptions supported by introspection. Interestingly, the maximin strategy rational individuals in the "original position" are predicted by the anti-utilitarian Rawls to adopt presupposes the same kind of psychological disposition. It is tantamount to a "diminishing marginal importance of primary goods," over and above some minimum. Unsurprisingly, it generates the same kind of egalitarian norm, a social "ought" deduced from a psychological "is."

4 Values and the social order[*]

FROM VALUE TO RATIONAL ACTION

The basic building block of social theory is practical inference, the logical relation we consciously refer to for understanding, explaining, and predicting human action. Aristotle introduced practical inference as a way of linking the good or desirable to the action that was good, right. Recent thought treats it as the appropriate form of reasoning from means to ends, goals.[1] Ends are broadly characterized by values, which must be, to put it at its lowest, one of the variables upon which the desiredness or goodness of ends depends. The notion that actions – or, more precisely, choices among feasible actions – are purposive is implicit in such reasoning, as is the possibility of using its premises, if sufficiently specified, for telling whether an action that applied some means to some end was rationally chosen or not, or how strong, how demanding a criterion of rationality it satisfied. Significantly, Anscombe (Anscombe, 1957) regards calculation as an integral element of practical reasoning. It would help clarify further thought if "choosing" an alternative were distinguished from the mere "taking" of it – a distinction that depends on the element of calculation and that revealed preference and empiricism do not find congenial.

Compared with practical inference, which can yield causal theories, even amply confirmed hypotheses of correlations, interdependencies, implicit functions lack ambition. They amount to potential evidence that can underpin social theory, but they do not constitute social theory. In this sense, the narrowly positivist tradition that is reflected in much of macroeconomics and macroeconometrics, and in structuralist and functionalist sociology, is a negation of such theory. Its self-righteous refusal to "look inside people's heads" and to see human choices as the calculated fitting of means to ends allows it to produce a range of things from forecasting models to mere strings of words, but precludes it from providing explanations.

* This chapter first appeared in *Values and the Social Order*, G. Radnitzky and H. Bouillon (eds) (1995), vol. 1, Aldershot: Ashgate. Reprinted with permission.

Unlike the physical sciences, inference presupposing purposiveness is proper to the study of reasoning beings and cannot be avoided without inordinate loss of content.

This, it seems to me, is what gives ends, and the values they carry, a special role in the social sciences. It is all very well "to take them as given," but if they are, can they avoid being unintelligible? – and is not the explanation of actions built on them cut short before it starts being interesting? An end presumably has attributes – properties that make it sensible for people to apply means in order to attain them. These attributes, some or all of which we may consider to be "values" serve as motives; in being imputed to an end, they are capable of qualifying the action aimed at the end as rational or not. Value, in this very broad sense, is an indefinite, open-ended, almost inchoate concept. It is not at all obvious that we can do better by treating it as referring to a narrower, closed class of "higher" moral attributes. In the present chapter, I will treat values both as moral reasons furnishing norms for conduct that could not be explained by individual advantage (or, as it is sometimes put, by individual utility-maximization) and as prudential reasons furnishing the substantive content of individual advantage.

Very useful work has been and will yet be done within the "scarce means to given ends" paradigm. In addition, this tradition imposes salutary mental discipline, of which there is never too much around. But it is patently limited, and the clear distinction it promises between the positive and the normative is somewhat fictitious. Who has "given" the ends? – how do we know that he has? – and if he did, did he do so for a reason? It is not always possible or desirable to shut out questions of this kind. However, if they do get asked – and social-choice theory, political philosophy, and history must now and again ask them, even if many branches of economics can get by without them – we find ourselves studying ends. The iron curtain between "is" and "ought" may then turn out to be more permeable than it looks from afar.

For if we put ends, their values, and the side constraints of action within the explanadum rather than outside it, the very distinction between ends and means may start looking spurious, or at least arbitrary, a matter of opportunistic convention. The choice of means may or may not be rational, explicable with respect to some end; but need one, or can one always, stop at the point where this end *ends*? It is always possible to go one step further and similarly explain, or fail to explain, the choice of the end in question. It can always be shown, by practical inference, to be the means to a "further" end, and that end, in turn, can likewise be unmasked to reveal its nature as a means to yet another, further end, and so on.

Either we face an infinite regress, a sort of endless spiral, or we finally run up against an end which, despite all our hermenuetic ingenuity, looks genuinely inexplicable, noninstrumental, valuable per se and hence "final." There is no third alternative, no "middle." But the two alternatives, the instrumental and the final, are not "out there" in the world of ascertainable facts, nor are they merely the consequences of our definitions. They are, to all intents and purposes, two opposing subjective judgments reached on grounds another reasonable person may but need not share. An end is final when we cannot plausibly think of another end, or an associated value, that would explain why it is chosen. But when do we give up trying?

Take the ends that are almost universally treated as noninstrumental, such as well-being, happiness, fulfillment, goodness, or (in another register) eternal salvation – whether our own or that of loved ones (including, for the more fierce kind of altruist, all humanity). If we find it hard to think of plausible reasons why well-being should be desired, happiness is worth pursuing, and goodness is an attribute of preferable states of affairs, we effectively sentence them to be dismissed as tautologies. The very attempt to explain them is fatuous. Happiness makes happy, goodness is preferred to badness, satisfaction satisfies. Nothing more informative can be said. On the other hand, if we persevere and look around for introspective evidence or other clues, we may decide that well-being is the means enabling us to transcend subsistence and address "higher-order wants;" fulfillment is the proper use of our faculties leading to their development, while eternal salvation is our contribution to God's purpose. Thus we provide at least verbal explications, albeit of disputable content, that transform final ends into instrumental ones. The exercise can go on and on until our patience is exhausted. The stop is where we put it.

What is true of "final" ends in this context seems to me to be true of unexplained, exogenously "given" constraints. It may well be just a matter of judgment whether to treat laws, rights, rules, and even perhaps certain physical features of the social landscape as being themselves "chosen" in view of their instrumental character. Endogenous and exogenous are separated by the scope of the inquiry. Tastes, final ends, unexplained values, exogenous institutional constraints begin where our inquiry stops, and not the other way around.

The stop may, of course, be called at any point in the chain, but some points are more convenient than others. Economics, in particular, has requirements that have given rise to two widely adopted, classic stopping points. One is profit in the theory of producers' behavior. It is the ultimate maximand, the final "value" for the purposes of the theory. This is no denial of the plausible supposition that the firm maximizes profit because its owners want the profit *for* something that is even more "final." But that is no longer within the theory; it is another story. The other classic stopping point is the preference-ordering of final consumption goods in value theory, though the ordering is avowedly wide-open to further analysis in terms of diverse "wants," physical and psychological dispo-sitions, from which the preferences for diverse goods could be derived.

Stopping points are used willy-nilly in any social theory that links ends and means. But when its scope is outside economics in the narrow sense, it is no longer very obvious where they can most conveniently be put. The question of their suitable place opens up deep divisions. One is between individualist and holist explanations, individual and collective values. The other is between cognitivist and noncognitivist meta-ethics. Which side of such divisions we come down on has consequences for the way we make sense of social orders, and the kind of order we would recommend. Alternatively, our preconceptions about the right sort of order may lead us to take one side or the other – for only by taking the "right" side can we render values, principles, and rules consistent with the ideology or *Weltanschauung* within which we feel comfortable. Either way, the stopping point matters.

COGNITIVE VALUES, REVEALED PREFERENCES

Holists and individualists are at daggers drawn as if the heresy of the ones were a serious threat to the faith practiced by the others. Much of this hostility seems overdone. The reciprocal threat is real in some respects only, and those are mostly confined to two fields. One is what Popper calls "historicism," and that also extends to "organicism," the other is what I would call value-holism. Outside these, ecumenism would be quite safe. Let me try and suggest the area of legitimate coexistence.

James Coleman, a sociologist with faultless methodological individualist credentials, observes a swarm of gnats made up of identifiable individual gnats and finds that it is acting as if it were a single entity directed by its own goals. He recommends treating it as an actor called a swarm.[2] It is quite conceivable that, with some knowledge of entomology, one could explain, by reference to the motives and opportunities of individual gnats, why the swarm darts this way or that, yet still holds together. But there would be little point in making the effort. The gnats are all the same; their roles are undifferentiated; and probably nothing would be gained or lost by making the methodological individualist hypothesis that they interact by each doing what it deems best on the assumption that the others will be doing what is best for them.[3] Here, holism is a handy shortcut. Whether such a thing as a swarm – or "society," "state," "com-munity," and other notorious holistic terms – "really" exists or, as Hayek insists, is a mere mental model (Hayek, 1952, p. 56) is, as far as I can see, beside the point. The words neither can nor need be avoided.

The mutual threat does not reside in holistic concepts, but in the use to which they are put in deciding whether the whole is or is not more than the sum of its parts. For individualists, it is not: they have Occam on their side. For holists, it is: they can invoke Aquinas. If it is, then certain theories about certain composite entities – such as the "large group," sellers and buyers interacting through a market, society, the race – can be adequate only if they cannot be decomposed, without leaving any residue, into theories about the actions of the individual members of the entity in question. Stating it the other way around: in the holist tradition, a theory about individuals as members of multiperson entities – no matter how carefully it differentiates between them by type, class, or role and however subtly it grasps their interdependence – will still fail to be a social theory worthy of the name. For holists, a theory about society built from the assumptions of methodological individualism can only be right by sheer, statistically improbable accident.

However, a holistic explanation of the "actions" (if one may call them that) of society must proceed by practical inference no less than the methodological individualist one, or it will describe but fail to explain. For, to be true to itself, it must maintain that its subject is a single actor in a more than metaphorical sense. Holist theory must not damage itself by claiming that the single actor in question is mindlessly staggering around the social scene, weaving patterns whose regularities are wholly independent of its motives, or that it has none. (Needless to say, if there are no regularities, there is no theory.) If its actions are purposive, they must be serving ends whose selection is, in some sense, instrumentally determined and is intelligible in terms of the values grafted on the ends. The holistic actor, in other words, has holistic values.

Now this need not be understood as a separate, unconnected value system wholly unrelated to individual values. On the contrary, the holistic actor is supposed to be motivated by values that many individuals also share. Communitarians and socialists, many of whom are holists though not many recognize it, do not profess ends that liberal individualists must reject or regard as bereft of value. If anything, it is the price communitarians and socialists would be willing to pay, and the deontological constraints they would transgress for these ends, which are unacceptable to the opposite camp, and no doubt vice versa.

If it nevertheless makes sense to call certain values that both holists and individualists profess "holistic," it is because these are attributes of ends no one can attain for himself alone. He can aim at them only by seeking either to persuade others in his group to aim at them too, or to have them somehow imposed on others in his group. Holistic values are indivisible:[4] an individual cannot finely regulate the "amount" he obtains by marginal adjustments in the "quantity" of means he devotes to them. If he reaches a holistic value, many others – typically all members of a compound entity – must reach it too, and ordinarily he cannot have more of it without many other people, too, having more of it, though not necessarily in the same proportions.

The disparate examples of holistic values that spring to mind add up to the daily bread of a community's politics. No one can shut sex-shops and sweep pornography from the streets, clean up corruption, restore the cathedral, elect a government of ecologists, nourish artistic creation, give the young access only to what is fit for them, and so forth, unless he can do it for the whole neighborhood, the town, the entire society. It is likewise impossible to have economic growth, the promotion of "strategic technologies," "industrial policy," "fair trade," and "stability" for any single individual unless all have it (whatever that means), whether they like these things or not and whether they gain or lose from them. Values attached to distributions, such as social justice, solidarity, or equality, are by definition holistic in that they cannot be enjoyed by one without being chosen for some whole, the distributive base over which the good to be distributed is reshuffled, churned into the requisite pattern.

In holistic parlance, it is the common good, the public interest, the public weal that require us to ban drugs and pornography, to promote high culture over low, to have virtue prevail, to plan the economy rationally, to bring about equality. Two possible interpretations can be read into such expressions. Under one, the values in question are good without having to be good for any one individual (they may be, but that is beside the point).[5] Their goodness is a matter of truth or falsehood; it is possible intersubjectively to decide which it is (a job often assigned to the "impartial observer"). Here, we inhabit the realm of cognitive meta-ethics,[6] in company with Aristotle and Aquinas, but also, in a less appealing tradition, with Bentham. It is worth remarking that Bentham first formulated his central proposition of utilitarian ethics in a manner independent of distributive considerations and added an egalitarian requirement in a later version, almost as an afterthought (Schwartz, 1986, pp. 95–6). This world is now peopled by closet-cognitivist utilitarians, from Pigou to Hare, Sen and Harsanyi, who believe that the good of several individuals can somehow or other be integrated (with due regard for algebraic sign) into a kind of whole and that such wholes can themselves be quantitatively compared with one another.

The other interpretation is basically noncognitivist, and therefore less demanding, more innocuous, but only at first sight – for in due course it leads to the same deep cognitivist trap: how do we know that the community wants a reign of virtue, a national industrial policy, compulsory health insurance, progressive taxation, subsidized opera, and folk dancing? The noncognitivist answer is that we learn it, so to speak, from the horse's mouth: it periodically reveals its preferences for these values through the political process, by some recognized method of social choice, for example, by voting for the corresponding programs. What better evidence is there that the public wants something than that it says so?

SOCIAL CHOICE: "NATURAL" OR RULE BASED

Voting, of course, is neither the only nor the most obvious, normal, "natural" method for reaching collective decisions. In antiquity, unanimous agreement preceded by persuasive oratory was the norm, and in many tribal societies, as well as in countless committee, jury and board meetings of our own age, this norm is still sought after, though not always with complete success. Early Roman law laid down (albeit only with regard to water rights) that *"quod omnes tangit ab omnibus approbetur"* ("that which affects all must be approved by all"); the principle was taken up in a wider context in the Justinian code and came to be widely applied in medieval Church government. The Emperor Frederick II invoked it, as did Edward I in summoning Parliament; it was frequently restated in the fourteenth and fifteenth centuries in many countries from England to Hungary by learned authorities, including Occam (Guénée, 1985, pp. 173–4). That decisions favored by members of a majority should be binding on a dissenting minority was an innovation that crept in, almost surreptitiously, through Church institutions. Perhaps its first important appearance was in the government of the mendicant orders in the thirteenth century (Guénée, 1985, p. 182), and the conciliar movement later practiced the method when all else failed. Subsequently, it spread from clerical to lay government. It is perhaps not flippant to remark that mendicant friars are quintessentially equal, and Church government is meant to be strictly nonviolent – two elements that go some way toward explaining why majority rule originated where it did.

The materially stronger part of any group can always make the weaker part agree to its decisions by beating it into submission. Since applying violence is costly, as is resistance to it, both parties are better off if the weaker part submits before violence is used against it. However, the weaker part would be even better off if it had neither to submit nor to resist violence. It may therefore be tempted, by a show of determination, to deter violence altogether and avoid the collective decision it dislikes. It could achieve this by inducing the stronger part into thinking that the cost of subjecting the weaker part by violence would be too high and exceed the benefit of the collective decision sought. This may be either facilitated or hindered (it is impossible to say which a priori) if neither party knows even approximately which is stronger, which weaker. In any event, there is obvious room for precommitment strategies, reputation building, bluff and counter-bluff, and the calling of bluffs by both parties. Even in the absence of miscalculation, violence may not be avoided, though there is clearly a good deal of historical evidence that often it can be. Consequently, if such situations are recurrent, this group may reach a cooperative solution by convention: all concerned may – tacitly or otherwise – agree in advance that the proposal of the stronger-looking part is to be adopted by both parts. Like in chess, where analysis of an unfinished game can induce a player to resign without playing it out, the parties in the collective decision problem may assess the forces ranged on either side, and without further pain and strain declare the question resolved in favor of the stronger force.

This would be the "natural" solution to non-unanimity. More precisely, it would be a first-order "natural" solution, supplemented by a second-order convention of nonviolence. The latter could also arise "naturally." (It is not wholly fanciful to suggest that this is what must be going on under the surface in cases of unanimity in well-run committees, where, after some preliminary debate serving to reveal the force of opposing positions, questions are resolved without voting. Those who find themselves on what looks like the weaker side may prefer not to manifest pointless dissent.) Under this solution, land (hence men at arms) in earlier times, economic influence and possibly also the means of mass persuasion in our own age, would have the decisive power over collective decisions and would largely determine the "holistic values" the community declared to favor and, by adopting the corresponding policies and laws, caused to prevail.

It is crossing the Rubicon to move away from an assessment of the opposing *powers and interests* in kind and count numbers of *votes* instead. In contrast to what I characterized as the natural solution, whether enriched by a violence-avoiding convention or not, this solution is an artificial one. It deliberately abstracts from all the naturally occurring elements of a decision problem bar two: the alternatives put up for question and the number of votes cast for each. Once the principle of simply adding up votes regardless of who cast them and regardless also of the intensity of preference or the weight of concern that causes each to be cast, has been agreed upon, the democratic die is cast as well. Minority rule is impossible, since within each electorate more than one minority could be constituted; hence one minority alone could not be decisive. Majority rule alone is possible; within it, there is a choice between qualified and simple majority. However, the smaller is the majority – hence the larger the minority – the larger is (all other things being equal) the majority's benefit from a collective decision, since the larger is the cost that can be imposed on the minority. This is patently the case in simple zero-sum redistributive decisions By maximizing the losing minority, the winning majority can maximize its redistributive gain. The same is true of positive-sum decisions that nevertheless have some redistributive character.

This being the case, any collective-decision rule requiring some qualified majority is vulnerable to erosion. Within any qualified majority, there is a smaller one that has a clear interest to decrease the winning majority and increase the losing minority. The potential gain from doing so can be profitably invested in the effort to change the decision rule accordingly, provided a residual gain is left over. Any decision rule is self-referring (whether de jure or only de facto), capable of being used for changing it. If the rule is that two voters can block a change[7] in the rule, it can be changed by overcompensating one of them for the loss he would suffer from the change. However, the change permits despoiling two; from the proceeds, it is necessarily possible to overcompensate one.

What is true of a blocking minority of two is obviously true of any larger number; the marginal blocking voter can always be overcompensated from the loss to be imposed on the extra-marginal ones. Equilibrium, in the sense of a decision rule that cannot be profitably changed, is reached where the potential gain of the winning majority is at a maximum, i.e., under simple majority rule. This is probably the underlying reason why the historical evolution of democracy has clearly been directed towards this terminal state and why simple majority rule is widely considered to be more "democratic" than any rule requiring a larger majority or permitting a smaller blocking minority.

Counting every vote as one and no more than one (equivalent to Arrow's Anonymity axiom) is one of the conditions giving rise to the well-known paradox of social choice, namely, that a social-choice rule incorporating this and a few other minimally democratic requirements is unable to order all feasible social states of affairs – "holistic ends" – in a coherent, nonself-contradictory manner. A rational, nonself-contradictory ordering will obtain if individual votes, i.e., expressions of preferences for alternative states of affairs, are weighted by the intensity of preference, interest concern of each particular voter. One-man-one-vote, however, is designed to conceal intensity. Its effect is to express ordinal and to suppress cardinal preference: Information about "how much better" the voter likes the outcome he votes for fails to transpire.

It is ironical that such suppression is held to be a virtue,[8] and the "natural" solution to the social-choice paradox is categorically rejected in democratic theory, which insists that letting some votes have more influence on the result than others would violate an important moral principle, equality. (We should pause to note that what it would violate is one possible version of equality. One can formulate other, equally plausible equality axioms that would, on the contrary, require giving some people more votes than to others, depending on the person or the question or to be decided, or both.)

The upshot is that the ordinal preferences of different individuals in a community, expressed as votes, are added together to produce one whole. This whole is then taken to have expressed society's choice. However, the aggregation involved in this procedure is no less dubious than in the consequentialist derivation of the common good from individual goods in the Benthamite tradition, touched upon in the second section of this chapter, which consists of adding up different individuals' utilities to arrive at "total utility," the "solution of the social welfare function." Arguably, both interpersonal utility-aggregation and vote-aggregation suffer from the same defect. Both propose to perform impossible arithmetic operations for the sake of justifying a holistic result. Justification is allegedly found in pretending that the result is in fact the compound sum of individual components. The latter have empirical, intersubjectively testable existence – they are "real" and so is their sum.

Democrats, and utilitarians, may concede that it is impossible to add up, or to deduct from each other, heterogeneous quantities, say plums and walnuts. Yet they might defend voting, as well as consequentialist reasoning, to find the common good, the public interest, on the grounds that what is heterogeneous at one level is homogeneous on the next higher one. On that higher level, so many plums and so many walnuts are, all together, so many pieces of fruit, to be counted, added, or subtracted as such, and the same is true of the preferences and interests of different individuals. For all people are homogeneous *as people*, and so are their preferences, ends, values, regardless of who, among equals, holds each. It is of the essence of democratic ethics not to recognize differences of subject or object among them. For democrats, the commensurability of different persons' preferences must be "analytic," a consequence of their equal worth,[9] and the legitimacy of their aggregation is nothing more than a necessary truth that follows from the definition of democracy. For this purpose, the right definition is that it is a collective-decision procedure designed to give each participant as much influence on the outcome as to every other.

This, of course, is an irrefutable defense resting on a quasi-tautology. Votes can be added up because they are homogeneous because they are equal because the voters are equal. The charge of value holism, or the graver charge of smuggling in a whole under the innocuous pretense that it is really only the sum of its parts, in fact amounts to a charge that democracy is not a satisfactory normative political theory. Underneath Arrow's paradox lurk morally and even prudentially[10] more substantial faults.

Such a finding, were it to be sustained, does not mean that any other theory is better. In the nature of the case, any argument in favor of one is forever bound to be inconclusive. Objections of comparable force can be marshaled against any normative political theory intended to justify any procedural – though perhaps not any substantive – rule for making collective decisions. Selecting one looks inherently, inescapably relativist.

Far from deflating any hope one may attach to thinking about alternative social orders, this conclusion is hopeful (in a manner of speaking). It points us toward the merits of what I have elsewhere called a "strict liberal" minimalist position. There is manifestly a great deal that is wrong with social choice as such. Whichever way it is reached, "democratically" or otherwise, there is a strong presumption that it wrongs some. The vague moral notion that wronging some is nevertheless right, or is doing good "on balanced," can only be supported by affirmation; no other support is possible. The real normative task of political theory is to delineate the category of social choices that are justified by their substantive *content*, provided there is any, if they cannot be justified by the *manner* in which they are reached.

Since nonunanimous social choice *eo ipso* imposes "dominated" choices on some part of the community, the problem is hardly procedural – *how* to impose such choices? – but substantive – *which ones* may legitimately be imposed?

From here, there is an obvious follow-up. How to avoid making all the other decisions that are perhaps not legitimate but ready at hand, temptingly available – especially as it is in the immediate interest of one half of society to impose them on the other half? If the odds are against good decisions, should one not seek above all to make *fewer* ones, as a kind of stochastic strategy of minimizing wrong?

The scope for legitimate collective choices may well be quite narrow. Deontological rules to keep the use of political power within limits that are correspondingly narrow would be well worth devising, though respect for them would be constantly threatened by the strong temptations to use politics broadly rather than narrowly, maximally rather than minimally.

RULES INFLUENCE OUTCOMES

Making prior consent to nonunanimous decisions, subject only to the satisfaction of procedural conditions, is obviously not neutral for the substantive content of the decisions that are likely to be taken by this procedure. On the contrary, perhaps nothing is more decisive in shaping the resulting social order. It will be a redistributive order.

Taken literally,[11] majority rule elevated to a sufficient condition for social choice – as is suggested by the ideas of popular sovereignty or the supremacy of parliament – transforms politics into a three-person "distribution game." In this game, the total payoff is the sum of what the three players initially possess. If any two can agree on any distribution of the total among the three, it shall be effected. Hence a majority coalition of two can, by agreeing, dispossess the third. Once the coalition of two has taken all from the third, it becomes vulnerable to a split. Whichever way the coalition members shared the payoff, the dispossessed minority can in the next game tempt one member of the majority to desert, form a new coalition, and agree on a new sharing at the expense of the deserted member of the previous coalition. The poorest player can always destroy an existing coalition, because he can always offer one of its rich members a large enough share of the possessions of the other rich member to make both the former and himself better off. The latter, now that he is dispossessed and poor, can in his turn split and destroy the new coalition by employing against it the same bribing strategy. Depending on the bargaining solution, redistribution may take place, not from the richest to the poor, but from the richest to the middling rich and only marginally to the poor.

The game can be repeated indefinitely, the role of dispossessed going round cyclically.

However, this is an unstable result. It can be stabilized in various ways, one of which is to enforce an agreement on an egalitarian distribution. Such an agreement, however, is vulnerable to defection in the same way as any other distributive one, because under the given procedural rule, any two players can change it in their own favor by ganging up on the third. Repeated experience of cyclical dispossession, with the sum of the supergame being nil or, in effect, negative – since the cyclical movement must have some negative utility – might then teach the parties to prefer the stability of egalitarianism and render the agreement self-enforcing.

A more likely – and life-like – noncyclical solution might arise if one player was, for practical purposes, a goose laying golden eggs in each game. This player would find herself the permanent loser, the others dispossessing her in each game of some freshly laid eggs, leaving her just enough to go on laying in the next game, and perpetuating the same redistributive solution.

The "golden egg" version serves, in fact, as the common nucleus of positive theories of redistribution. In such theories, some part of society uses a (procedural) decision rule to gain income, wealth, or opportunity at the expense of another part. This may happen through the manner of raising revenue – shaping the pattern of taxes – or through expenditure – transfers and public goods targeted at particular classes of the population – or nonbudgetary reallocations of rights and privileges – affirmative action, restrictions on the freedom of contract including price and rent controls, etc. – or through combinations of these methods. Some theories assume that redistribution, whatever else it is designed to do, must redistribute from rich to poor; redistribution within income categories, from rich to rich and from poor to poor, is often overlooked. Some of the most interesting results, however, are produced by analyzing this type of redistribution; public-choice theory has produced many such.

Further insight into the nature of redistributive social orders is gained when to the interpersonal dimension an intertemporal one is added. A coalition satisfying the procedural-decision rule can redistribute income in its favor at the expense of some – perhaps unspecified – part of the next generation, by failing to match public expenditure with revenue. There are macroeconomic limits to how far this can go, but – as the persistent large deficits of such countries as Greece, Italy, Belgium, or the United States show – they are remarkably nonstringent. Microeconomics, that is, ordinary utility-maximizing behavior, is supposed to set limits, too; for the utility of present income must be equated, at the margin, to the utility of the present value of future income. Government dis-saving crowds out private capital formation, hence reduces future income. At some point, the gain of present income by way of more government services and public goods, transfers, or lower taxes is offset by the loss of future income due to lack of investment. This limit, however, is lifted if enough people fail to think of their descendants, or feel no concern for their material welfare.[12] Those who have no descendants or who feel only a little concern for them, even if they were not the majority, can provide a sufficient building block for the formation of a coalition that will redistribute intertemporally, for prima facie they can, inside the coalition, compensate their partners with interpersonal gains in exchange for getting their way with intertemporal ones. A deficit will then be run even if most voters think that, taking their concern for their descendants into account, they would be better off with a balanced budget.

A case can be made that a pure, substantively unrestricted majoritarian democracy would end up by "churning," taking much – and, in the limit, all – of everyone's income under one set of redistributive measures and simultaneously returning the same income to everyone under a different set of measures, whether in money or in kind. Some would be making (small) gains, others (small) losses, most of the gain being purely "optical," illusory, self-deceiving, owing to particular benefits of redistribution being more concentrated and conspicuous than its general costs – a factor amply explored in the public-choice literature. Basically, most people would be paying for most of their own redistributive benefits, but not all would realize that this was the case.

It is perhaps easier to conceive of this scenario than of its contrary, namely, that a society unhampered by restrictions on its democratic decision-making power will, for utility-maximizing reasons, endogenously generate a political self-denying ordinance, a barrier to redistribution (Bouillon, 1991). Here, the basic argument is that, if progressively more radical redistribution earns for the winning coalition a progressively larger slice of a steadily diminishing pie, its slice would reach some maximum and then start to decrease well short of the point where redistribution is transformed into a frenzy of unrestrained and destructive churning. Hence, in order to maximize its slice, the winning coalition would seek to moderate redistribution both from rich to poor,[13] majority rule, and between special interests within the rich and within the poor.

One of the reasons why it is difficult to put one's trust in an endogenous barrier of this kind is that the choice that has to be postulated between a given slice of a large pie and the larger slice of a smaller pie cannot be made by any one individual for himself. It is only intelligible through practical inference of the holistic kind; the winning coalition as such must exercise restraint on behalf of its members. This is running the risk of committing a "fallacy of composition." We see that it is in the interests of a holistic entity that restraint be exercised; but can we translate this into the interests of the individuals who must each decide to vote accordingly? It is true for the holistic entity that it would maximize its ends by adopting the means of a barrier; but why is it true of any particular individual who makes the effective choice? There is no direct passage from such global magnitudes as the economy-wide elasticity of work effort with respect to the income tax rate or of risk-taking with respect to the capital gains tax rate, to the relevant practical reasoning of each individual who matches his "means" – the political support he can swing behind a particular redistributive programme – to his "ends," post-tax real income and the nonbudgetary advantages he thinks he can derive from redistributive policies, such as price controls regulation of various kinds, and "rents." It is implausible to present the representative individual as succeeding correctly to balance, at the point of marginal equivalence, his putative redistributive gains against his personal share in the loss of national income due to redistribution.

An endogenous, utility-inspired barrier would be more likely to spring up, in rather a jack-in-the-box fashion, after things have gone a long way past any maximum for the winning coalition – never mind the median voter who can always find compensation *within* the coalition. When a large mass of voters finally turns round and comes to blame redistribution and all its works for the palpable damage it has done to the economic environment and its moral underpinnings, there may be a wholesale backlash that has nothing marginal about it, as happened in recent years in England (1979), the United States (1980), and Sweden (1991). By that time however, redistribution had long overshot the theoretical equilibrium. The problems involved in an attempted pull-back, a "rolling back" of the size of government and the share of public expenditure are well known, as are the reasons that cause redistributive coalitions fairly promptly to re-form and start all over again. The upshot is, in all probability, a continuing historical pattern, made up of a forward creep of ever more complex, ever less transparent redistribution periodically pulled up short by painful, wrenching conservative stops.

SOCIAL CHOICE MADE "TOO EASY"

Getting a purely procedural social-choice rule established is rather like eating the fruit from the tree of knowledge. It is fateful knowledge that cannot be unlearned. Using the knowledge is the sin of one part of society, as it imposes its ends on the rest freely, costlessly, without risking repercussions in the earthly short term – for resistance, let alone the use of force, against the "common will" is inconsistent with prior consent to accepting any outcome, provided it is the product of due process.

Social choice, making decisions collectively for both self and the dissenting minority, becomes easy. Like venial sin, it stirs little or no remorse. It can become a compulsive habit, too. For the very existence of the choice rule – the accessibility of forbidden fruit – is a permanent temptation. It keeps provoking society to split into two virtually equal halves, one of which will turn out to be the winning coalition. Success in forming it has richly rewarding distributional consequences. They go far beyond anything known under predemocratic "social choice"; feudal strife, the matching of baronial against royal power, contests between town leagues and territorial lords, church–state rivalries over the revenues of investiture, conflict between the landed and the commercial interest, have only scratched the surface of the distribution of property and income. They had a strong effect only in the very top layers of society; the middle and the bottom used largely to keep their share, if only because, closer to subsistence, they offered too thin a margin for redistribution as potential victims, and their power was insufficient to put them among the potential victors. One-man-one-vote has, of course, changed all that.

Under democracy, the winning coalition is entitled to define the common good for society as a whole, and by relatively simple recourse to the collective choice rule, it can legislate for all, one holistic end after another, while shifting the resulting burdens at least to some extent on to the losing coalition.

The operation of the choice rule is protected from criticism by its automatic association with holistic values few have the courage (the gall?) expressly to denigrate. Redistribution is always, though not always accurately, identified with the service of equality, social justice, compassion, "caring," solidarity and sometimes even of prudential considerations like social stability, the willingness of the less privileged to tolerate the existing social order, and so forth. The "objective" function – as Marxists used to say – of these values is to legitimize precisely those democratic choices which, by overriding the very property rights that a social order is intended to protect, are most in need of legitimation. In this sense, these are the democratic values par excellence; they lift democratic outcomes into a moral dimension. Yet equality and social justice, not to speak of the rest, inescapably fail the Paretian test of an "improvement," in that in realizing them, the interests of at least some persons must be sacrificed to the interests of others. Whatever may be their intrinsic merits, it is strange to have them called "liberal values."

In the light of such considerations, the recent Hegelian speculation about "liberal democracy" representing the "end of history" appears particularly inane. Only the attention it has received is more so. "Liberal democracy" is a curious conjunction to start with. However, if it stands for a world where everyone can assume prior consent by everyone else to all democratic decisions, that world is surely anything but a final resting place for history. It is singularly fertile in ceaselessly producing and reproducing distributional conflict; for property rights are never "given," known quantities in it. Instead, they are permanently "in play" as stakes in democratic politics, which can recast them to fit the public interest, the common good, the will of the majority. Admittedly, all this happens nonviolently. Surely, however, in historical change, movement need not always be violent. If anything, it may be more febrile, more unstable if it is sheltered by an agreed and all-powerful choice rule from the risks and costs of change brought about by violence.

ON THE ETHICS OF CHOOSING "SOCIALLY"

Contrary to what might be thought, a purely procedural social-choice rule is consistent with a purely consequential – hence substantive, content-dependent – evaluation of social states of affairs. An omnipotent majority and consequentialism, even in its narrow, utilitarian version, are comfortable bedfellows.

Ethics either universally valid, applying to all human action if it applies to any, on – as Bentham would have it – the public good is in one sphere, private ethics in another, and actions in the two spheres need to be judged by different yardsticks (Lyons, 1973, 1991, pp. 199–219). Were one to take this position, most of the ethical problems of good government would be swept under the carpet. However, the position would involve countless morally indefensible judgments, besides being crushingly banal. Yet, if there are to be no two different ethics at the same time, individual and holistic values must find their relative places, however large or small, within one. Should this prove to be altogether impossible, the social order these values motivate may itself be ethically inconsistent. Putting it differently, if it were held that any feasible social order must both protect individual rights and promote equality in some relevant sense, the two requirements could not be fulfilled. One could only redistribute by violating certain individual rights, that is, metaphorically speaking, by sinning. Sin, of course, is an ubiquitous, everyday phenomenon, but it would be absurd to frame deontological rules to govern the social order that made a virtue of it, and granted it a legitimate role.

A consequentialist type of ethics might take the view that all purposive action, including social choice, contributes to certain goals to some degree. The goodness of actions derives from the hierarchy of values that make these goals the chosen ends. Social choice helps attain the ends of many individuals, and its value is some composite function of all the values these individuals associate with the ends reached by it. The consequentialist reconciliation of private and public ethics is nothing but the formation of this composite. It is, as utilitarians would put it, the incorporation of all relevant values in the arguments of the social welfare function.

He who says composite, however, says aggregated, made into a whole in some manner, and these facile words beg a question instead of proposing an answer. Earlier in this chapter, I argued the logical absurdity of calculating the algebraic sum of votes, or, in the same vein, of the gains and losses of different people, and calling the result "the balance of good." Essentially the same absurdity surrounds the albeit wider consequentialist attempt to evaluate social states of affairs by weighing each one by the individual values, including the most abstract as well as the down-to-earth, that the members of society attach to them.[14] The non-cognitivist enterprise to find out the goodness or otherwise of social consequences, so to speak, from the horse's mouth, "from society itself," fails for lack of a horse, let alone a horse's mouth that would speak.

A half-way house between the noncognitivist position, which pretends to no knowledge of the good except insofar as it is the good of someone and gets trapped in the impossibility of aggregation, and the cognitivist one that claims directly to divine the worth of whole states of affairs, is the recourse to the "impartial observer," who takes account of everyone's good from one moral point of view.[15] However, there is nothing to compel agreement that the moral point of view he takes is the right, or the only one among several right, points of view – unless of course we share it to start with. The impartial observer taking a moral point of view is, on a close look, indistinguishable from a mere observer merely taking a point of view.

A remaining avenue open to consequentialism – I take it to be the only one – is cognitivist, and consists in adhering to the belief that we can both recognize, and justify to others, the ranking of good, better, and best states of affairs on intrinsic grounds, without having to refer to the persons for whom they are good. It is also "value-holist," maintaining that it is rational for society, or the race, the ethnic community, the Vaterland, to choose a state of affairs regardless of which particular individuals in society would or would not choose it. Risking to be called to order by classical philosophers for misinterpreting Aristotle, I should call this double position Stoic, Spartan, and Aristotelian, as distinct from the Athenian one that pays more heed to individuals. It is satisfying aesthetically but precarious intellectually, for neither is it self-evident nor can it be argued for. It supposes a prior commitment to virtues. More disturbingly, it leaves room within its terms for widely differing kinds of social orders, some of which look glorious and noble; others, inhuman and awful. It is possible to see these orders in all kinds of lights[16] and this may be the very reason why this ethic and the political philosophy derived from it are not only faulty – for aren't they all? – but more at fault than others. One is moved resignedly to echo Adam Ferguson that we must try and rely on law, since, unlike in the age of Spartan simplicity, we cannot rely on virtue.[17]

NEED ORDER HAVE AN ETHIC?

Lord Devlin, in a much-commented lecture (Devlin, 1965), once sought to establish the true role of law as an instrument of social survival rather than of the realization of ethical principles, a guide to the good life. He contended that law is needed to enforce some morality, whatever it may be, without which society would disintegrate. While "disintegrated" is obviously a subjectively twistable word, and not two people need agree whether a society – say, inner-city America or postsocialist Russia – has "disintegrated" or not, the drift of the argument, nevertheless, makes perfect sense. Devlin's particular point was that it did not matter what morality the law sought to enforce as long as it enforced one. The threat to social survival was moral and legal laxity, indifference, indeterminateness, and fudge. Diametrically opposed to this diagnosis is Hayek's theory of cultural selection, which predicts that societies adopting one morality and one type of law – and other basic social institutions – survive better than those adopting some other type. The test of institutions is a natural selection culminating in survival for the best. The best, in fact, turn out to be spontaneous orders; they have the highest capacity for survival.

In neither the Devlin nor the Hayek view, however, do human preferences for particular values have a role in the selection of the social order. Is this possible, and plausible? – and if it could be the case, what would it entail?

Positive law influences behavior by setting norms for it, providing for redress and sanctions in cases of their breach. Its central subject, so to speak, the mold in which the norms are formed, is the system of rights. On one view, the law creates them. On another, it discovers the rights that are there, or ought to be there, and by legislative and judicial action transforms them into legal rights, which it undertakes to uphold. Simplifying, we might consider Bentham, Austin, Kelsen, and most of the modern legal positivists as holding the former view: For them, the legislator and the judge create rights, and no one else can. Most moral philosophers, natural lawyers, and common lawyers tend to take the latter view. They see rights as prior to law, as moral truths derived from human nature of from God's intentions, or as implicit in the purposes underlying social arrangements. It follows, then, that law is as capable of violating rights as it is of upholding them. Bruno Leoni and Hayek incline to feel that law made by the legislator is liable to violate rights, whereas law found by the common law judge tends to clarify them.

Clearly, however, any sharp distinction between "created" and "found" law is somewhat unreal, as is the one between statute and judicially made law. We "create" what we can and wish to, but we "discover" what we are looking for and are predisposed to find. It is commonly accepted now that discovery is a child of preconceived notions, theories. Perhaps a more important and more genuine distinction is one between laws that do and laws that do not restrict people's admissible and Pareto-superior options, i.e., do or do not stop them from bettering their lot if they can do so without worsening anyone else's. It is not evident to my mind that this is quite the same distinction as the one between "made" and "found" law, though there are reasons to expect "found" law to favor Pareto-
superior outcomes.

For the granting of a right – whether it is supposed to be made *ex nihilo* or as the legal recognition of something that was implicit in morality, custom, or expediency – entails the creation or recognition of the concomitant obligation without which the right would have no valuable content, and could not even be exercised. While the right is a benefit to some, the obligation is an (actual or contingent) burden on others.

In creating the right for adult citizens to elect their legislators and political office holders, an obligation is imposed on the latter to abide by the election's result, even if it means submitting to loss of office. This obligation may be no hardship in the eyes of most of us who do not hold political office, for why should office holders have security of tenure instead of being exposed to our displeasure? Admittedly, in civil life many people do claim some right to a degree of job security, and the right is sometimes recognized in that employers assume the corresponding obligation. There are good reasons why this should not be the case in politics; our obligation to grant them job security would contradict our right to elect and recall politicians, a right to which they have at least implicitly agreed.

On the other hand, in creating or, as some would say, in giving legal recognition to, a right to work, a right to a formal education, a right to have one's artistic creations exhibited, performed, bought, a right to be healed when ill, a right to compensation for drought or flood damage and so forth, a different, onerous set of corollary obligations is imposed. It may be said that the obligor is "society," the whole community or the state; stating it in such lullaby language may obfuscate but does not change the fact that the obligation will be borne by as yet undesignated individuals, who must be taxed, or otherwise deprived of their resources, when the rights in question come to be exercised.

The right, then, is implicitly justified by consequentialist reasoning in precisely the same manner as other redistributive measures not based on rights. Both amount to a change in the social state of affairs that is not a Pareto-improvement; it is good for some, bad for others but still assumed to be "good on balance" – whether the balance is struck by the old-fashioned utilitarian pseudo-arithmetic or by some, intellectually more respectable, comparison of reasons for and against. Both are inspired by the values of whoever was in favor of granting the right, and both are justified by giving values such weights as will ensure that the aggregate benefit–burden balance turns out positively.

Making a change that is not a Pareto-improvement may be a vice on the off-cited Kantian ground that if one person is made better off by making another worse off, the latter is used as a means. It may also be condemned on the different ground that the latter person's rights must not be violated whatever the good this permits to be done to others, for rights are "trumps" that must prevail over the common good – at least sometimes.[18] It seems to me, however, that imposing changes that are not

Pareto-improvements, involves a possibly more fundamental, epistemic vice: There is no way of supporting the assertions that the good done to one person is "greater" that the bad that must be inflicted on the other to bring it about. If such outcomes are nonetheless to be legitimized, this must be done, not by pretending to measure the incommensurate, but by invoking holistic values that do not depend on comparisons of the good of some to the bad of others.

Equality, social justice, solidarity, human fulfillment are the most often cited holistic values in support of rights that are not self-justifying on simple Paretian grounds. A notable feature of most of these holistic values is that they not only compete with individual ones as do all alternatives. They in addition attack and undermine individual values, dislocating them in the preference ranking of individuals. Solidarity, to take one of them, depreciates responsibility for oneself, if only because it reduces its relevance in the face of hazards, hard knocks, adversity. Equality is antagonistic to achievement. Security saps thrift. Social justice impairs the respect for agreements. Equality and social justice may also act as anti-values to the value of prosperity, material ease (if the latter count as values), spoiling them with remorse. One may, of course, recognize such antagonistic pairs, values acting as anti-values upon others, without taking a view of which are better, those that chase or those that are chased. What one should not do, however, is to feign a belief that all these values are mutually consistent and tolerant, capable of thriving together in a good "pluralist" society.

The observant reader may, at this point, feel that he is hustled through a brutal change of scenery with insufficient warning. For he was made to pass from rights whose corollary obligations were being voluntarily assumed by the obligor "for value received," to rights that "society" gives to some and to obligations that others are made to assume involuntarily. The former is the world of civil society; the latter, of collective choice, of politics. In civil society, law is meant to protect and eventually clarify rights rooted in original possession or subsequently created by contract. In the world of politics, law creates rights and obligations that are reflections of the intent not of the parties but of the political authority; in enforcing them, law shapes and upholds a social order of its own making.

The passage from civil society to politics, then, is from an order that is value-neutral in that it has, at first blush, no involuntary feature,[19] to one where some value is invoked to justify the imposition of obligations for the sake of rights. This world cannot tolerate value neutrality; it would lose legitimacy if it did.

By a roundabout route, we have come back to the question raised with regard to the social orders seen by Lord Devlin and Friedrich von Hayek, each in his different way. These orders, made for or tested by survival, are, in a manner of speaking, value-neutral. At least, values do not play a determining role in their functioning – either because, as in Devlin, any value will do as long as it is firmly respected, or because, as in Hayek, no one seeks to shape the order in the image of any particular value, nor is anyone trying to justify anything in value terms. If the emergent order, nevertheless, turns out to favor certain values over others, this will be the wholly unintended outcome of cultural selection, in which values prevail according to their contribution to the survival of the "host organism." Macedon overshadows Athens; the barbarians topple Rome; Confucian East Asia gains economic supremacy over the slothful and feckless Occident – or not. Time will tell. But whatever happens and whichever order prevails for the time being, it prevails for reasons that have nothing to do with anyone's preference for the values that characterize the order.

A social order that is value-neutral in this accidental, ad hoc sense may be feasible and have good chances of survival. But if this is all there is to it, it is an unattractive proposition. Unlike nature, humanity has always demanded more than survival and "nondisintegration," and no doubt always will. Survival is a prior condition, not the sole object of the exercise. Looking for more, for a social order that goes some way toward letting people choose what they think they would like may be a Utopian ambition, but it is probably an irrepressible one. If it cannot be repressed, it is no doubt best to indulge it consciously, with open eyes, and with the warning flags fluttering. For, like Hippocratic medicine, the first commandment of social philosophy is surely: "Avoid doing harm."

THE FEASIBLE, THE ADMISSIBLE, AND THE RIGHT

Making sure to avoid doing harm before trying to do good forbids what I called, throughout this chapter, "balancing" – offsetting the interests, values, and votes of one person, group, or class against those of another and determining which should weigh more. Doing so is the original sin inherent in "social choice," and though people will not cease sinning or give up the practice of collective choice, and though a social order cannot possibly eradicate this sin, it should not encourage it by provoking brazen temptations. Least of all should it dress up sin as a virtue.

There are, as I have kept on insisting in this chapter, compelling reasons for abandoning the effort to evaluate social orders by evaluating their full consequences.[20] Modern political thought, in accepting some of these reasons, has increasingly turned to alternatives that it is pleased to call "rights-based."

Much of this thought is, to put it bluntly, confused and confusing. It seems to me that it is best understood if we adopt, at least for the present purpose, a threefold classification of the subject of rights-based theories. This classification has one merit – namely, that it groups like with like from the point of view taken in the previous section about choices that better some and wrong no one. There are, then, distributive rights, redistributive rights, and (for lack of a more respectful term that would fit) redundancies. Distributive rights are matched by voluntarily assumed obligations. Redistributive rights have involuntary, collectively imposed obligations as their counterparts. Redundancies are not rights, properly speaking, and entail no concomitant obligations, but merely signify the absence of any obligation if the corresponding right is absent; but this goes without saying.

With this triple classification at the back of our minds, let us address the problematical nature of the greater part of "rights-based" political theories. Their general approach is to propose a panoply of rights selected so as to correspond to the essential nature of the right-holder, to his basic aspirations, to his needs and interests that are worthy of respect, and so forth. There is little or no explicit reference in their selection to the essential nature, needs and interests, basic aspirations, and so forth, of the bearers of the matching obligations.

The imposition of involuntary obligations is justified on the standard consequential ground that the benefit the rights in question confer on some is greater, or morally more valuable, than the burden they impose on others. There is, as far as logic can take us, only a hole where this argument sees grounds. But even if the grounds were there, they could hardly bear the weight of a *right*, whose nature entails that it simply must not be violated. Respect for a right *qua* right cannot be justified on consequentialist grounds, which represent the "balance of reasons"; like Dworkin's card-like rights that are sometimes trumps over the public interest and sometimes trumped by it, depending on the *merits of the case*, consequentially justified rights stand when, but only when, the balance of expected consequences favors them. They do not stand by virtue of a deontological rule that is derived from the very nature of rights. (The muddle over "consequentially justified" rights parallels the muddle over rule-utilitarianism. In the latter, we are supposed always to choose the act that conforms to the good rule – e.g., "always honor your promise," even if keeping the particular promise in question did not increase aggregate utility. Surely, however, it *must* do so, for if it did not, the rule would not be a good rule on utilitarian grounds. Always keeping the rule increases the credibility, hence the social usefulness of promising. This is the reason why rule-utilitarianism recommends that *every* promise be kept. If this is a good reason, however, keeping the particular promise in question must be utility-enhancing; breaking it would be utility-reducing – and act-utilitarianism would have to come to this conclusion anyway. It would not need the additional help of rule-utilitarianism to reach it.[21] Utilitarianism cannot both judge acts on the balance of reasons, and serve as the *raison d'être* of rules that must be kept independently of the balance of reasons, so to speak reflexively.)

Let us, at this point, pull back to the Archimedean fixed point of distributive rights, that is, rights backed by obligations whose basis is rock-solid both epistemologically and morally. We really have it from the horse's mouth that they do exist, because the obligor himself says so. They are indisputably legitimate, for the very individuals who must bear the obligations have, by executing valid contracts, each separately declared their agreement to bear them in exchange for value received. This, then, we know on clear evidence. What else is sure?

In a broad sense, rights created by *voluntary* contracts are all property rights. (Note, for precision, that not all property rights are created by contract. Some result from unilateral gifts and bequests, and a historically not unimportant category originates in "finding," invention, original occupation, homesteading. Some kinds of intellectual property belong to this category.) They distribute benefits from possession, use, yield – or more precisely, the powers of disposition over these benefits – among individuals. In this broad sense, employment contracts, too, give rise to property rights to the extent that they create powers to dispose of another's labors in exchange for income, though the power is severely circumscribed. The sum of all these rights determines a distribution.

What seems to distress most theorists of "rights-based" social orders is that what I call here distributive rights seem to be a bleak, cold-hearted, and narrow base on which to build a society. They sense a great vacuum, and proceed to fill it with "bills of rights," "human rights," "minority rights," perhaps also "gender rights," "cultural rights," rights to "equal respect and concern," but also welfare rights, and why not rights to "worthwhile options," "meaningful life chances," and so forth. The list is lengthening as time goes on and as we find new reserves of magnanimity and ingenuity for repairing gaps in the web of rights.

Evidently, however, the list is a heterogeneous mix of redistributive rights, redundancies, and mere pious wishes that have no practical meaning. As Sen disarmingly admits regarding his own proposed additions to the list – "goal-rights" and the subclass he is particularly interested in promoting, "capability rights" – the attempt to integrate goals and rights "rather blurs the distinction between rights that relate to so-called positive freedom and those related to negative freedoms such as liberty and noncoercion" (Sen, 1982, p. 200). In fact, the distinctions that are blurred, if that is the right word to use, are of a different and more fundamental order. Consider in detail one of his "capability rights" that must enable the economically deprived "to make claims on the state" to rectify their deprivation (Sen, 1982, p. 199). It is not altogether clear whether they ought to have the right to *make* such claims or the right to have the claims *met*, i.e., their deprivation rectified. The latter entails redistribution in favor of the poor. But if this is done, it is done anyway for another reason. "Social choice" is made by the winning coalition; and it often happens to be one of the conditions for the coalition to function that there should be redistribution in favor of the poor (as well as, and perhaps more so, in favor of other interests): The "capability right" to have deprivation rectified adds nothing to this.

Partisans of proliferating rights, however, might point out that it is one thing to get redistribution and quite another to get it "as of right." Given a "capability right" to have redistributive benefits conferred, they depend on the right-holder, i.e., the poor, and not on coalition forming or other contingencies of the political process. What if power relations shift in ways unfavorable to the poor?

Much of this objection is casuistry. It is true that continuing redistribution depends on politics. But it is equally true that continuing to have the right to it depends on the same politics. Both are contingent on the constellation of political forces being favorable to the "goal," and if they are not, there is no "capability,"[22] and for this reason, all redistributive rights have a certain phoneyness about them, dressing up as matters of right something that is a matter of the political balance.

The other possible interpretation of the "capability right" we are trying to understand is perhaps less trite. Sen suggests this interpretation by relating the right to the freedom of speech. The economically deprived must be capable, "as of right," to make claims. If they could not and did not, public opinion might pay no attention to them and the redistributive process might pass them by. They must be able to speak up, to demonstrate in the street, to lend their support to one political entrepreneur rather than another depending on who was most likely to satisfy their claims, etc. Note, however, that they must be able to do all these things, not if and because they were granted a *right to make* claims, but if and because nobody can prove to have *contradictory rights to stop them* doing any of these things. The economically deprived can go on "making claims" in the same way as they can walk, speak, sleep, remember, and exercise their other faculties. All their feasible options must be admissible unless they prove to be inadmissible; and to prove that they are, somebody's contrary right must be proved. Only then would the economically deprived have an *obligation to refrain* from some form of claim making or another, like squatting on somebody's property. Failing proof of contrary right, the capability right is redundant – it is a "right" to do what it is admissible to do. Its obverse, no less redundant, is an obligation not to do what is forbidden.

We can, of course, also seek to grant a right to do what is inadmissible to do by virtue of another right somebody else happens to have, like empowering the hungry poor to steal from the rich; but in that event what we must do is to invalidate the latter's right, not to give the former one that would violate that of the latter.

The important point is that people do, as a matter of definitional, necessary truth, dispose of their feasible options in the absence of a contrary right that would render them inadmissible, and need no separate "capability rights" to some particular subset of the feasible set. The same argument holds with respect to any other "rights" such as "human rights," which affirm no more than this: What people are legally able to do because no one has a right to stop them, they ought to be legally able to do. This is obviously a redundancy. If, on the other hand, some other-than-legal ability is meant, perhaps money or knowledge, it is a categorical mistake to treat the matter as one of rights. Rights define the frontier between the feasible and the admissible. The feasibility of an action is not to be confused with the right to do the feasible.

Neither redistributive rights nor (a pleonasm) "rights to liberties" fill a vacuum, because there is no vacuum of the kind they could possibly fill.

Some feasible options are inadmissible because they would violate a right, and this is perhaps the most evident source of the constraints that go into the making of the social order – for if a right is a right, it must not be violated. Constraints, however, come in other colors and hues and from other, perhaps less evident, sources as well. What characterizes the system of constraints that would go best with the type of social order that causes the least wrong and is the most commendable? – and can a system of constraints be justified without relying on excessive presuppositions about values?

JUSTIFYING DEONTIC ORDERS

For reasons that should progressively emerge, I call an "excessive presupposition" about values the attempt to use them as justifiers of any feature of the social order preventing Pareto-improvements or imposing outcomes that are not Pareto-improvements.

It can be readily seen that all purposive actions of a person that do not inflict a loss on another are designed to bring about Pareto-improvements – for this follows from the action being purposive and from its causing no loss. Thus, a freely agreed-upon contract that inflicts no loss on a third party is designed to be a Pareto-improvement. The scope of the concept extends to schemes of social cooperation: It includes firms that are networks of contracts, and also the enforcement of "imposed" Pareto-optimal solutions in noncooperative games of the prisoner's dilemma type. Prisoners' dilemmas are treacherous terrain, as are externalities, for it is relatively easy to allege that a social situation requires a coercive constraint, either because the participants are caught in a prisoner's dilemma or because they create a harmful externality. In both cases, the constraint would arguably help correct a Pareto-inferior outcome; but it is far from certain that such cases occur as often, or are as important, as it is alleged. There is no place here to explore the grounds for believing this; it suffices to remark in passing that a social order should not make room for coercion at the drop of a hat, i.e., on the a-prioristic identification of certain standard situations, such as public goods, with prisoners' dilemmas. Some attempt at testing, or some other substantive proof, should be required that a certain situation does have the characteristics of such a dilemma. Orthodox, received public goods theory, for one, is quite insufficient to establish the case that without coercion we could have no public goods, or only "too few" of them. Without testing it, one can at best reserve judgment.

Constraints, however, that are in all probability necessary to ensure that our actions and interactions are Pareto-improvements, are *eo ipso* justified. Inasmuch as they forbid actions that would harm others or violate their rights, they demarcate, within our feasible options, the inadmissible from the admissible in such a way that everything admissible either is an improvement or is indifferent. The principal constraints that function in this way are, of course, distributive rights and rule-like, self-enforcing social conventions that facilitate coordination and cooperation by setting norms. They are all, taken globally, self-justifying.

Obviously, not all constraints are self-justifying. A simple example is legislation restricting the freedom of contract or otherwise curtailing the exercise of property rights; such legislation is patently capable of frustrating certain transactions that should be Pareto-improvements, as well as of causing outcomes that are not. Redistributive social choices are probably the most important of such Pareto-inimical constraints. In a well-designed[23] social order, this effect, which is at least controversial, would not be countenanced unless it were justified.

The justification, however, runs into precisely the same difficulty as the evaluation of social states of affairs – which, of course, is what we should have expected. Two approaches are possible. One is straightforward consequentialism, or one of its special versions like utilitarianism, propped up by undeclared cognitivist meta-ethics. With this approach, one would say that the law, convention, or other constraining institution may not be intrinsically good (and we wouldn't know it if it were), but it is good because it favorably influences the interests of the people who are affected by it. Since, however, the constraint in question has been defined as having effects that are not pure Pareto-improvements, it cannot be good for all. If it is good for those who gain from it and bad for those who lose, the justification must hold on the balance of reasons or not at all. However, as we have argued above, "the greater good of the gainers outweighing the lesser bad of the losers" is, strictly speaking, gibberish because it compares incommensurables. Hence it cannot justify the constraint except by a latent, unspoken cognitive assertion about what is good.

The other approach, an overtly cognitivist justification, is at least coherent, potentially rational. Here, we would argue that a constraint is conducive to a value that has intrinsic worth independently of, or over and above, the gains and losses of the individuals its operation affects. As far as I can judge, these values must be holistic, preferred by a part for the whole.[24] Chosen by some decisive part of society or, of course, by the legislator acting on its behalf, such values impinge on everyone whose options are restricted or rendered more costly by the constraint. Perhaps unexpectedly, the analogy with the arguments of the fifth section continues to hold in the cognitivist context as well: equality, distributive justice, universal love, solidarity, the intrinsic worth of art or, why not, of "multi-culturalism" that cannot survive on individuals' voluntary support alone, national greatness, and such other values as the occasion may call for, can all, without logical difficulty, serve to justify any configuration of nonself-justifying constraints. It suffices to impute a great enough intrinsic worth to the particular value the constraint favors.

Tempting as it would be to stop at this point, the story has an ending it behooves us to reach. He who says constraint says enforcement. Some constraints are self-enforcing in the special sense that enough of the constrained individuals find it worth their while voluntarily to invest efforts or other resources to deter violations, without a specialized agency (e.g., the state) having powers to force them to contribute the resources in question. Other constraints may require enforcement in the everyday sense of coercion, threat of sanctions, and compulsory contribution of the wherewithal needed for enforcement. The problem is a case in public-goods theory and is not directly relevant for the present. More relevant is the adequacy of any enforcement, voluntary or coerced. Whether the respect for the law can be mainly, let alone wholly, a matter of fear of sanctions is a question legal philosophy tends to answer in the negative. What is true of law is probably even truer of rule-like conventions whose sanctions are usually less reliable. Moreover, respect is somewhat broader and more demanding than mere obedience. Even if a large measure of obedience can be secured by enforcement alone, a corresponding measure of respect probably cannot be.

Apart from sanctions, people can have two kinds of reasons to respect constraining institutions. One is dependent on content or context or both. I stay within a rule because, all things considered, it is useful, beneficial, and in most circumstances it is not "too" constraining but only "reasonably" so. If this were not so in a particular case, I would not wish to observe it and might try to violate it, depending only on the risk of being found out. The other kind of reason is content- or context-independent or both. I obey the rule because it is a moral duty to respect rules that qualify as such by virtue of the authority of the rule giver, the object the rule is meant to secure, or because everybody else respects it. My obedience does not depend on the merits of the case. I do not refrain from killing a person because I think he deserves to live; or from maiming him because he "owns his body"; or from stealing his property because he earned it or needs it more than I. I refrain from all of these things because it is my duty to not to do them. Arguably, *all* proper, genuine rules are deontological in this sense, because if they were to be observed only according to the merits of the case, they would demand no more than what ad hoc pragmatism dictated anyway and would serve no purpose of their own.

It is easy to accept as deontological rules the constraints that we find to be self-justifying. Acceptance goes with the grain; it is "natural" inasmuch as self-justifying constraints refer to a bare handful of minimal first principles, and little else. People must be left to choose what they prefer if they can do it without violating anybody else's rights. Rights are matched by obligations. Obligations arise from torts and promises. Torts must be avoided or redeemed. Promises are made to be kept. Property is created by finding and contract.

Each of these basic precepts is undemanding in terms of the moral theory that supports it. Most of them, in fact, lay down behavior norms that seem to be part of our genetic heritage; part of it we share with our simian cousins. A social order whose nonphysical constraints can largely, if not wholly, be derived from such undemanding principles is likewise undemanding. Constraints requiring justification, on the other hand, may or may not be assimilated to deontological rules by all concerned. The holistic values they depend on are presuppositions that conform to the moral intuitions of some but not of others. Such presuppositions are "excessive" if, as I believe to be the case, they are meant to elevate the constraints in question to the rank of deontological rules. It is not a moral duty to surrender some of our resources in order to promote equality. There is nothing morally binding about "social choices" by virtue of the fact that they are "democratic."

NOTES

1 G. E. M. Anscombe, 1957, states, "... the thing wanted is at a distance from the immediate action ... [which] is calculated as the way to getting ... the thing wanted" (p. 45).

2 Coleman 1982, p. 114. Also J. W. N. Watkins, 1952, in Ryan, 1973.

3 I.e., that the swarm is in Nash-equilibrium.

4 For Charles Taylor, a notable adversary of philosophical individualism, one cannot both admit that not all "ultimately valuable" goods are divisible and adhere to "social atomism" (Taylor, 1979).

5 Cf. T. M. Scanlon, 1978: "I depart from the classical utilitarians and many of their modern followers in rejecting subjective preferences as the basis for the valuation of outcomes. This role is to be played instead by an ethically significant, objective notion of the relative importance of various benefits and burdens" (p. 76). Also Scanlon, 1975.

6 Cf. Kliemt, 1987, pp. 502–6, who stresses that for the cognitivist, normative standards can be categorically justified; somebody can have a legitimate claim to know what is good without knowing such contingent elements as the circumstances under which it is good, and *for whom*.

Cf. also, for a position that is tentatively both cognitivist and holist, Scanlon, 1977, repr. in Waldron, 1984, p. 143, and footnote: "Their value does not rest on their being good for particular individuals ... Perhaps all convincing appeals to these notions can be reduced to instrumental arguments, but I do not at present see how."

7 Of course, if fewer than two could block it, it would be a unanimity rule, not a collective decision rule.

8 Pope Boniface VIII decreed that "zeal should not be added to zeal nor merit to merit, but only one number to another." His reason was opportunistic: He sought a means to overcome squabbling about the relative zeal and merit of bishops standing for opposing points of view. Over the centuries, however, any *differential* influence over collective decisions has come to be seen as reprehensible, morally wrong, a falsification of the "true will" of the people, hence of the result that "should have been" obtained. Why this has come to pass is a question that would repay study, but is well beyond the scope of this chapter.

9 Incommensurables are, of course, neither greater nor smaller nor equal to each other. For "greater," one can read better, worthier more important. Equals are necessarily commensurable; it suffices to declare people and their wishes to be equal to solve the aggregation problem. It could, of course, also be solved by declaring them to be unequal yet homogeneous – but this might be harder to get accepted.

10 It is a "prudential" fault of democratic decisions that they do not seem well designed to serve the interests of the voters, except those in the uncommitted middle, whose adhesion is sought by both of the two competing halves of an electorate. In practice, this tends to take the form of redistribution from both the rich and the poor towards the middle. (Health and education services, and the provision of many public goods, are widely considered to have a redistributive effect in favor of the middle-income groups.) In abstract models, the median voter theorem expresses the same phenomenon: Both those above and below him get the short end of the stick.

11 It is possible, however, that no such rule can be taken literally, and simple majority rule in particular cannot. If the winning coalition ruthlessly abuses the potential offered by the rule, the losing coalition will cease to abide by it and will rebel, strike, sabotage, emigrate, send its capital abroad, or whatever. We can then revert to what I called above the "natural method" of making collective decisions, where the result approximates that which would be obtained if one part of society had to "beat into submission" the other half in order to obtain it. The result, in other words, will reflect all the relevant power relations, including of course the reluctance of shouldering the cost of violently using power.

This idea of the ultimate contestability of procedurally correct decisions that defy underlying power relations is put forward in a most original essay by Patrick Minford (Minford, 1991). Society's "cord," for Minford, is a coalition that no alternative coalition could defeat by any means (including violence). In the core, the distribution of power (and property) is stable. Any other distribution will in the long run be overcome or overthrown by enough citizens using their capacities and endowments to that end.

12 Under rigorous assumptions, if cumulative deficits increase, people increase their savings pro tanto to maintain the wealth (real income) they intend to bequeath to their descendants (Barro, 1974). Alternatively, they can stop voting for deficits. As opposed to the Barro theorem, there can be a case where people would rather leave no bequests, or best of all negative bequests if that were possible. They are then "bequeathed-contrained" and will *cet. par.* vote for growing cumulative deficits (Cukierman and Meltzer, 1989).

13 The tradeoff between redistribution and the national income available, combined with the median voter theorem, provides the equilibrium distribution

of posttax income, the share of national income absorbed by government, and the degree of inequality in Meltzer and Richard, 1981. They assume that taxes are proportional to income and the amount of taxes collected is redistributed in the form of equal lump-sum transfer payments to rich and poor. There is a tradeoff between the national income available for redistribution and the degree of equality, for redistribution is a negative-sum "game." As the tax rate is raised, and posttax incomes become more equal, a point is eventually reached where the median voter's gain from a greater lump-sum payment is just offset by his combined loss from a higher tax rate and a lower available pretax income. Any further increase in redistribution would produce a net loss for him and he would not vote for it. Meltzer and Richard conclude that this is the equilibrium degree of redistribution.

If, however, the winning coalition at this point can, by "tilting" tax rates or biasing transfer payments, still increase its total redistributive gain, it need not be stopped by the loss that a higher degree of redistribution would inflict on its marginal member i.e., the median voter. Its incremental gain is available to overcompensate the median voter for his incremental loss. Other ways exist for keeping him in the winning coalition. By making taxation unequal (e.g., moving from flat to progressive rates) and/or by making transfer payments unequal (e.g., giving all to the poor), the winning coalition can keep the median voter just satisfied, and go on increasing its total gain, by imposing a loss on the losing coalition that is progressively larger than its own gain. Thus the negative sum of the "game" would be increasing without the median voter becoming worse off. Equilibrium would be reached at the point where, because of the exhaustion of its taxable capacity or an imminent withdrawal of its consent to majority rule, the losing coalition could no longer be made to absorb more than the whole of any further increase in the negative sum. There is no reason to suppose that this point would coincide with the equilibrium point defined by Meltzer and Richard.

14 As Phillipa Foot reminds us, "J. S. Mill notoriously found it hard to pass from the premise that the end of each is the good of each to the proposition that the end of all is the good of all" (Foot, 1985, repr. in Scheffler, 1988, p. 241).

15 Harsanyi, in Sen and Williams, *Utilitarianism and Beyond*, 1982, p. 39. The impartial observer has "ethical preferences" that are, so to speak, not his own. His evaluations are, in the jargon, "evaluator-neutra." Unfortunately, this condition cannot ensure that another impartial observer should arrive at an evaluation that is even approximately the same. The "ethical preferences" of the two observers may be both impartial without being unique, and their evaluator-neutral evaluations may well differ – which leaves one wondering what "evaluator-neutral" really amounts to.

16 Apologists of the nation state as valuable enough to be worth any individual sacrifice, and many ideologists of totalitarian systems, evidently see them in one light – agnostic value relativists in another – there are, no doubt, other lights seen through other prisms.

17 Cited by Rawson, 1969, p. 349.

18 Cf. Dworkin, 1976, who invokes rights as cards that are sometimes trumps over the card of the common good, sometimes not – which card takes the trick depending on which is backed by the weightier argument. Dworkin remains blissfully unaware of the vacuity of his finding that the weightier reason weighs more.

19 This is perhaps an unusual way of stating the sufficient condition for value neutrality. It springs from the idea that when each chooses what he prefers, no choice is swayed by a value other than that of the chooser. Obviously,

values do influence choices in a truistic sense, without this necessary truth contradicting value neutrality. "To each, his own values" makes the social order value-neutral.

20 As Phillipa Foot puts it by way of concluding her elegant analysis: "we [must] accustom ourselves to the thought that there is simply a blank where consequentialists see the best state of affairs" (Foot, 1985, repr. in Scheffler, 1988, p. 242).

21 "To justify a rule is, among other things, to justify not acting, on occasions, on the balance of reasons" (Raz in Hacker and Raz, 1977, pp. 220–1).

22 It is possible but not certain that it takes a bigger shift of political forces to legislate away, or curtail, the redistributive "entitlement" of a group (e.g., to reduce tax-free benefits) than to alter the discretionary dispositions of the budget and cause the same group a comparable loss (e.g., to tax the benefits). This rather second-order possibility is hardly the goal the advocacy of redistribution "as of right" has in mind.

23 Without professing complete confidence that society as a whole can develop and function as a "spontaneous order," I should certainly not wish to exclude it either. Hence I am not implying that "well-designed" must be a matter of conscious, "constructivist" design. I must leave the matter open for now.

24 If a value were unanimously preferred, even forcing it down our throats might be a pleasant experience for all of us. The constraint that forced it would, in some bizarre sense, be Pareto-optimal. It would, however, presumably be redundant.

REFERENCES

Anscombe, G. E. M. (1957) in Raz, 1978.

Barro, R. J. (1974) "Are Government Bonds Net Wealth?," *Journal of Political Economy*, 82.

Black, R. D. Collison (ed.) (1986) *Ideas in Economics*, London: Macmillan.

Bouillon, H. (1991) in Radnitzky and Bouillon, 1991.

Coleman, S. J. (1982) *The Asymmetric Society*, Syracuse, NY: Syracuse University Press.

Cukierman, A. and Meltzer, A. H. (1989) "A Political Theory of Government Debt and Deficits in a Neo-Ricardian Framework," *American Economic Review*, 79.

Devlin, P. (1965) *The Enforcement of Morals*.

Dworkin, R. M. (1976) *Taking Rights Seriously*, London: Duckworth.

Foot, Philippa (1985) in Scheffler, 1988.

Guénée, B. (1985) *States and Rulers in Later Medieval Europe*, Oxford: Blackwell.

Hacker, P. M. S. and Raz, J. (eds) (1977) *Law, Morality and Society*, New York: Oxford University Press.

Harsanyi, J. (1982) in Sen and Williams, 1982.

Hart, H. L. A. (1983) *Essays in Jurisprudence and Philosophy*, Oxford: Clarendon Press.

Hayek, F. A. (1952) *The Counter-Revolution of Science*, Glencoe, IL: The Free Press.

Kliemt, H. (1987) "Unanimous Consent, Social Contract, and the Skeptical Ethics of Economists," *Rechtstheorie*, 18.

Kontos, A. (ed) (1979) *Powers, Possessions and Freedom*, Toronto: Toronto University Press.

Lyons, D. (1973) revised 1991, *In the Interest of the Governed*, Oxford: Clarendon Press.

Meltzer, A. H., and Richard, S. F. (1981) "A Rational Theory of the Size of Government," *Journal of Political Economy*, 89.

Minford, P. (1991) "A Positive Theory of Rights," in Minford, *The Supply Side Revolution in Britain*, Aldershot: Elgar.

Radnitzky, G. and Bouillon H. (1991) *Ordnungstheorie und Ordnungspolitik*, Berlin u. Heidelberg: Springer.

Rawson, E. (1969) *The Spartan Tradition in European Thought*, Oxford: Clarendon Press.

Raz, J. (1977) in Hacker and Raz, 1977.

—— (ed.) (1978) *Practical Reasoning*, Oxford: Oxford University Press.

Ryan, A. (ed.) (1973) *The Philosophy of Social Explanation*, Oxford: Oxford University Press.

Scanlon, T. M. (1975) "Preference and Urgency," *Journal of Philosophy*, 72.

—— (1977) in Waldron, 1984.

—— (1978) in Scheffler, 1988.

Scheffler, S. (ed.) (1988) *Consequentialism and Its Critics*, New York: Oxford University Press.

Schwartz, Pedro (1986) in Black, 1986.

Sen, A. K. (1982) in Scheffler, 1988.

—— and Williams, B. (eds) (1982) *Utilitarianism and Beyond*, Cambridge: Cambridge University Press.

Taylor, C. (1979) in Kontos, 1979.

Waldron, J. (ed.) (1984) *Theories of Rights*, New York: Oxford University Press.

Watkins, J. W. N. (1952) in Ryan, 1973.

5 The twistable is not testable

Reflexions on the political thought of Karl Popper[*]

> ... nobody has shown that there are only two possibilities, capitalism and socialism.
>
> Karl Popper (p. 142)[1]

Critical rationalism that its founder describes as "the minimum concession to irrationalism" (p. 232) requires that no proposition should be held immune from criticism, not even the proposition that all genuine propositions are open to criticisms. One can therefore scarcely do less, in homage to Sir Karl Popper, than to expose his propositions to the acid of the very method of which he is the champion.

These reflexions are meant to be a critical commentary, of Popperian inspiration, on the political philosophy which, though not properly his (for Popper has never set out to develop a political philosophy of his own), nonetheless accords closely with his *obiter dicta* on the social predicament and his critique of some Hegelian and Marxian positions.

In his own mind they amount to "a kind of critical introduction to the philosophy of society and of politics" (p. 259).

Genuine propositions are capable of being corroborated, and are criticized by a process of confrontation with the ascertainable facts of the case. This is the test of falsifiability, for which Popper is perhaps best known. Statements that are not propositions about ascertainable facts of the case cannot be criticized in this sense. However, they do not escape scot-free, for they can at least be tested for consistency. A proposition that is a deduction from another proposition must obey the rules of logical inference and a mistaken deduction, a *non sequitur*, is as a rule not allowed to survive adversarial debate.

A statement of preference or, more broadly, a subjective *ordering* along some value dimension is harder to test. Yet, contrary to the well-known and somewhat facile injunction against the disputing of tastes, it, too, can be "tested." The test is not the demanding one of truth or, in Popperian

* This chapter first appeared in English in *Journal des Economistes et des Etudes Humaines*, vol. 2, no. 4, December 1991. Reprinted with permission.

fashion, provisional acceptance pending further challenges. It is the less demanding one of formal consistency. Admittedly, it is absurd to claim that John is "mistaken" in putting tea before coffee, Stendhal above Flaubert, justice ahead of welfare. But if his ordering can be shown to be incoherent (he prefers Stendhal to Flaubert, Flaubert to Maupassant and Maupassant to Stendhal), he can be confronted to this prima facie self-contradiction and his explanation of it, if he has one, can be tried by the canons of rational argument. Moreover, if he professes preferences that, taken together, make nonsense of any possible hierarchy of values – he wants property to be inviolable, political power to be limited, and economic inequality to be abolished – his inconsistency can be discovered and demonstrated with the aid of fairly elementary economics and jurisprudence.

What is ultimately unfalsifiable, immune to rational criticism and useless except as a piece of gratuitous self-expression, is the stand-alone, ad hoc value judgment. The latter tends to be pragmatic, eclectic, and is not inserted into a coherent hierarchy. Not only can stand-alone value judgments not be tested for their empirical content; they would not be value judgments if they could. More awkwardly, they cannot be tested for formal consistency either, because they are not part of any system and need in no way fit in with the logical structure of one. They escape the requirements of coherence, of mutual consistency.

The upshot of this for political philosophy is that we should treat protestations of pragmatism, disavowals of doctrine, negations of ideological bias as the shrillest of alarm signals. They should warn us that we are being stalked by the unfalsifiable. They foreshadow the stealthy creep of a programme of piecemeal action radiating irrefutable good sense and good will; a programme that is easy to accept and churlish to disparage; a set of least-cost, least-pain solutions to our ills that risks to be debilitating in its cumulative effects. I am, of course, referring to social democracy.

HOW TO BE A DEMOCRAT

If he were pressed to order his wishes and values into a hierarchy, Sir Karl Popper would almost certainly prove himself to be a democrat first, a socialist a distant second. His commitment to democracy, however, takes a form that almost obliterates the question of what comes first. It helps him bypass the problem of conflicting priorities. Unlike many other social democrats, he does not seem to be worried by the dilemma: "where do I stand if the democratic process generates reactionary, anti-social outcomes?" The reason why the question does not seem to arise for him lies in what seems to be the "twistability" of his image of democracy.

Popper, of course, is not impressed by the pedantic virtue of "defining his terms." He is comfortable with robust meanings that take care of themselves without needing finicky definitions. He has little patience with conceptual analysis and would rather leave a degree of freedom to interpretation than encourage what he regards as barren Aristotelian essentialism and definition-mongering, the cause of "the medieval backwardness of our social science." Engagingly, he remarks that "everybody knows what truth, or correspondence with the facts, means (as long as he does not allow himself to speculate about it)" (p. 379) Nor does he find it necessary to define what he means by democracy.

In a general way, two meanings are current. One is *procedural* and *deontic*. It refers to a set of particular rules for reaching collective decisions that, if duly followed, make for a regime we agree to call democratic. The other is *substantive* and *consequentialist*. It refers to the sum of collective decisions that, if duly reached, amount to a democratic regime.

The deontological meaning would oblige us to accept the "verdict of the urns" no matter how idiotic or vicious we judge it to be; it is the democratic decision and we are deemed to have the duty to respect it. American liberals are perhaps the most typical adherents to this interpretation, while classical liberals would be provoked, by deplorable "verdicts of the urns," to question the rules, the electoral laws, unqualified franchise, campaign financing, or other parts of the collective choice process.

The consequentialist meaning, on the contrary, leads us to identify a decision procedure as democratic if it produced the right *result*, undemocratic if it did not. Thus for Rousseau, and for his heirs Robespierre and Lenin, there is a "general will" (or its equivalent under other names) which society either recognizes or not, and must be enlightened or forced to recognize if it does not do so spontaneously. For socialists, a decision giving effect to the "real" interests of the working class is democratic, one that does not is manipulated, misled, extorted by media pressure, beset by false consciousness.

Popper's own use of the term falls between the deontological and the consequentialist in a way that can cause unease. "By democracy I do not mean something as vague as 'the rule of the people' or 'the rule of the majority,' but a set of institutions (among them especially general elections, i.e., the right of the people to dismiss their government) which permit public control of the rulers and their dismissal by the ruled, and which make it possible for the ruled to obtain reforms..." (p. 151); "democracy ... is the only known device by which we can try to protect ourselves against the misuse of political power; it is the control of the rulers by the ruled. And ... political democracy is also the only means for the control of economic power by the ruled" (p. 127).

Democracy, then, is "a set of institutions" that produce various desirable results and conditions. They are stressed in contradistinction to persons who may be arbitrary and abusive (ch. 7). But the institutions remain unspecified and play no visible role. *How* do they "control" power? – and do they really succeed in doing so? Confident in the power of reason, Popper is not troubled by the question: institutions are "designed" to achieve what we expect of them (p. 131). Democracy is not rule-obedience in general or majority rule in particular. It is the getting of the right results, and if our institutions do get them, they have proved themselves to be democratic. If they fail to get them, we can always adjust their design. For democracy is not a predetermined institutional design; it is a set of consequences that are independently specified (e.g. control of the rulers, control of economic power, reform) and can then be used to determine the dependent variable, the institutions that must somehow or other yield the required consequences.

The parity of reasoning with Rousseau, and with socialist orthodoxy as well, is striking. A set of institutions must lead to recognition of the general will, or realize the true interests of the working class, or conform to the laws of social development (not to say "historical necessity"). If it does not, it is the wrong set, in need of redesign.

Consider the implications. What constitutes "control of the rulers" is not a question of fact, but of subjective opinion. Opinion is seldom unanimous, any more than it is unanimous about what constitutes the interest of the working class, or social justice. Suppose that under a given set of institutions some of the ruled would like to, but cannot, get rid of their rulers; the reforms they desire fail to get adopted; or the economic power of big business looks oppressive to them. Can one say that the institutions that produced this unsatisfactory result were not democratic? – and can one say that they were? One hypothesis is no more falsifiable than the other. Neither contains a genuine proposition stating an intersubjectively testable fact about which no two observers, whatever their leanings, can honestly disagree. "Oppressive" economic power, "uncontrolled" rulers or "failure to adopt sensible reforms" are essentially twistable evaluations. By borrowing the Popperian nondefinition of democracy, it will always be possible for some to reject the capitalist USA of the interwar years as undemocratic (there was a good deal of economic power concentrated in "few" hands, the Supreme Court was blocking popular reforms), and for others to call the October 1917 "revolution" democratic (the ruled had got rid of the rulers, all power passed to the soviets).

Likewise, nobody will ever show, to revert to the motto of this chapter, that there is no "third way" between capitalism and socialism, as well as perhaps a fourth and a fifth. Nobody can possibly show this, nor its contrary, if only for the simple reason that the words "capitalism" and "socialism" do not refer to definite states of affairs which ascertainably prevail, or fail to prevail. Can it be "shown" that socialism ever did, or did not, exist in Russia and its orbit in the last half-century? Of course the same leeway exists regarding capitalism.

The present writer, when a subject of a "people's democracy," used to taunt his political masters that capitalism had never existed anywhere, that it was yet to come, it was the "wave of the future" – a taunt that reduced them to fury but naturally failed to provoke any refutation. This sort of game, however, is more than playing with words. Pseudo-descriptions positively ask for being twisted in this way. Room for play with words is a sign that the words are out of joint, unconnected to each other and to reality, perhaps adding up to effective rhetoric but falling well short of being bona fide statements, testable for their information content or their consistency with the context.

There is a setting, though, where describing democracy by the results we should like it to produce does not lead to the clash of one irrefutable rhetoric with another. This is the setting of the social democratic consensus. One is tempted to find that Popper's notion of democracy is relative to this consensus, and is hardly comprehensible outside it. Within it, all are broadly agreed about what it means that the ruled control the rulers (it means that the government is unseated when it does "too little" or "too much"); that the economic power of the state protects freedom rather than menacing it (it means that power is exercised in an "institutional framework," not according to the "arbitrary will" of bureaucrats); and that no citizen is reduced to "practical slavery" (it means that the "economically weak" are never "forced to sell themselves" on the labor market). Anyone who is not already a social democrat at heart will not be persuaded that these terms really describe a recognizable world. They are twistable and not testable; they evaluate rather than specify; only for the like-minded do they mean one and the same thing.

For the others, they leave a large question unanswered: how compatible is democracy as seen by Popper with a conservative or a liberal ideology? Putting it differently: how to be a democrat without also being "social"?

HOW TO BE A HISTORICIST

If there is a link between Popper's philosophy of knowledge and his view of society and its politics, it is his rejection of historicism. Were it not for this link, his scattered remarks on good and bad government, rational politics, equality, social justice, freedom and its protection could easily be taken for the ad hoc opinions of almost any well-meaning, progressive lay citizen whose politically formative years extend from the Great Depression to the early welfare state and the "mixed economy" – opinions that have no very obvious theoretical underpinning and spring spontaneously from meliorist sentiments. His emphatic anti-historicist stand, however, appears to provide a unifying principle, helping to organize disparate pieces of social diagnosis and therapy into something like a political theory.

Sir Karl's boundless contempt and loathing for Hegel leave him, if not exactly speechless in the face of the historicist creed, at least short of the patience fully to explain why historicism, had it been developed by a better philosopher[2] would still be unacceptable to critical rationalism. I believe there is some room for doubt that it *would* be; for it is possible to read Popper on politics as if he were saying, not that historicism is always wrong, but rather that the trick is to know how to be a historicist.

Historicism at bottom treats "history" as a series of events ("social developments") displaying certain regularities that are more predictable than most. This view can be traced to the basically nonHumean, inductivist hypothesis which asserts that known past events can constitute a sufficient body of evidence from which valid extrapolations can be made to future events, even where both the past and the future events in question are *singular* ones, being of a once-for-all, nonreproducible, "historical" character (pp. 264–9, 363–4). Consequently, history or social development has *laws* that can be *discovered* and *exploited*.

Popper will have none of this. For him, history has no "meaning," no "tide" and no "wave." When pushed, he does not hesitate to say that there *is* no such thing as "history," only histories of particular classes of events. Above all, there are no historical laws. Historical determinism is naive or wicked superstition, and so are theories of "social development." Not only are they morally defective and defeatist, they also lack any basis in the theory of knowledge.

Yet, if historicism has no rational foundation, how is social engineering nonetheless possible?

For the Utopian historicist, it is of course possible and desirable. Sir Karl very properly dismisses building Utopia as the nonsense and romantic delusion that it is (ch. 9); for him, however, social engineering is something different altogether, and it is perfectly capable of achieving certain desired, less-than-Utopian, results (e.g. p. 129).

For the historicist of Marxian stamp, though social engineering is possible, it is largely unnecessary. It can be applied in conformity with "the laws of social development" rather than trying to buck them. This is the thesis of the "impotence of politics." Engineering to bring about the social changes that are bound to happen anyway is of limited utility (it can at best "ease the birth-pangs"), while engineering to change the necessary course of events is futile and counter-productive.

For the consequent anti-historicist, social engineering ought to be impossible for the fundamental reason that we cannot knowingly engineer society without relying on a falsifiable hypothesis of its "physics"; but any such hypothesis would be a historicist one, and as such it would prove to be unfalsifiable, meaningless.

One strong thread in Popper's thought appears to be consistently anti-historicist, in the sense of the above dilemma. He gives pride of place in social theory to the unintended and unforeseen consequences of human action; it is these consequences that make social theory a distinct field of study and stop it from collapsing into "methodological psychologism" (p. 88, and ch. 14). He is very conscious, too, of "the unwieldiness, the resilience or the brittleness of the social stuff, its resistance to our attempts to mould it" (p. 94) – a poor outlook indeed, one would think, for undertaking engineering jobs meant to mold it just the same.

One would think so, but one would be wrong. Far from despairing of it as we would expect from his epistemology, Popper is very much confident of social engineering. Moreover, he sees it as far more than just blind, trusting-to-luck tinkering with an engine that is acting up and needs fixing, whether or not we understand how it works. Unlike Hayek, he does not want to stop at trial-and-error, the method we supposedly employ when we have no clue to what we should be doing. He is deeply persuaded that we can be more ambitious than that.

A well-grounded understanding of the engine is both necessary and possible: "*A social technology is needed whose results can be tested by piecemeal social engineering*" (p. 222, italics in text). The value of the engineering is not only that it may, more often than not, help to fix the engine when it is "broke." It is, in addition, to help build up, by repeated tests, a whole "social technology," a body of unfalsified hypotheses about the working of "the social stuff": "a technology for the immediate improvement of the world we live in, the development of a method for piecemeal engineering, for democratic intervention" (p. 143).

What, then, is the difference between the "laws of social development" which Popper despises, and the body of hypotheses about how society works, which he believes possible and useful? Is he, or is he not, a historicist? For the obvious difference, namely that "laws" are "true" while surviving hypotheses are tentative propositions that remain forever open to falsification, is merely the basic difference between *all* empirical knowledge as understood *before*, and all empirical knowledge as understood *since*, Popper's *Logik der Forschung*. Popper did not tell us to steer clear of historicist fallacies because they embraced a mistaken, fruitless inductivist concept of knowledge. *All* scientific theories used to do that to his way of thinking. Sir Karl had another, more particular objection to historicism: that it reasoned about a subject matter made up of unique, singular events as if it consisted of repeatable, reproducible ones. The life of society, the "social stuff," did not lend itself to scientific theorizing in its pre-Popperian inductivist, any more than its Popperian fallibilist, version. Yet, in postulating a "social technology," Popper seems to be asserting that the "logic of scientific discovery" is perfectly applicable to social development which we can understand, predict, and mold.

But why is *historical prophecy* baseless and false, and *social prediction* and the engineering that is based on it, rational and to be encouraged?

The naughty answer seems to be that even historical prophecy is right when it predicts correctly. "We must demand that unrestrained *capitalism* give way to an *economic interventionism*. And this is precisely what has happened" (p. 125, italics in text). Marx had actually prophesied that it would, and "we must say that he was right" (p. 193). But if historicism is epistemological nonsense, wasn't he right for the wrong reason, by some pure fluke? Or doesn't it matter?

The belief in a social technology is uncontestably a belief in a form of historicism. However, as the terms Popper uses to characterize historicism on the one hand, and social technology on the other are somewhat twistable (one twists to determinist prophecy, the other to a set of predictive hypotheses suitable for testing), they can look as if they were poles apart. But this is only so because the same linguistic operation is described by Popper either as *metaphysics* or as falsifiable *science*, depending on what it predicts, or why, or how far ahead.

Clearly, there are kinds of prophecy that are essentially unfalsifiable. "The kingdom of God shall come" or "the exploitation of man by man will cease" do not have any observable information content. I can always claim that this kind of prophecy has in fact been fulfilled, and no one can call me a liar. Sir Karl relegates such claims to the realm of apocalyptic fantasies. Similarly, the statement "socialism will be realized in the end" never risks being refuted, both because we may never feel compelled to agree on what socialism is, and what it means for it to be realized, and because even if we did agree, "jam tomorrow" would forever remain consistent with "never have jam today." This trick is old hat, and if historicism were no more than irrefutable prophecy, we could pass on to other things. However, when a prediction is not metaphysical but "observational," is it the hocus-pocus of historicist prophecy or the scientific prediction of social technology?

Popper implies that it is hocus-pocus when it is large scale, and scientific when it is piecemeal. (The latter is tested by success or failure at bearable cost.) But the key word "piecemeal" is nothing but a key question-beggar in this context.

As far as I could ascertain, Sir Karl nowhere defines "piecemeal"; to read the word as if it referred to the size or scale of engineering jobs would clearly be false; step-by-step or bit-by-bit are too subjective and twistable to let us tell a social measure that is piecemeal from one that is not.

In fact, Sir Karl uses the word as a *synonym* for "testable." An act of piecemeal social engineering is one whose effects can be discerned and judged in the finite future, preferably before we are all dead. Presumably it is also economical in terms of its cost–benefit relation and the risk we run if it fails. But if this is how we must understand and use "piecemeal" it is a *petitio principii*, begging the question that it is supposed to resolve. Social engineering is testable when it is piecemeal; piecemeal means testable; social engineering is testable when it is testable.

A hypothesis about the likely consequences of some policy measure is a part of social technology when it is exposed to the test of success or failure, hocus-pocus when it is not. *Both*, however, are historicist in that they presuppose a science of society; the possibility of knowing *what* makes it tick in a certain way as well as of *making* it tick differently. "Socialism will liberate the workers" is hocus-pocus, for there is no possible test telling us whether the workers *have* been liberated or not. "Public ownership of industry will raise its efficiency" is not hocus-pocus if there is an intersubjectively applicable method of correlating efficiency with private and public ownership respectively. However, as is well known, such multiple correlation analysis is notoriously tricky and rarely yields unambiguous results.

The unreliability of correlations, however, is neither aggravated nor relieved by the *scale* of the social phenomena we are trying to link into a cause-and-effect chain. Social engineering via the nationalization of industry is certainly not "piecemeal" in the sense of little-by-little, cautious or tentative. It is almost impossible to do it otherwise than boldly, by large segments if not in one fell swoop. Yet its status is no different, in terms of the fallibilistic philosophy of knowledge, from small-scale fiddling with, say, customs duties or welfare benefits, for the effects of the latter are similarly difficult to determine with any confidence.

Effects upon the "social stuff" are testable or not, regardless of the scale of the engineering experiment; and if large-scale and small-scale are equally testable, they both belong in the toolbox of social technology, where some tools may well be big and powerful, others small and delicate. When Popper talks of "piecemeal," what he intends to say is "exposed to the tests of experience" or "to be judged by success or failure in application." He does not really mean "small" as opposed to large, "step-by-step" as opposed to sweeping, except insofar as these actually signify testability.

Nor is it convincing to read into the insistence on "piecemeal" a prudential, maximin-type strategy of doing less damage if the hypothesis underlying the attempt at engineering turns out to be false. A year's worth of legislation and policy-making can probably do as much damage by countless "piecemeal" interventions as by a few major measures. For Sir Karl, "piecemeal" appears to suggest that the measure in question is rapidly vindicated by its result, that its ends "can be realized within a reasonable span of time" (p. 367). But the time-scale of social experiments is unrelated to their size or depth; a radical and large-scale reform may quickly prove to be an unworkable flop, while the poison of minor measures may take a long time to work its way through the system. The latter, indeed, may be the more dangerous, for their effects are less likely to be spotted and provoke effective protest.

There is, in short, little in Popper's epistemology that would legitimize his own practice of historicism, to wit, the reliance on social engineering. Invoking a social technology as its base does not really change matters. If Sir Karl is to persuade us to separate the social democratic sheep with its carefully tested social engineering from the totalitarian goat and its historicist bungling, he must marshal independent arguments.

HOW TO DO GOOD AND NOT FORCE OTHERS TO BE HAPPY

One of the characteristic political themes of the *Open Society* is the strong recommendation to limit the scope of political power and the reach of our political goals; this is what leads many liberals (in the nonAmerican sense of "liberal") to regard Sir Karl Popper as one of their own. In two chapters (chs 9 and 24) he argues eloquently against trying to make people happy: "the politician should limit himself to fighting against evils instead of fighting for 'positive' or 'higher' values, such as happiness" (p. 276); "the attempt to make heaven on earth invariably produces hell. . . . The fight against suffering must be considered a duty, while the right to care for the happiness of others must be . . . confined to the close circle of their friends" (p. 237).

However, anyone who takes this injunction for a normative *limit on the scope of politics*, is liable to be disappointed. The fight against evil and suffering is, of course, a perfectly twistable description of political action, it means what the consensus wishes it to mean, and so does the counsel against trying to make people happy. If Mill's more rigorous Harm Principle could be twisted until it came to mean a call for the welfare state (for *not helping* people is to *harm* them), what cannot be read into Popper's "Fight Against Suffering, Not For Happiness"?

In any event, before interpreting Popper as advocating limited government, limited power for the state and a limited domain for collective choice, one would have to reconcile these negative constraints with the positive demands he makes, or finds that citizens can legitimately make, upon the state and hence upon each other. Not only is the list of such demands open-ended, but each demand, taken in isolation, is able to serve as the warrant for coercive state action, subject to no other limit than the risk of taxpayer exhaustion and revolt.

It suffices to reflect on some of the requirements we should expect the state to fulfill suggested by Sir Karl Popper in manifest good faith:

"We must construct social institutions, enforced by the power of the state, for the protection of the economically weak from the economically strong. The state must see to it that nobody need enter into an inequitable arrangement . . ." (p. 125). "Weak," "strong," and especially "inequitable" are, of course, almost infinitely elastic adjectives. For some, (to take a pedestrian example) the very institution of collective bargaining suffices to make all labor contracts equitable; for others they are all inequitable because they leave room for exploitation. These essentially subjective, value-laden terms have an agreed, consensus meaning only within a fairly homogeneous "speech community," to wit among social democrats. The normative content of these phrases is indeterminate: they can legitimize virtually limitless intervention on behalf of the "weak" and to uphold "equity." Social life, no matter what institutions are "constructed" to canalize it, ceaselessly reproduces conditions that can be described as the weakness of some, the strength of others, and the inequitableness of the arrangements they would conclude if left to themselves. These descriptions are, of course, "unfalsifiable." They can generate literally any policy prescription, including "unlimited" government.

In practice, policy norms will be constrained, strictly or loosely as the case may be, by the consensus meanings of "weak," "strong," and so forth. The state, in other words, would have a Popperian mandate to do what the consensus (through its interpretation of what was weak, strong, equitable, etc.) wanted it to do – no more and no less.

What, then, is the real content of such commandments? How are they translated into firm limits, frontiers for political action? They are empty in the sense that *any* state playing *any* role can safely be said to be conforming to them, provided only that "consensus" is suitably defined to mean "sufficient agreement with what the state is in fact doing." (If agreement were insufficient, the state would of course have to change the role it played, since this is how the word "sufficient" operates here). A social democratic consensus would plainly not fail to generate social democratic policies – but we know this anyway. If the consensus were perchance "neoconservative," "libertarian," or New Left, the state would presumably adopt the matching measures, reflecting the very different meaning that would be given to "protecting the weak" or "inequitable."

We have, however, still not been offered clear reasons why the consensus of men of good will ought to be social democratic, rather than conservative, liberal, socialist or whatever.

Moreover, the social democratic consensus is itself difficult to identify without ambiguity. When are social democratic institutions neither "too Left" nor "too Right" but just dead center? In what specific way should they respond to the demand for equity and protection for the weak? In one place, Popper calls for compulsory disability, unemployment, and old age insurance, and for a statutory guarantee of a livelihood for everyone willing to work (p. 126). Obvious "twistability" characterizes even these down-to-earth specifics: what level of benefits constitutes adequate insurance against the hazards in question? – what does the "willingness to work" mean? – to do what work? – and what counts as a livelihood? Admittedly, not all norms of what a state ought to do are easily quantifiable. Not all can be translated into precise commitments. And only of precise commitments can it be claimed that the state has successfully fulfilled them, or failed to do so, or has exceeded its mandate, for otherwise such claims would be empty rhetoric, mere irrefutable assertions. Therefore even the descent from lofty generalities, from "planning, step by step, for institutions to safeguard freedom, especially freedom from exploitation" (p. 143) to the relatively humdrum level of the actual institutions we must construct to achieve this, does not save the Popperian political discourse from the danger of being twisted so as to justify almost any stand and be filled with almost any empirical content – even if it was manifestly meant to be filled with a moderately social democratic one.

It remains to note that having placed our confidence in social engineering, based on the possibility of an evolutionary social technology, it would hardly be rational to put some kind of limit, exogenous to the technology, upon its scope. Doing so would presuppose that while the technology was good, there was above it something better, a source of knowledge overriding the technology itself.

If the technology suggests that on the balance of the evidence it is feasible to do some good somewhere, it would be curious to declare that it would be better still not to do it. It follows tautologically from the very concept of a social technology that if the cost–benefit balance of a policy is expected to be positive, it is better to execute the policy than to drop it. In this light, it is difficult to interpret Sir Karl's injunction against trying to make people happy, or realizing certain values they either hold dear, or will no doubt hold dear once they have become realized. If a piece of social engineering cannot merely redress injustice and alleviate suffering, but contribute to some people's happiness, why not go ahead with it? And doesn't the removal of injustice and suffering in any case contribute to happiness? Where does one stop and the other begin?

There seems to be some inconsistency between the advocacy of social engineering and the injunction against furthering happiness. Could it be overcome by arguing that a mandate to make people happy is too apt to be twisted into one to *force* them to be happy, – hence the technology needs to be constrained lest it should be employed to do "coerced good"? Some such interpretation, however tenuous it is, would link Popper's "anti-happiness" constraint with J. S. Mill's rule against coercing people for their own good. However, the corollary of Mill's rule is that it is wrong – morally, deontologically wrong, and not merely self-defeating, dangerous, inadvisable, or inefficient – to coerce people except to stop them from harming others.

There is no visible trace in Popper's *oeuvre* of any such deontic rule. His stand against the potentially totalitarian tendency to force people to be happy is, as far as one can judge, consequentialist, as is his entire social engineering. If social engineering is anything, it is a series of political decisions making people allocate their efforts and wealth otherwise than they would if allowed to do it as they saw fit. The coercion they are subject to in order to comply is one Mill would not have countenanced;[3] it is, however, positively welcome in Popper's political thought, where the problem of its justification does not arise from the simple reason that for Popper the consequentialist, "good on balance" or "the benefit exceeds the cost" *ipso facto* legitimizes the coercion employed to bring it about. If "balance" is correctly struck and "cost" correctly assessed, they already subsume the undesirability of coercion, and imply that it is outweighed. There is then no need for something *else* to legitimize it, as it were, a second time round. *"May the state do good?"* is, in this scheme of thought, a nonsense question.

HOW TO BE A SOCIAL ENGINEER

With this finding, we have almost certainly reached the nub of the matter. Popper, as we have seen, is in the habit of making his normative statements in terms of the consequences that he requires politics to generate. Democracy must enable the ruled to remove their rulers and to control economic power. Our institutions must prevent the exploitation of "the less gifted, or less ruthless, or less lucky" (p. 127) and "prevent even bad rulers from doing too much damage" (p. 131). Political life must be cleansed of "the crime of anti-equalitarianism" that would give some men "the right to use others as their tools" (p. 236). Social engineering must improve our life and make social and economic arrangements more efficient and rational. Admittedly, "interventionism ... leads to an increase in state power and bureaucracy. But ... his is again *merely a problem of social technology* and of social piecemeal engineering.... We must plan for freedom, and not only for security" (pp. 193–4, italics in text).

How could anyone disagree with such aims, and how could one *not* applaud the institutional design that can bring them about? It is all the more easy to agree as approving the aims does not commit us to anything at all. The consequences we are encouraged by Popper to seek when making political choices, are such that whether we are going forward or backward, left or right, we can always claim to be pursuing them. Who can ever prove that we are *not* planning for freedom? – or that we are committing the "crime of anti-equalitarianism"?

The hard part in political theory is to excogitate, not what we ought to want, but *how to get it*. It is easy enough to call for institutions "designed to" do this, that and the other. The puzzle and the pain begin when the institutions that *will* do these things have actually to be "designed," and (even before the design could start) specified in hard engineering language that has a "falsifiable" information content. What are the rules collective choices must obey in order to qualify as "democratic"? Which bargains count as "equitable" and which are the laws we need to uphold equitable bargains while overturning inequitable ones? What is it we must do, or refrain from doing, to make an economy perform "efficiently"? For it is not good enough to say that the institutions must be just, or rational. All our institutions are that – or none is, depending on the observer's pleasure. It must, at the end of the day, be stated in untwistable language, in what precise way they are supposed to meet which precise criteria.

There is nothing in consequentialism to require a consequentialist to talk in terms of a wish list, an inventory of the consequences he thinks good institutions ought to produce. He can perfectly well make the backward leap, and argue instead in terms of the specifications an institution must meet in order to be good – where his "good" is still a consequentialist, instrumental one, derived from the aims he wants the institution to serve. One could hazard the guess, however, that such a leap does not come naturally to the consequentialist. That even Sir Karl Popper, the great advocate of social engineering, and the scourge of empty assertions masquerading as testable statements, resorts to a list of demands for what well-designed institutions must achieve, instead of telling us *how to design them*, corroborates the guess in a small way.

The silence on how to design the institutions that will give us our dearest wishes, permits another guess: that there is really nothing very much to say, that getting what we want is not primarily a matter of "designing" institutions and if it were, we would not know how to do it.

A quite fundamental doubt underlies this guess. If it should turn out that there *is* no epistemological basis on which to build a *social* technology, that in reality "there just ain't no such thing," nothing sensible *could be said about the means* we should choose to produce the social *ends* that Popper recommends us to pursue. All we could tell the social engineer is that we want the engine to run sweetly and reliably, but we could suggest no way for him to find out *how* to make it run so. Random tinkering, whose purported effects ("greater justice," "less exploitation") cannot be intersubjectively ascertained, or are untestable for other reasons, may never give rise to a technology. It will very likely ruin the engine before it does.

It is not a priori foolish to criticize propositions purporting to tell us something about the world, for they *could* be mistaken. Nor is it foolish to challenge an alleged hierarchy of preferences, for it may be internally inconsistent and fail to be a true hierarchy. It would, however, be quite foolish to reject Sir Karl Popper's political thought for failing to be a coherent hierarchy of aims or an engineering manual for improving society. Clearly, he did not intend to produce either a credo or a manual.

However, it would be fascinating to see the same Sir Karl Popper setting out the deontology of the state, working out from first principles what it *must*, *may*, and *must not* do – rather than listing the many desirable results we expect from its actions. When is it right – if it ever is – for some people, whether dictators or democratic majorities, to coerce others into accepting their choices? What makes coercion legitimate? When is it our duty to obey the political authority, and when is it proper for us to use it for securing advantages at the expense of our fellow citizens?

These are, it seems to me, the fundamental questions of political philosophy. Even the consequentialist, in order to have coherence among his objectives, must try to answer them at least implicitly. Explicit answers are better still, for they are more open to scrutiny and criticism. Sir Karl Popper is not a liberal in the cis-Atlantic meaning of the term. He is a social democrat, even if one is not altogether sure of the reasons why. He is under no intellectual obligation to produce a deontology of political action, and if he did produce one, I should be the last to try and predict what it would be like. But how I wish that, liberal or not, he should find the leisure and the interest to provide us with some leads for guessing!

NOTES

1 All page references in brackets in the text are to Popper, 1962, vol. II.
2 The historicist torch passed from Hegel to Marx; but though Popper considers Marx a much better intellect, he does not consider him a philosopher (any more than the great majority of historians regard him as an historian, or of economists as an economist).
3 Mill the liberal, who would admit coercion only to stop people from damaging each other's interest, is himself in danger of getting into a consistency problem with Mill the socialist, who would re-order the distribution of the social product once it has been distributed in a process arising from the exercise of valid property rights by willing sellers and buyers.

REFERENCES

Popper, K. R. (1945) *The Open Society and Its Enemies*, London: Routledge & Kegan Paul, 4th edn (revised), 1962, vol. II.

6 Hayek: some missing pieces*

Has Hayek a theory of the social order, a comprehensive view of society as a determinate and self-reproducing system, in the same way as Hobbes or Marx, though perhaps no one else can be said to have an (albeit simpler) theory of the social order? The question has some weight, since if it is true that Hayek is the most influential twentieth-century advocate of liberal government, the strength and penetration of normative liberal doctrine must to no small extent depend on the persuasive force of his positive social theory: the less coherent it is, the more modern liberalism is vulnerable to erosion and invasion by incompatible elements.

It is hard, probably harder than it looks at first sight, to be sure what we mean by a social order. Hayek himself mostly uses the term "order" in the context of his ideas about the spontaneous order. However, he intends order as such to mean something akin to a pattern or schema, such that by looking at a part or a phase of it, we can make good enough conjectures about the whole (1973, p. 36). It is as if, by finding a piece of a jigsaw puzzle that depicts a cloven hoof, we could tell that the puzzle, if it were all fitted together, would in all likelihood represent a cow, a goat, or perhaps the devil, but certainly not a lady with her parasol.

My thesis, putting it at its sharpest, is that Hayek shows us pieces of a complex jigsaw that are intriguing and inspiring, but they do not suffice to let us predict whether, if we had all the pieces, the completed puzzle would show a cow, a goat, or the devil. If I am anywhere near right, he has no complete theory of the social order to back up his liberal recommendations. They are in any case a little incongruous, since he predicts that whichever kind of order is superior will duly prevail through group selection, hence recommending it is somewhat out of place even if we could know that it was not superior, and *a fortiori* if we could not. Does Hayek show us how to tell?

There are, it seems to me, at least three areas of the puzzle where he has left out important pieces, and where pieces he did place do not really fit together. One is the distribution of the social product, the other is

* This chapter first appeared in *The Review of Austrian Economics*, vol. 9, no. 1 (1996), pp. 107–18. Reprinted with permission.

public goods, and the third is the spontaneity of the very spontaneous order that gives the whole puzzle its character.

MAKING THE FREE SOCIETY ATTRACTIVE

One of Hayek's most widely known normative ideas is that there can be no such thing as social, or distributive, justice. The concept is simply a category mistake: "there can be no distributive justice where no one distributes" (1978, p. 58). It is certainly doubtful whether one can defend, from arguments drawn from justice, the popular belief that certain participants in arm's length transactions are responsible for the distributive shares that accrue to other participants; that rich employers should pay higher wages to poor employees, and that supermarkets should not drive small shopkeepers out of business.

Hayek holds, reasonably enough, that the terms of voluntary exchanges are determined objectively, they are not matters of anybody's good intentions, nor of what richer parties think the poorer parties ought to be getting: nobody distributes. What he calls the "market order" entails a distribution that is neither just nor unjust. It is, however, efficient. As such, it has instrumental value and can serve other valuable ends. These ends, for Hayek, cluster around the maximum chance for the randomly chosen individual to conduct his own life successfully. Distributive justice does not figure among the ends the riches created by the free market order should serve. A long line of others, from John Stuart Mill to A. Mueller-Armack and beyond, have of course taken the well-known position that the market order conforms to "economic laws" and is neither just nor unjust, but the wealth its efficiency creates can be devoted by "society" to satisfying, among other things, the requirements of distributive justice.

Both Hayek's and Mill's position, different as they are from each other, stand in sharp contrast to the more rigorous thesis that the market order does in fact produce a distribution that *is* just if the distribution of ownership in a selected initial position were just, and subsequent exchanges were free from force and fraud.

Hayek, in his insistence that the whole issue is categorically irrelevant to the market order, leaves a blank where others put distributive justice. Its missing piece is an unintended invitation for them to fill the void.

However, while disputing the very sense of the concept of distributive justice, Hayek is nevertheless concerned with distribution. He notes that modern societies without exception do organize welfare states – is this cultural selection at work? – and that this evolution is consistent with respect for "abstract rules of just conduct." It is more than a historical shift in the spontaneous order, more than an unintended result of human actions directed at other purposes: deliberately helping it along is a positive "task of the defenders of liberty" (1960, p. 259). "[T]hough a few theorists have demanded that the activities of government should be limited to the maintenance of law and order, such a stand cannot be justified by the principle of liberty" (ibid., p. 257). The welfare state is a conglomerate of many diverse elements, some of which may "make a free society more attractive" (ibid., p. 259). For one, government must provide for "the minimum of sustenance" for the helpless, and this minimum should be, not absolute, but relative and rising with the general standard of living (ibid., p. 285). For another, such provision cannot be confined to the deserving poor, but must be extended to all (ibid.). As a corollary, it becomes the recognized duty of the public to compel all to insure or otherwise provide against the "common hazards of life" (ibid., p. 286).

It is clear enough that a guaranteed minimum income, once granted, will not for long be kept down to the level of absolute physical subsistence, but will creep upwards and take on features of a defense against "relative deprivation." It is also clear that if people no longer have an incentive to provide against bad luck and old age, a case is created for compulsory social insurance. What is less clear is why Hayek considers, not only that these things are bound to happen, and to happen on a scale that expands with economic progress, but that it is no bad thing that they should. Their object is not to conform to any moral imperative, whether of compassion, fellow-feeling, let alone distributive justice, which he rejects as the product of muddled thought. Nor is it because a distribution brought about by the market order can, along the lines of Benthamite and Pigouvian utilitarian thought, be "corrected" to generate a larger sum of aggregate utility, for Hayek to his great credit never embraces the idea of interpersonal aggregation of utility. In fact, his advocacy of such quintessentially redistributive measures as the guaranteed minimum income is accompanied by injunctions that such measures must not have a redistributive purpose! Barring both justice and utility as their object, all he leaves us with by way of justification is that some redistribution, (if it is not intended to be redistributive) "makes a free society more attractive."

Why, however, should one seek to *make* the free society more attractive? Is it not going to prove itself more attractive anyway in cultural selection, by its superior aptitude to prevail over less free societies (assuming that the ambiguities of what it means to "prevail" have been resolved)? Manifestly, Hayek thinks it can do with a bit of help. Embellished by the institutions of a moderate welfare state, presumably more people will opt (vote) for it, or fewer people will desert it for the totalitarian alternative he abhors. Does this mean, however, that the free society is not the social order that prevails because its intrinsic properties make the groups that adopt it more numerous? – does it mean that the free society is a social order that prevails over others if and because its properties are adjusted to what people from time-to-time find attractive (even if it does not make the groups adopting it more prosperous and numerous)? If the latter is the case, what distinguishes Hayek's social theory, or at least the part he has made explicit, from the theory of democracy as the system where social choices are made by adding together votes for alternatives being acknowledged as superior, not by virtue of its intrinsic capacity to make its host group grow, but by virtue of attracting more votes?

Enough pieces are missing from the jigsaw to permit either interpretation, though Hayek would no doubt protest quite sharply against his cultural selection being, by a piece of impudent distortion, equated with procedural democracy. However, his missing pieces leave room for a "conglomerate of elements" that may well be mutually inconsistent, part cow, part goat, part devil, leaving it to the spectator to call which is which. What exactly is a free society? On what grounds can Hayek predict that it will prevail? Above all, what is the point in its functioning of the unplanned interplay of individual decisions whose collective effects are unintended, and what of consciously formed collective choices carried out by the agency of the state? Hayek's *obiter dicta* on redistribution seems to me to leave the question largely open. This void is only deepened by his treatment of public goods and the role of the state in providing them.

THE PIVOT BETWEEN ORDERED ANARCHY AND STATISM

There is a measure of unself-conscious irony in Hayek's call for a "much more clear-cut attitude towards [public goods] than classical liberalism ever took" (1978, p. 144). Classical liberalism would entrust to the state the provision of only one, very special, public good, to wit, "the enforcement of general rules of just conduct" (ibid.). There is, however, a multitude of other "highly desirable" public goods that "*cannot* be provided by the market mechanism" because they "*cannot* be confined to those who are willing to pay for them" (ibid., my italics). Therefore the means for providing them are either raised by the coercive power of the state, or not raised at all. The liberal may wish that the way be left open for private enterprise to provide them if a method is discovered for it to do so (1978, p. 145), but pending such discoveries, it is legitimate and indeed mandatory for the state (or local authorities) to tax society in order to enable it to enjoy these highly desirable things.

Is Hayek's position "much more clear-cut" than that of classical liberalism? Public goods are of central importance to social and political theory. If they *cannot* be provided in voluntary transactions, but we must and want to have them, the state is necessary and Pareto-superior. If they *can*, ordered anarchy is possible, and the state usurps the space that, in its absence, would be filled by Pareto-superior, voluntary transactions. It may be held that property and contract enforcement is a necessary condition of voluntary transactions. It may be further held that such enforcement is a public good only the state *can* provide. This, in brief, is the classical liberal position of the minimal, protective state. It may or may not be good theory, but it is clear-cut enough. More recent theory suggests that even contract enforcement *can* be provided voluntarily by those who expect to benefit from respect for their contracts, and there is no evidence that organizing a state for the enforcement is more efficient, less costly in terms of total transaction costs, than its decentralized, private provision. In this view, even the minimal, classical liberal state is a needless blemish upon ordered anarchy, let alone the modern liberal state subsumed by Hayek, which has a mandate to tax society for the sake of providing goods and services as long as they are both public and desirable.

Hayek seems strangely unaware of the pivotal role of public goods theory between ordered anarchy and statism, and treats it cursorily. Hardly realizing its consequences, he accepts the textbook division of the universe of goods and services into two exogenously determined halves, public and private. Private goods are *excludable*, hence *can*, public goods are *non-excludable*, hence *cannot* be produced in voluntary transactions, where goods are forthcoming against equivalent resources or not at all.

In reality, there is no such exogenous division. Nothing is "excludable" without further ado; for nothing can be sold without the seller incurring costs to exclude from access those who would not pay the price. Exclusion cost is no more avoidable in a good destined to be sold than is the cost of production or transport. Everything is excludable at *some* cost that may be high or low, depending on a host of circumstances, of which the physical characteristics of the good is only one. Over the universe of goods, exclusion cost is a continuous variable. Where society draws the dividing line between public and private goods is an endogenous decision, for social theory to define. Providing a good publicly saves exclusion cost. This advantage may be partly, wholly, or more than wholly offset by costs arising from wasteful use of the good the consumer can have without paying for it, and from other, less direct risks. If social choice were usually "collectively rational," goods would be provided publicly if the saving of exclusion cost outweighed the disadvantages and added costs of publicness. As it is, whether a good becomes public, or stays private, is decided by the "public" through a political process that is not set up, and is quite unlikely, to be "collectively rational" in the above sense. Certain goods become public goods because it is held that people ought not to *have* to pay to have them, others because they *won't*. All this is well understood now, and was already understood when Hayek expressed his view that the state ought to provide "highly desirable public goods."

The half-universe of public goods is in fact one *we* fill. It thus comes to contain innumerable goods that are desirable *if* and because they are public, so that their marginal cost to the individual consumer of the good is nil or imperceptible, and they amount to a "free lunch," to something for nothing. If so, the observation that they are highly desirable is a product of circular reasoning. As long as the good remains a good (i.e., short of saturation) every potential consumer of it will readily vote for its public provision if it is not yet so provided, and for its provision on a more generous scale if it is provided but sparingly. Where should the line be drawn? How should a liberal society count the votes for more of everything, and the votes against the taxes to pay for it? Whichever way it counts them, it has relatively little chance to stay liberal.

There is only a missing piece in Hayek's theory where the principles should be that a liberal society would adopt to draw the line between public and private, to keep it there, and stay liberal in the process. Unlike classical liberalism, which confines the state to the provision of a single public good, law enforcement, Hayek's social order is less, rather than more, clear-cut: it permits, if not positively mandates, the state to produce any number in any quantity; the state's place in society is consequently ad hoc, open-ended, indeterminate, and no amount of dire warnings against socialism, fatal conceit, and loss of freedom will make it more determinate.

A theory of social order is incomplete if it makes no serious attempt at assessing the long-term forces that make the public sector grow or shrink. This can hardly be done without relying on a defensible theory of public goods. Hayek feels no necessity for one. Strangely, the question seems to have held no interest for him. By way of making good the missing piece, one must insert some account of the conditions under which goods will remain private, produced only for restricted access against payment in full, as opposed to the conditions that will favor their production for unrestricted access by any member of a given public, with the necessary resources being raised either by voluntary association under contract, or by involuntary taxation. The relative weight of these three alternative solutions is perhaps the decisive influence on the extent to which a society is political ("politicized" is the pejorative word usually employed for it), shaping its life by collective rather than by individual choices. The question is of abiding interest to Hayek. He does not answer it, though he fervently wishes throughout his massive *oeuvre* that the answer should favor individual choice.

WHO ENFORCES THE ENFORCEMENT?

Why does it matter to Hayek, or anybody, whether an order is spontaneous or not?

The attraction of spontaneity is both moral and prudential. Though it is not clear whether Hayek saw more than instrumental value in it, he stressed that the elements in a spontaneous order "arrange themselves" rather than being arranged by "unified direction" (1960, p. 160). When the elements are human beings, their property and their choices, nobody's dispositions are imposed on him by another's command. Everybody chooses for himself what seems to him the best, given that everybody else chooses likewise. All choices are interdependent, and made mutually compatible by property rights and their voluntary exchanges. None dominates and none is subordinated. This lends the order in question a moral *laissez passer*, while nonspontaneous orders, constructed by imposing some alternative on the participants by authority or the threat of force, are morally handicapped by their coercive element. If they are to pass for legitimate, they need to show some compensating merit. Spontaneous social orders, in other words, have a prima facie moral standing. Constructed orders must first earn it, or do without.

The prudential attraction of spontaneous orders springs from the belief, strongly held by Hayek and fairly well supported by historical evidence, that since the knowledge required for successfully designing a complex order is either irretrievably dispersed or latent or both, the constructed order runs a high risk of being inefficient if not grossly counterproductive.

Game theory calls "coordination game" an interaction where, if all or most players adopt the same norm of behavior (strategy), all get a payoff that is no worse and may be better than if they adopted different norms. Compliance at least weakly dominates deviation. Hayek's spontaneous order is at first sight a coordination game: he speaks of rules that, if they are generally observed, make all members of a rule-following group "more effective," "because they give them opportunities to act within a social *order*" (1978, p. 7, Hayek's italics). The rules are randomly generated, by analogy with genetic mutation. Some are positively selected in a process of "cultural transmission ... in which those modes of conduct prevail which lead to the formation of a more efficient order" (ibid., p. 9), because the more efficient order helps the group living within it to "prevail" over other groups. A classic and appropriately Austrian example is the use of money, a more efficient "norm" or "rule" than barter. No member of the money-using group can do better by reverting to barter once most others trade against money. Compliance dominates deviation.

All would be well if Hayek confined his concept of the spontaneous order to cases of voluntary rule-following that are coordination games, i.e., where the emergence of the order depends on some members of a group adopting the same rule of behavior, but once they do, the order is self-enforcing: all members have a continuing incentive to adhere to it and can only do worse for themselves if they deviate from it. Patently, however, there are important rules that do not function like this. Once they are widely followed, they generate an incentive for the individual member of the group to violate them. Perhaps the simplest "spontaneous" order, as Hayek would call it, that operates in this perverse way is the queue. Every member of the group that has a rule of queuing rather than milling around and pushing each other, gains from every other member following the rule. However, the member who jumps the queue gains more than the one who stands in it; he can abuse the decent restraint of the others. Queue-jumping dominates queueing. The same is true of the spontaneous order that is at the center of Hayek's theory, the "market." It will not function to the advantage of every participant unless at least two key rules of conduct, respect for the property of others and performance of reciprocal promises, are widely followed. However, if they are followed by some, this *ipso facto* tempts others to steal, usurp, trespass, and default on contracts. These favorite deviations offer a higher payoff than compliance with the rules, which of course renders compliance a potentially self-destructive mode of conduct. Neither queueing, nor the market, nor many other ostensibly spontaneous orders are truly spontaneous, i.e., coordination games along the benign, self-enforcing lines of using money, speaking the same language, or driving on the same side of the road. They are thinly disguised or overt prisoners' dilemmas.

Though he steers clear of game terminology, Hayek is quite aware that this is so, and that those of his putative spontaneous orders that are in effect prisoners' dilemmas, and have deviation as their dominant strategy, need something more than the efficiency of their rules of conduct if they are to survive. Not being self-enforcing, they need some support from rule-enforcement. At one point, he suggests that the successful group, though it does not realize to which rule it owes its superiority, "will accept only those individuals as members who observe the rules traditionally accepted by it" (1978, p. 10). Hayek's group, then, expels robbers and cheats. It uses ostracism to punish and deter violations of its rule. Ostracism is one of the several time-honored voluntary enforcement mechanisms that have been employed, since the dawn of civilization, to ensure the survival of beneficial but fragile conventions, including adherence to the customs and laws of property and contract, where the convention itself generates an incentive to break it. Ostracism, like other defenses against violation, can thus be understood as an auxiliary convention, a satellite serving the fragile, nonself-enforcing main convention. In the absence of such supporting conventions, the emergence and widening of the division of labor, trade, and capital accumulation would be incomprehensible. So would be those cultural, legal, and political institutions whose material wherewithal was produced by these developments.

There is some excuse for holding that a spontaneous order that needs to be enforced is still a spontaneous order, if its enforcement itself is spontaneous, the norm of a voluntary convention. Its adherents follow it by voluntary choice: they "prefer" to carry out costly and often unpleasant actions to exclude, punish, and deter violators, and do not need to be threatened with exclusion, punishment or other deterrents to be induced to do so. More realistically, they may not actually "prefer" to act against violators, but wish to avoid disappointing the conventional expectations of fellow members of their group who rely on their help, and on whose help they wish to be able reciprocally to rely. (Splitting hairs, I am treating the threat of a sanction and the risk of disappointed reliance on an expected benefit as different in kind. If they are not, the distinction I seek to make between spontaneous and enforced enforcement becomes blurred, and difficult to sustain.)

It is, however, stretching spontaneity beyond the breaking point to call an order spontaneous if it depends on "enforced enforcement," i.e., if members of the group or a subset of them punish and deter violators of the rules, not because they think it is in their reciprocal interest or simply because it is right to do so, but because they are threatened with exogenous sanctions if they fail to do it. In the latter case, with enforcement at one level depending on enforcement at the next higher level, who ultimately enforces enforcement?

Hayek is convinced that as civilization evolved, the scale of human coexistence changed by an order of magnitude, from small to great. There was a passage from the "face to face" society of small groups to the "Great Society" of the large group. Members of the small group were related to each other by ties of many kinds, and these relations gave rise to group solidarity. Members of the large group are unrelated and anonymous. They succeed to profit from the division of labor and the economies of scale made possible in their "extended order," not by relying on personal relations of trust, reciprocity and sympathy, but by respecting a suitable set of "abstract rules of just conduct."

Who, however, enforces the rules of just conduct? Respect for property and contract are not self-enforcing. On the contrary, they generate incentives for their own violation. Failing reliance on reciprocity, there is no voluntary convention for enforcement, except for saying that in classical liberal doctrine it is the sole field where coercion is legitimate (1978, p. 109). In fact, if the Great Society works the way he believes it does, anonymously and at arm's length, enforcement cannot be supplied spontaneously, for it is undermined by the free rider problem and perverse incentives in exactly the same way as property, contract, and other prisoners' dilemmas. Enforcers must be coerced to enforce. Calling a spade a spade, one would say instead that enforcers must be paid to enforce, and for this to happen taxpayers must be coerced to pay taxes. There must be at the end of a regress of enforcement-enforcers, an ultimate, sovereign enforcer. There is no doubt whatever that when talking of the need to enforce rules of just conduct, it is the state that Hayek saw as the necessary, sufficient, and legitimate enforcer.

Here, too, vital pieces are missing from the jigsaw. Take the market order whose unique efficiency helps the large group to prevail. It is a web of exchanges of all kinds, most of them indefinitely repeated. In some instances, the two sides of the exchange are performed simultaneously. These are in most circumstances self-enforcing, and the parties to them might as well be anonymous (though usually they have names). When, however, performances are not simultaneous, executory contracts ⁚ some complexity are often required, and they are not self-enforcing.

How could strangers with no name and no established reputation enter into such contracts with each other, the state's enforcing facilities notwithstanding? Do they ever do so? Who will be prepared to perform first when facing a nameless unknown? Yet, how, if you are anonymous, can you do any business at all except by performing first, unless somebody, broker, banker, insurance underwriter, middleman, lends you his name for love or money? In the Great Society, most people may well be anonymous to most others, because they have no profitable occasions to get acquainted; but since they have no such occasions, it does not matter much that they are anonymous. However, few people or none can remain anonymous to the handful of others with whom they interact in making the market order go round. That handful gets selected spontaneously, and it is always a "small group." There *is* no anonymous, large-group interaction because it would be too numerous to admit it. Its individual members interact in several "small groups" whose membership may be partly overlapping, partly different. Thus, each small group is open to other small groups and memberships are intermingled at the edges.

The truth of the matter about the Great Society is that few or no large groups are completely homogeneous. Their membership can always be disaggregated, sorted into smaller groups by a variety of selection criteria. As the large group is always *the sum of small groups*, the converse goes as well: small groups can always be aggregated to form what is, from a chosen point of view, a large group. Its dimensions are in the eye of the beholder.

If one chooses to see it only as a large group, as Hayek does, something must be said about the existence problem of the nonspontaneous order which its specifications entail: if Hayek won't tell who enforced the enforcement, others will expound it with a vengeance.

For the effect of leaving out pieces from the jigsaw puzzle of social theory is that the vacuum is only too naturally filled by a false conception of the state. This conception is hardly compatible with liberal principles. Indeed, it is hardly compatible with the very market order that Hayek wants to be spontaneous, and culturally selected to make groups that adopt it succeed, and groups that deliberately deform it fail. For although it does not logically exclude other alternatives, Hayek's theory leads straight as an arrow to the facile conclusion of an indispensable state that alone upholds property and contract. They exist by the grace of society acting through the political authority. They function as society chooses that they should. The massive chorus we have been hearing from the left and center, chanting that property is a bundle of separable privileges granted or withheld by society, and the freedom of contract is subordinate to public policy, is vindicated by the very theory that should have prevailed over such a chorus with a clearer, a more powerful voice.

REFERENCES

Hayek, Friedrich A. von (1960) *The Constitution of Liberty*, Chicago: University of Chicago Press.
—— (1973) *Law, Legislation, and Liberty*, vol. 1, *Rules and Order*, Chicago: University of Chicago Press.
—— (1978) *New Studies in Philosophy, Politics, Economics and the History of Ideas*, London: Routledge & Kegan Paul.

7 The rule of forces, the force of rules[*]

All is not well with our politics. Never before in history, perhaps with the exception of ancient Greece, has civil life been politicized to quite the same extent as today. It might appear that society should be better, more fully served by its government than ever before. Yet few would think that this is the case. The principal products of more intrusive, more caring, and more comprehensive politics seem to be disaffection with, and dysfunction of, government. Where the process has gone furthest, under "real existing socialism," failure reached staggering dimensions. But whether governments now profess to live by democratic or socialist precepts, or by the near-ubiquitous, ungainly crossbreed of the two, their relations with the governed are sour.

The causes of this state of affairs are by now quite widely understood. They have become the commonplace wisdom of political science and political economy. The study of public choice convincingly explains why political decisions are biased toward self-defeating, perverse effects and suboptimal, "negative-sum" outcomes, and why we, as rational players in the political "game," nevertheless keep asking for more of the same. Given the rules of the game, any other outcome is unlikely as long as enough people behave prudentially, in the sense of maximizing some not wholly implausible combination of material ends. Selfless voters or suicidal politicians could, of course, produce less depressing solutions, but they seem to be a rather rare breed. Failing a wholesale change of hearts, one possible solution to the dilemma suggests itself: change the rules. Hence the rising interest in constitutions as they are, and as they should be.

Seeming to be close to a state of despair by the very public choice logic that he coinvented and whose workings no one grasps better than he, James Buchanan (1993, p. 1) put it pithily:

How could the constitutional framework be reformed so that players

* This chapter originally appeared in the *Cato Journal*, vol. 14, no. 1, Spring/Summer, 1994. Reprinted with permission. An earlier version was presented at the Mont Pélèrin Society meeting in Rio de Janeiro, September 1993.

who advance generalized interests are rewarded rather than punished? . . . The response is clear. *The distributional elements in the political game must be eliminated.*

WHO GETS WHAT, WHO PAYS WHAT?

Any constitution that would eliminate the distributional element would, in truth, abolish politics itself. The reason for holding that politics is quintessentially distributional is fairly simple. When all benefits and all related costs come in finely divisible pieces, rather than in great indivisible lumps, each person's benefit can be made contingent on his paying a price that fully covers the cost of production, including the cost of excluding nonpayers. Individuals, in free contractual or quasicontractual interactions, will then profitably produce reciprocal benefits for each other, each paying for what he receives. There is no need for any collective decisions. If, and only if, important indivisibilities exist or are felt to exist (e.g., on the grounds that if peace, justice or security from life's risks is to be produced at all, it must be produced for all at once), do some politics become inevitable. Though it is quite a step from "some politics" to the fully fledged state, it is basically from our "need" for indivisible public goods (of which public order is a special case) that many political thinkers derive the need for a coercive supreme authority. Costless, non-scarce goods call for no decisions; each can take as much as he wants, and so can the person coming after him. However, public goods that cost something to produce involve political cost-allocation and political benefit-sharing. No matter how austere a notion of "need" for such goods we adopt, even a bare night-watchman service assuring public safety must involve collectively deciding who shall bear what part of the cost. Setting a global standard for the common benefit to be provided is, no less inevitably, a political matter with distributional consequences. Seen broadly, these decisions affect not only the present, but prejudge the future, too, through the grant of unrequited rights ("entitlements") and the assignment of the corollary obligations to involuntary obligors. Within this view of politics, arguing that political choices must not be about distributions means to argue that political choices must simply cease to be made.

On a closer view, however, Buchanan's postulate turns out to be, not that questions of distribution should be purged from politics (which in strict logic would be a contradiction in terms), but that they should be resolved in conformity with the principle of "equal treatment" or generality, applicable in politics no less than in law. Buchanan (1994, p. 2) suggests that eighteenth-century constitutions duly gave effect to this requirement. However, I believe that such a view gives these constitutions more credit than, at least judging by the American experience, they can rightly claim. With the passage of time, the US Constitution, far from enhancing the safeguards of property as its Lockean inspiration called for, has proved to be very apt to accommodate redistributive group politics and sanctimonious, busybody, legalistic modern American liberalism.

I will come back to the content of the equal treatment principle presently. For now, it suffices to note that, if the principle were true to the promise its name seems to hold out, it would not abolish politics, but would assuredly take out some of its appeal; for if equal treatment really meant what at first blush it seems to mean, its adoption would change the world. No longer could politics enable some to gain at the expense of others, no longer could majorities despoil minorities, no longer could organized groups take turns to exploit each other, trying to get from politics what the economics of property and contract denies them.

A constitution that succeeded to hold nonunanimous collective choices to the purportedly straight and narrow path of the equal treatment principle postulated by Buchanan would by the same token drastically lower the stakes in the political game. Most of the fun, and most of its point, would be gone; it would hardly be worth playing. Welfarism could not favor particular groups. Interventionism would be unable to pander to its natural constituency, the corporatist interests.[1] Constitutional rules effectively ensuring equal treatment would utterly transform the incentive structure of public life. The net effect would be a reversal of the trends of the past century or more, and the relative places of state and civil society would start moving back toward the classical liberal ideal. Can any constitution achieve this much? And can it, for that matter, achieve anything significant at all?

CONTRACT OR VOW?

There are only two ways of reaching nonunanimous collective decisions that are binding on all. One is for the greater force to prevail over the lesser, bending it to its will. It need not always twist the weaker party's arm, and humiliate it into open surrender. Mutual recognition of the relative forces often suffices to produce a semblance of unanimity. There is always a presumption in favor of avoiding actual tests of strength, for the use of force to bash one side into submission is costly to both sides. Also, the risk that bullying and arm-twisting will get out of hand and escalate into a mutually wounding all-out fight is a deterrent to making too many controversial "social choices," and to multiplying them immoderately and even frivolously, simply because each one seems a good idea to the stronger party of the moment.[2]

At the same time, the stronger party to this shadow arm-twisting, or to the real fight, does not have much chance to remain the stronger faction for long. History tells us that shifting alliances usually preserve, or restore, rough balance between opposing coalitions. No group retains quasi-permanent superiority, if only because imbalances create incentives to break up coalitions, whose members are induced to change sides until a rough balance of power is reestablished.

Let us call this somewhat informal method of reaching decisions in the face of incompatible interests or preferences "the rule of forces." To this day, it is this rule that governs the *modus vivendi* in international relations. However, in medieval Europe, as well as in modernity until the emergence of an effective monopoly of the use of force in centralized nation-states, basically the same balance-of-power rule governed the respective spheres of decision. Principally, these spheres were concerned with the roles and prerogatives of the prince and the "live forces" of civil society, such as major feudal lords, the estates, and the leagues of towns, some of which were allied with the prince, while others opposed him as contentious issues arose. The "constitution," to the extent that it existed, was no more than a summary expression of the balance of these social forces.

The alternative to the "rule of forces" is the "force of rules." Under the former, collective decisions obey, roughly speaking, the will of that coalition within society which could beat, or is seen as capable of beating, the rest into submission by using armed force, economic power, or moral ascendancy.[3] The "force of rules," on the contrary, rests on a prior commitment by all the parties concerned to abide by unwelcome decisions provided they have been arrived at in a manner laid down and agreed upon in advance.[4] The "rule of forces" prevails in a Hobbesian world of two principals, government and society, in a partly cooperative, partly adversarial arm's length relation that has the essential features of a tacit contract. In this state, the provisions of a constitution are substantive, for it is meant to lay down, though not in so many words, what government must and must not do if it is to earn obedience and avoid rebellion. The "force of rules" fits the fantasyland in which dwell the General Will of Rousseau and its successor, the to-be-maximized social welfare function of contemporary social choice theory. Here, government is not a principal, not a party to an implicit contract with society enforced by forces located on both sides. There is only one principal, society. Government is its subordinate agent. There is the usual principal–agent problem between them, but it is not of first-order significance. The purpose of the constitution is no longer to smooth the rough edges of an adversarial relation, but to elicit the General Will by specifying the procedure for identifying it. As we now prefer to say, it is to provide an agreed-upon method of "social preference-revelation and aggregation." Constitutional rules are thus invested with a putative moral force, since they are the instrument through which "social preference" manifests itself.

Two consequences follow as a matter of strict logical entailment from this distinction. One concerns the respective functions of the two types of constitution, the one resting on forces, the other on rules. Forces yield to each other, when they must, on matters of substance, but they need not bother about procedure. Procedure is unimportant unless a procedural decision has a foreseeable effect on a substantive result. In that case, however, the apparent matter of procedure is in reality a matter of substance, albeit once removed. Conversely, rules for deciding in advance which alternative shall be accepted by all as the "socially preferred" one are by the nature of the case procedural.[5] They say, or can be made to say, that if an alternative was selected by certain agreed upon rules about how selections are to be made, that alternative is to be taken *by* all as better *for* all *on balance* than any other that could have been selected but was not.

Procedural rules go with the democratic grain; substantive rules go against it. At first sight, there is something incongruous about the idea that society should adopt a constitution that rules out certain alternatives – for example, interference with the freedom of contract – since by doing so society may bind itself to choosing an alternative that, come some future day, it might not prefer. Though good enough sense can be made of such a resolution, it takes a mental and moral effort that may not always be forthcoming. Substantive rules that tangle up the social choice machinery in apparent self-contradictions of this kind do not sit easily with democracy. I cannot think of a way of proving that he is right, but I unhesitatingly follow Buchanan (1994, pp. 2–4) when he affirms that it is substantive, not procedural, rules that make a liberal constitution. I would wish, though, that he would press home this judgment a little more dogmatically than is his wont; for it touches a serious question about the systemic compatibility of democracy and liberalism. More on this presently.

The second consequence is that a constitution that is not the expression of some balance of power between principals who hold each other in check on specific matters, but a mechanical procedure for collective decision-making in all things, has the incentive structure of a vow ("a contract with oneself") rather than of a contract properly speaking. It may be that not all contracts are honored, but they are contingently enforceable, depending on the forces directly or indirectly interested in their fulfillment. (All who have occasion to rely on contracts have an indirect interest in any given contract being honored.) Vows may be kept, but they are not enforceable. "Society" might respect a constitutional "vow" stopping it, on some occasion, from choosing a tempting alternative. But should it wish to yield to the temptation, all it has to do is suspend, reinterpret, or amend its vow. There is no greater force protecting the integrity of a vow than the strength of character of the individual (or in our case "society") that made the vow. Assume that a procedurally proper decision is reached, e.g., by majority vote, whose substantive content would be unconstitutional, vow-breaking. The sole force that could be devoted to upholding the "vow" is, according to the rules, directed by the very procedural "social choice" that is proposing to break it. The case need never arise, for there are usually ways of twisting a political vow so as not to have to break it. But if such a case were to arise, it is hard to see what could be done about it, except to protest impotently or look the other way.

A constitution that rests on the "force of rules" rather than, as of old, on the "rule of forces," has something of the character of a benign confidence trick. It is respected by most, in the spirit of David Hume, as long as most believe that it is respected by most. But under majority rule, the trick must be adapted to the majority view, the majority taste, the majority interest. This is why, under the system of judicial review, constitutional rules *evolve*. Failing it, they could hardly survive. The changing fortunes of the "takings" clause and the commerce clause in American history are telling examples. The few existing constitutional rules that could have inconvenienced "social choice" have in time all been reinterpreted out of recognition. As an example, one need only reflect on the fact that Italy is constitutionally held to a balanced budget.[6]

EQUAL OR DIFFERENTIAL TREATMENT

Take, however, a substantive rule that looks powerful, has not (to my knowledge) been tried in application, and promises to change the whole perverse incentive structure of politics for the better, deflating its sphere of competence instead of inflating it as at present: the rule of equal treatment proposed by Buchanan (1994). Buchanan is aware that putting this principle into practice would pose many problems of detail. By and large, however, he clearly believes that it could be translated into readily understandable guidelines that governments would find hard to flout openly.

They would be forced, for instance, to impose taxes at uniform rates; differential rates among persons, organizations, locations, industries, products, or other possible classifications of taxable subjects, would be ruled out (Buchanan 1993, p. 5). At least formally, no less than four types of taxation, each with a uniform rate of its own, conform to this guideline. We could have a uniform lump sum tax on natural and legal persons alike; or a poll tax on all natural persons, rich and poor, and another lump sum tax on all legal persons, large or small; or a flat rate tax on all incomes, high or low; or a tax at a uniform rate on all capacities to pay (this would be our progressive income tax under a different name). Nevertheless, while all four tax regimes may appear uniform, it can be argued that they are, in fact, differential: they all treat some members of a given class of taxable subjects worse than others.

Another possible guideline mentioned by Buchanan would lay down uniform subsidies for every industry. However, a uniform subsidy on labor employed distributes state aid among industries one way, a subsidy on capital employed another way, one on physical output or sales yet another way. Analogous arguments can be found to show that guidelines meant to tighten the nexus between benefits from public goods and their costs (e.g., "The region receiving the new major road should pay for it") can, given the political will, always be circumvented by unfalsifiable claims of large, bountiful external benefits. Financing more and more education, a benefit to local families and their children, from central rather than local revenues would be a likely result of heeding such claims – the same result we are apt to get anyway, without an equal treatment guideline.

The long and short of it is that every "equal" treatment is equal with respect to a selected category or class of cases and unequal with respect to another. Giving the same stipend to all able or all deserving students treats all able or all deserving students equally, but treats all students – some of whom are not able and not deserving – unequally. Equal treatment of all poor old people is unequal treatment of all old people (poor and rich) and of all poor people (young and old). The inequalities generated by achieving equality for some category of subjects or cases are countless. Their number depends only on the richness of our vocabulary for formulating ever more and finer categories, within each of which the same treatment must be accorded to all.

Of course we have known since Aristotle that what we call equality is really equiproportionality, a fixed ratio between every member of one class of entities and every member of another class. A uniform proportion between each member of the class "families" and each member of the class "income dollars" yields "equal family incomes," but unequal "incomes per head," "per gainfully employed person," or "per dependent child." This is a relatively innocuous case of different distributional results being obtained by strictly adhering to "equal treatment," but shifting the reference class. One can trust the ingenuity of lobbyist lawyers and politicians worried about the next election to think up others whose distributional bite is sharper and deeper, while still conforming to some plausible construction of equal treatment and generality.

CHOOSING PROCEDURE, CHOOSING SUBSTANCE

A little more needs to be said about procedure, substance, and the prospects for a liberal constitution. Constitutional rules are not Moses's tablets. They are not made in heaven, and even if they were, men on earth would soon unmake them. It is a strange supposition that politics goes on within constitutional constraints, but that the constraints themselves are somehow above politics, determining it without being determined by it like any other product of collective decision-making. This is why, alas, no constitution is a 'fixed' one. As values change, and views of how the world works – and the social forces associated with those views – change, constitutions also change. Either their letter is amended or their spirit (their "intent") is reinterpreted. No great technical difficulty obstructs these developments. Any obstacle to change – for instance, a restrictive rule protecting property from expropriation – is maintained because it is in the blocking minority's interest to have the rule. Its removal permits a redistributive gain whose value, in a world of no frictions and no "leaky buckets," approximates to the value of the interest. The prospective gainers can buy off part of the opposing interest (unblocking the blocking minority) and still have something left over. Relaxing the rule that protects property releases resources whose new distribution can dominate, politically defeat the old, in the same way as every existing distribution can be defeated by a new redistributive bargain, in obedience to society's apparently circular preference rankings.

Each set of constitutional rules permits an associated maximum of redistributive gains to be made by a winning coalition. Under a liberal constitution, the greatest possible gain is likely to be relatively small. That it minimizes the scope for redistributive policies is, in fact, as good an operational definition of a liberal constitution as I can think of (though the reader will perhaps decry it as question begging; for it supposes that constitutional limitation of the scope of redistribution is a feasible result). If it chooses according to the motivation usually attributed to it in modern political science, and notably in public choice theory, the winning coalition will seek to get the set of rules adopted that will maximize its potential redistributive gain. What is sauce for the goose is sauce for the gander. Choosing the rules that maximize the winners' gains from politics is fully on par with maximizing the gains once the rules are given. If the latter is a realistic assumption, so is the former, and thus we must say goodbye to the ideal of the minimal protective state.

Substance – a heavily redistributive state with everyone subsidizing everyone else, and strongly intrusive politics – can be "chosen" by choosing procedure. The smaller is the winning coalition that can decide a given issue in its favor, the greater is the residual losing coalition and, consequently, the greater is the total of spoils the winners can extract from the losers. Under democratic equality, where every person and his vote weighs the same as every other, the smallest possible winning coalition is one-half of the voters and a tie-breaker, the median voter. Hence the procedural rule that will best deliver the desired substantive result is one that makes a simple majority decisive for every issue. So does the analysis of constitutions show liberalism and democracy as inexorably divergent, like the up train and the down train, running in opposite directions on parallel tracks.

NOTES

1 Politics would be left with one irreducible constituency, the diehard intellectuals who cannot help believing that one must "reinvent government," because social engineering is a force for good that must never willingly be surrendered.

2 In contrast, collective decision-making by rule, when all have the duty peacefully to accept whatever comes out of the vote-counting machine, is not a deterrent but a positive incitation to social choice-making: the risks of strife and rebellion are removed, only the victors' rewards remain.

3 Though given the perceived capacity to do so, the need to use this force will seldom arise.

4 Of course, this agreement must also be respected after the fact by all.

5 Norman Barry (1989, p. 279) notes that today liberalism is often interpreted "as embodying agreement to procedures irrespective of the outcomes that might emerge from them." This is the position Barry (1989, p. 277) attributes to Hayek, in that "there are no *substantive* limitations on what legislatures may do, only strict procedural ones" in Hayek's constitutional proposals. Substantive rules seek to prejudge "end-states," which is now widely held to be an illiberal ambition. Only procedure, "procedural justice" and "process" (as in "the peace process," as distinct from peace) are politically correct objectives. Here is another example of trendy jargon clouding thought. Barry's diagnosis seems regrettably exact.

6 I owe this startling item of information to Antonio Martino. The Italian budget is, of course, balanced like every other by the proceeds of vigorous treasury borrowing. Everyone who votes for this state of affairs must be trusting that his children, when they grow up, will manage to shift the burden of debt to other people's children.

REFERENCES

Barry, N. P. (1989) "The Liberal Constitution: Rational Design or Evolution?" *Critical Review* 3(2): 267–82.

Buchanan, J. M. (1993) "How Can Constitutions Be Designed so that Politicians Who Seek to Serve 'Public Interest' Can Survive and Prosper?," *Constitutional Political Economy* 4(1): 1–6.

—— (1994) "Notes on the Liberal Constitution," *Cato Journal* 14(1): 1–9.

Part II
Emergent solutions

8 Before resorting to politics*

INTRODUCTION

The good of some and the bad of others

Why does anyone want to resort to politics and why does anyone put one kind of political order above another? Those who are both very earthy and very frank approve the one they believe is doing the most good for them. "The way truly to understand history is the way of Princess Mathilde [Bonaparte]. She would not forgive those who spoke ill of Napoleon because, as she explained, 'without that man I should be selling oranges on the wharf in Marseilles.' The good or the bad done to us, there is the grand criterion of history" (Bainville, 1941, p. 16; my translation). However, it takes more effrontery than most of us possess to be *this frank* and *this earthy*; and at all events Princess Mathilde's "grand criterion" of political hedonism, by which I approve of the system that favors mainly me, and disapprove of the one that favors mainly others, has no hope of generating a semblance of basic agreement about the respective merits and consequences of political systems over and above the fairly low common denominator of democracy, namely the shared redistributive advantage of a winning over a losing coalition.

Once, therefore, we try to advance toward a beginning of Kantian generality and universalizability, seeking to justify political arrangements by reference to arguments that are morally more compelling than the advantages for some bought at the cost of setbacks to others, the "grand criterion" ceases to be of help. What makes matters worse is if a type of political order not only has a clear propensity to cause some to gain and others to lose, but if the gainers and losers are always much the same persons, divided by permanent cleavages. "[It] is difficult to see why a loser in the competitive struggle should support the market system when it encourages the development of character traits whose existence in

---

* This chapter, now slightly amended and abbreviated, first appeared in *The Shaftesbury Papers*, vol. 5, edited by C. K. Rowley (1996), Cheltenham: Edward Elgar, pp. 1–53. Reprinted with permission.

others works to his disadvantage and which he himself does not possess"
(Buchanan, 1985, p. 51). If this argument holds for the market system, it
holds equally for the system of the welfare state, a putative antidote to
the "market system," under which burdens are imposed on one class of
person and benefits awarded to another, and which is believed, not
without reasonable ground, to help develop character traits in one class
which work to the permanent disadvantage of the other.

The pursuit of values

What is true, in a crude and obvious way, of the system of political
hedonism that expects the state to cater for some interests to the relative
neglect, if not the actual harming, of the others, is true, albeit less con-
spicuously and more subtly, of any other political order that fosters one
value, or a few, to the relative neglect of the others. Not all values
are compatible; most must compete with one another. Secular historical
experience largely bears out that liberty has a cost in terms of security,
security in terms of progress, progress in terms of equality, equality in
terms of respect of rights, and so forth. There are, to use the economist's
jargon, marginal rates of transformation between each, indicating, for a
particular society and age, "how much" of one must in effect be sacrificed
to get a little more of another. At the same time, every individual with
a fairly developed awareness of his own preferences and with some
capacity to act upon them coherently, can be construed and understood
as having, to use the same jargon, marginal rates of substitution between
values, indicating "how much" of one he would be only just willing to
give up for a little more of another, if the occasion arose.

Values, of course, are very large, poorly defined and abstract categories,
and it is perhaps contrived language to suggest choices, substitutions, and
transformations between them, rather than between the objects to which
they are attached. To suggest, in addition, that values lend themselves to
meaningful quantitative measurement for their substitutions and transformations into one another to have recognizable "rates" (so many
"units" of one for one "unit" of the other) may be thought of as an even
worse aberration. Nevertheless, people as well as political societies do
visibly trade values off against one another, and sometimes do so consciously, on purpose, overtly reasoning about such marginal choices, and
that is all the quantitative character my present argument really needs.

A political order "reveals" its hierarchy of values by what it promotes
and demotes. It selects policies that produce more of one value and less
of another *as if* it sought to equate its marginal rate of substitution
between them to the marginal rate at which they can be transformed into
one another in the real world. The latter is a matter of the social and
economic facts of life that are given, at least in the short run. To say that
policies are chosen to adjust the marginal rate of substitution of any two

values to their marginal rate of transformation is to say, tautologically, that the policies are chosen rationally. It is also to say that if the tradeoffs they brought about were not the ones sought, the policies would be rejected and different ones adopted.

It is an empirical question whether these marginal rates of substitution between, say, liberty and other valuable ends coincide with those of many, or indeed any, denizens of the society whose political order we are discussing in these laborious and tediously technical terms. Plainly, if they are like people everywhere, namely different from each other, the coincidence will be less than perfect,[1] and the value-oriented political order will be a less than perfect match for the people who live within it and must live with it.

This is, indeed, exactly what we should expect on a little reflection. The design of teleological political orders, intended to equip them for the pursuit of some end, mimics the "model" of a single actor pursuing some end. However, a single actor making choices that bind others, no matter how sympathetic and well attuned he may be to the interests and preferences of those for whom he acts cannot possibly pursue the same ends, practice the same tradeoffs, and replicate the same choices as a multiplicity of actors would severally like to make, except if the latter are all alike in all relevant respects, a condition that is neither likely nor desirable. One cannot both uphold the teleological design that biases the particular order to favor, say, liberty over equality or vice versa, and avoid overriding the value preferences of some constituents who are invited and expected to accept this order. There is nothing, no discernible mechanism, that would make global social choice coincide with the best available choice of each individual consistent with the best available choice of every other – which is the equilibrium solution of ordered anarchy.

The pursuit of happiness

Some communitarians first of all, and probably socialists too, would say that this is as it should be. It is only right that politics should serve to promote certain values at the expense of others, and that this should leave some people adhering to values the community rejects, less than satisfied. Politics must serve the common good. We may disagree about what the common good happens to be, that is about the "object level" political question. We may even disagree about the meta-level question, that is the proper manner of ascertaining the common good. We do agree, however, that it is not any kind of sum of the good of everyone, nor any kind of game-theoretic equilibrium in which each does as well as he can consistent with everyone else doing so. Value neutrality, if it were possible, would be wrong.

Opposed to the idea of the common good is a traditional liberal view, little changed since it was handed down by the Philosophical Radicals, though no longer regarded as an essential indefeasible part of liberalism. In this view, the best political order is one that is most apt to give people what they most want – some kind of "greatest happiness," no matter which values it is derived from and in what proportions – and that formalizes this goal in the value-neutral terms of utility maximization. Of course, in properly understood "utility theory no one aims at utility as such or even cares about it. Utility is postulated as the mathematical expression of the rank or strength of the material ends people do pursue. So long as the relation between material ends can take any logical form at all, . . . there is no harm in this view, and very little bite" (Fried, 1978, n. 13). Except for the word "material" (for there is surely no restriction whatever about the ends utility theory handles, be they tangible or intangible, material or moral, or, in Bentham's words, "pushpin or poetry") there is much to be said for this explanation of Charles Fried's. It makes it clear that utility is not a *rival* of other values. It is *all* the values a person has, taken together, and ordered after having undergone the tradeoffs his relative preferences tell him to effect among them.

Translating into common utility language the multiplicity of values that motivate any *one* person's choices does nothing, however, to bring about value neutrality *among* persons. For it is impossible to pursue "utility" or happiness as such. One can only pursue specific objects functioning as ends that are expected to make greater or lesser contributions to "utility." It is possible to seek ends that are likely to contribute to the "utility" of two persons at the same time, or for that matter to that of a whole society. But it is impossible to do it "value-neutrally." For a collective choice that is a practice of tradeoffs between values can conform to the value hierarchy (marginal rates of substitution) of one person and not of another unless, once again, they think exactly alike.

Whichever way we twist and turn the "social welfare function" or the "social choice rule," we cannot square the circle. Value neutrality, where there is not too much of one thing and too little of another, can be achieved by the individual for himself, but not by a political order for many, let alone for everybody.

The "debacle and ruin" of liberal theory

These seem to me among the most fundamental, almost tectonic, reasons for the growing loss of credibility of modern liberal theory as a whole. They are inherent in its basic design. The upshot is twofold. First, liberalism is easily colonized by a variety of incongruous doctrines, notably about "rights" for desirable things and favorable treatment people are asserted to have, to the effect that the adjective "liberal" is becoming useless, signifying very little that is distinctive of one doctrine and not true of almost every other. Second, liberalism, misstated from the outset as a theory of the superiority of liberty over other "political" goods, cannot any longer sustain its strong original claim to moral ascendancy over other blueprints of the political order. A former liberal, and perhaps the most prolific present-day commentator of liberalism, now diagnoses "[t]he debacle of the project of liberal ideology" in which there is not anywhere a "compelling demonstration of the priority of liberty over other political values" (Gray, 1989, p. 261); he finds that "the liberal ideal itself becomes indeterminate in the absence of criteria for identifying freedom and unfreedom" (p. 141) and that "the strong indeterminacy in liberal principles . . . spell ruin for fundamentalist liberalism" (Gray, 1993, p. 313).

"Debacle" and "ruin" are strong words. They seem to claim too much too dramatically, for the case of liberalism is not lost, though I believe it will have to be pleaded along new, firmer and safer lines. Yet its loss of identity, loss of moral vigor, and vulnerability to dilution are persuasive evidence that something is seriously amiss that cannot be put right merely by a return to the orthodoxy, such as it is, of the classical sources.

For this reason the present chapter, though one of its objects is to deal with what seem to me some of the most potent fallacies that have colonized and perverted liberalism in recent years, seeks above all to look for the rock-bottom of liberal logic. It proceeds by laying bare what seems to me implicit in this logic and proposes three, admittedly sketchy, "principles of politics." I claim them to be principles that are entailed in the liberal ethic. Any liberal theory must incorporate them in its foundations and whatever else it contains must be consistent with them. Any such theory will, in that case, be simple, rugged, fairly though not absolutely undemanding in its assumptions about the nature of man and society, and undemanding in terms of its meta-ethics and epistemology. Above all it should be resistant to parasitic ideas alien to its ethic.

Armed with the nucleus, if not with the fully elaborated substance, of such a theory or perhaps theories, I shall in what follows seek to review some contemporary theses about the scope of government, democracy and property that, to my mind, contradict the logic of liberalism, while claiming to be developments and extensions of it.

IN DOUBT, ABSTAIN

Consequentialism "on balance"

Taken at large, this section pleads for an injunction to restrain consequentialism to its legitimate sphere, which in politics is very small indeed. Consequentialism, reduced to its simplest expression, assesses the worth of an action by its results; as a guide to action, it tells us always to take from a set of mutually exclusive options the one that will bring about the best consequence unless there is a sufficient reason for doing otherwise.

However, mainstream consequentialism is more absolute than this. For if the reason for not aiming at a certain consequence is sufficient, the consequence cannot be the best, and the real reason why we ought not to aim at it is that *on the balance of reasons* it is better not to do so. Consequent consequentialism, in other words, vanquishes all before it, because it reasons on the balance of *all* reasons. There may be under the widest, most general version of consequentialism, though not under its narrow and strict form, reasons for or against an action that are not its consequences. They are arguably not caused by it yet are its corollaries, so that we cannot seek "the" result if we do not override the reason that speaks against the action in question. Doing good by lying would be one example incorporating two reasons to be balanced against one another in wide consequentialism; the narrow version would ignore the wrong of lying if it did neither harm nor wrong to anyone. It is nonetheless the case that consequentialism, wide or narrow, proceeds by *adding up* widely or narrowly conceived arguments with due regard to their algebraic sign, positive or negative. The distinction between wide and narrow forms of consequentialism is confined to the kind of arguments that are admitted to the exercise of summing. Utilitarianism, the oldest and most prominent version of narrow consequentialism, operates only with arguments about the extent to which actions cause the preferences of individuals to be satisfied.

The scope of government as the scope for doing good

Within the logic of consequentialist ethics, it is incoherent to want to limit the scope of government. For as long as the beneficial consequence of the best available political option exceeds its opportunity cost (which is of course the benefit expected from the next-best option), it is incoherent to say that the best option ought not to be exercised. It is like saying that the net increment of good ought to be thrown out of the window, cheating society of it.

A constitution may be no more than a set of procedural rules laying down how political decisions are to be reached – perhaps, more precisely, the conditions that must be fulfilled for a political decision to be binding both for the officers of the state and for its ordinary subjects. These are, to use Herbert Hart's term, the "rules of recognition" writ large. Beyond them, the constitution may also lay down substantive rules about the admissible content of political decisions. Their effect is to render certain procedurally quite irreproachable decisions inadmissible. For instance, the effect may be to forbid and void a majority vote by secret ballot for indefinite detention without trial, for press censorship, or for the taking of property without just compensation. Any such substantive limitation is but "vain breath" in consequentialist ethics, for it amounts to a *vow* not to do certain things even if, one day, there was sufficient "on balance" benefit from doing them. However, by what Thomas Schelling calls "a stunning principle of social organisation" (Schelling, 1984, p. 99), but what seems simply an entailment of the meaning of "promise," a promisee can always release the promisor from his promise, and if they happen to be the same person the promisee cannot coherently both demand and refuse the release. If, then, the action that is inadmissible under the constitution appears to hold out better consequences on balance than any alternative, a consequentialist society cannot, without self-contradiction, allow the power for doing good of its politics to be frustrated by self-imposed constitutional limitations. Limiting government, as it were on purpose, would only be rational if the scope for doing good were itself limited, which no doubt it is not.

"Balancing" incommensurables

Why, despite its pleasing logic, is all this wrong? There are two independent reasons. The first is relatively mundane: it is that we ignore the full consequences of many of our actions. This, for an individual responsible only to himself and his family dependents, imposing his will on no one else, dealing with them only by means of voluntary exchanges or gifts, is not a very grave moral problem. Politics, however, is different. It involves the use of what is, for practical purposes, an irresistible power, "the monopoly of the legitimate use of force," to impose the will of some on all, including on those who would reject it if they could. For politics, therefore, the Hippocratic precept applies with particular stringency: *first, avoid doing harm*. A state that acts on the consequentialist logic, and ignores out of hubris, bad faith, or sheer lack of perspicacity, its own ignorance of the consequences which may in time turn out to be far from good, will fritter away the legitimacy of its monopoly of force – if indeed it ever had it.

The second reason is more fundamental and, to my mind, if anything more compelling. It is that among the multiple consequences, functioning as multiple reasons for or against, only some are commensurate. Those that are, suffer from our partial ignorance of what they will in fact turn out to be: but this handicap could in principle be attenuated if we learned more about the future. Those, on the other hand, that are not commensurate, defy any consequentialist logic even in principle, and even if all knowable knowledge were known. Between the good and the bad consequence, where neither is either greater or smaller than or equal to the other, no balance can be struck, and consequentialist reasoning is simply out of place.

The central place where consequentialist reasoning is incompetent to penetrate is the interpersonal balancing of "utility." This is more than somewhat ironical, since nine political decisions out of ten have such balancing as their unspoken justification; a policy is adopted because, though it imposes costs on some, it brings greater benefits to others.[2] The cost, seen comprehensively and taking everything into consideration that the policy influences unfavorably, is the diminished utility of some. The benefit, reckoned in the same comprehensive way, is the increased utility of others. The reason why we cannot proceed to a straightforward addition, with due regard to sign, is not (as many astonishingly still persist in thinking) that we "lack sufficiently detailed utility information" and don't know how much to add and how much to deduct, but if only we had the "information" we could strike a balance. The reason is that there is no information to be had and no balance to be struck. The good of different persons is incommensurable.

Avoid doing harm

Let us be very clear about one thing. The value judgment that it is better if a certain subset of a society gains and another loses than if neither gains and neither loses is just that – a value judgment and a perfectly legitimate one at that. So would the contrary judgment be. Neither has more analytical or empirical support than the other. The "ought" is not derived from any kind of epistemic "is," for before making the value judgment between two policies, we have not measured nor compared differences between the utility gains and the utility losses of two groups of individuals. Once again, we have not done so, not because we "lack the data" but because the project of comparison is nonsensical and could not be proceeded with. Policy recommendations that insinuate some kind of "is" backing up their "ought" – the classic example is the more or less tacit suggestion that a more even distribution of national income "must" have a greater utility – lack either honesty or intelligence. Policy recommendations courageously disclaiming support from facts, surmises, or reasoned forecasts, and resting squarely on some overt and partisan value judgment alone, must stand up against rival value judgments. This is a contest that cannot be decided inside consequentialism, if it can be decided at all. Its result must, at all events, be subordinated to the moral precept about the use of the fearful instrument of legal coercion: first, avoid doing harm.

Commission and omission

Nothing that I can see authorizes the setting of the commission of some harm on the same footing as the omission of doing some good. On the contrary, harming and benefiting the same person, let alone different persons, are sufficiently heterogeneous to be held prima facie incommensurable in any relevant and nontrivial sense. An action whose consequences combine such "incommensurable" elements cannot, then, be characterized by *one* on-balance consequence, and compared with another action and its consequence, because a combination of nonhomogeneous consequences resulting from an action cannot be expressed as a single net balance.

The consequentialist calculus, in other words, is inapplicable wherever a consequence of an action within a set of alternatives contains incommensurable elements. By and large, commissions and omissions, and interpersonal gains and losses, defy such calculus. Choosing one alternative from such a set is a value judgment, and must never pretend to be a judgment of fact.

It is dubious in the extreme that a political authority is entitled to employ its power of coercion for imposing value choices on society, on its subsets, and on individual members. Its sole guiding principle in such cases can only be: *when in doubt, abstain.* That the choice could be justified by a value judgment shared, for example by a voting majority, does not remove doubt, especially if outside the majority rival value judgments are held. It may be observed that the respect of this guiding principle, unless it were complemented by other deontic rules about what governments must do irrespective of the consequences (and unless these rules mandated government actions even if the consequences were not unambiguously welcomed by all concerned), would compress politics to the vanishing point.

Cognitivist authority

If consequentialism were to be a valid rule of choice in all cases, the value judgment by which the choice is in some cases (in fact in most cases that really matter) made, would itself have to be a valid one. But whether one judgment putting a valuation on a consequence, among rival judgments putting different valuations on it, is valid or not is itself a question to be resolved, under consequentialism, on consequentialist grounds. It can normally only be resolved by a value judgment which has, in turn, to be validated. This leads us into an infinite regress. To avoid it, we can close the loop by postulating a valid value judgment that, on cognitivist authority, finds in favor of on-balance reasoning in evaluating consequences. (One such possible value judgment could, for instance, assert that we ought to impute interpersonal levels or differences of human well-being to levels or differences of some measurable, homogeneous resource endowment, electing the latter as a proxy for the former.[3]) The doctrine then rests on circular logic, for the alleged correspondence between two sets of interpersonal differences, one measurable, the other not, is not a finding of fact, but a judgment about how we should evaluate such differences.

The presumption against coercion

If consequentialism is circular, depending in all cases involving harm or interpersonal comparisons on a value judgment about its own validity, the standard argument for letting the state do all the good we can find for it to do, and accordingly allowing politics to have unrestricted scope, falls to the ground. Its collapse releases and activates the basic presumption against coercion, a presumption that can be derived either from an axiom about the practice of choice, or from a social convention of "live and let live," of letting each do what he will if doing so involves, roughly speaking, no harm to others. Accepting, and acting on, this presumption also presupposes a value judgment, but it is one that demands far less of our moral credulity than any consequentialist alternative I can think of.

The presumption against coercion must always mandate *some* restriction of the domain of politics, removing at least some alternatives from the reach of social choice. Otherwise the presumption would have no effect on the use of coercion, and it is difficult to see precisely what would be meant by it in that case, unless it were that while coercion can legitimately be used to realize any socially chosen alternative whatever, in the face of the presumption social choices should only be made upon strong provocation and strong justification, while in its absence any justification would do. This difference is verbal, slippery, and vague, it does not work intersubjectively, and has no place in a political doctrine that is meant to be resistant to Princess Mathilde's and other interested parties' attempts to twist it in their own favor.

Giving real effect to the anti-coercion presumption, then, means at least some nonprocedural, strictly substantive limitation of social choice. It takes too much faith in political man's rectitude to believe that such limitations will generally, let alone always, be respected; after all, they are "only" vows, promises to ourselves, and temptations to break them come dense and fast in public life. It is a very unsafe political order that must rely heavily on a substantive constitution. The major danger, as the history of constitutions and especially of that of the USA convincingly shows, is not.the open breach of a substantive rule, but its "evolution," its reinterpretation, small step by small step, its twisting out of all recognition in the span of a few decades.[4] In view of this experience, some kinds of constitutional limitations look more likely than others to stand up against the temptations of the times, simply by virtue of their lesser twistability. An indiarubber rule, for instance, that subjects government actions to the test of fairness, and makes statutory distributions of burdens and benefits unconstitutional if they do not respect the condition of fair shares, must be practically unbreakable, for the understanding of what are fair shares is sufficiently flexible and malleable to accommodate the whole range of politically feasible distributive policies. By comparison, a fixed bar on aggregate public expenditure of all kinds, limiting a certain definition of it to a fixed maximum share of a certain definition of national income, however blunt and arbitrary it may be, is less twistable. It can no doubt be circumvented in relatively minor ways by stretching the definitions, but probably not in massive proportions; if public expenditure as defined exceeds the permissible percentage of national income as defined, the rule is openly broken, ringing the alarm bell, provoking at least some embarrassment, some blame, and some modest impetus for a revision of policies.

Lowering the stakes

The "when in doubt, abstain" principle will more effectively guide (and curb) the state in a body politic that is not yet permeated by, or has already shaken itself free from, consequentialist ethics and cognitivist meta-ethics. Such arcane matters in the realm of thought may not seem burningly relevant to practical politics. However, in the long run they probably matter more than they seem. The liberal disposition so attract-ively demonstrated by the Scottish Enlightenment, by Humboldt, Constant, and Bastiat, was inspired by implicit deontological rules of liberty and property. In the edifice of liberal ideology erected by nine-teenth-century philosophers and economists, an edifice whose design was wide open and, as I would contend, positively invited invasion by alien squatter elements, the deontology was largely replaced by essentially utilitarian justifications. Liberty and property became instrumental, means to other, more nearly final ends and values. As other means came to be seen as equally or more efficient in maximizing the same values, or as the hierarchy of values appears to have shifted, liberty and property, and the conventional rules upholding them, progressively lost their morally inviolable character. It would be extravagant to affirm that the hubris of consequentialist and cognitivist thought caused the loss; but it is plain that it gave intellectual coherence and ethical backbone to the process.

At first blush the "in doubt, abstain" principle looks not a liberal but a conservative one; for cases of reasonable doubt about policy abound, and if instead of resolving them, in doubt we abstain, it is the status quo we may be thought to protect. The theorem that "utility" is intersubjec-tively incommensurate, hence interpersonal comparisons presented as findings of fact are gibberish, appears likewise to justify the status quo at least by default.[5] However, it is an unwarranted diagnosis. For cases of reasonable doubt abound, not only about policy changes but also about policies already in force. Civil society is tightly shackled and heavily steered in its legal, cultural, and perhaps most particularly in its economic dimension by literally countless institutions, statutes, rules, state proper-ties, regulatory interventions, and administrative practices that are imposed on it by fiscal or other coercion. A benign view of government sees them as self-imposed by the citizenry, "socially chosen," but even so for some reason needing to be enforced by a dominant central coercive power that, by virtue of its monopoly, is different in kind, and not only in degree, from the lesser coercive powers scattered across civil society. With regard to such of these institutions as are, in the light of the foregoing arguments, in reasonable doubt, the principle calls, not for leaving them as they are, but for dismantling them. In that it is not a conservative, but a liberal principle.

Dismantling certain state and state-enforced institutions by repeal, privatization, and, at the margin, by reduced scope and reduced budgets for continuing programmes, has an interesting and I believe far-reaching byproduct: it lowers the stakes that can be gained or lost by exerting some influence on the redistributive aspects of governing. (I speak advisedly of the "redistributive aspects" of governing, instead of referring to the government's "redistributive measures," in order to exclude the inference that there can be government measures that are not redistributive. Every policy measure either produces benefits that have an incidence on individuals or imposes burdens that must be allocated among them, or both at the same time; and it is not logically impossible but hardly imaginable that they could leave the distribution the same as it would be if the measure had not been taken. This is a fact of life, whose truth does not depend on any redistributive intention. Whether redistribution is the primary objective of some government activity or its more or less accidental by-product, is often impossible to determine anyway.) The more the stakes are lowered, the more the nature of such policies as subsist is transformed. This is the converse of the case of a large role of government in the regulation of industry and commerce, in taxation, transfers, and the production of public goods, very fully explored by public-choice theory under the heading of "rent seeking." When potential "rents" are getting progressively more miserly, interest groups have less of a stake in preserving the stakes, the industry of seeking rents goes into decline, which ought by a feedback effect to reinforce and accelerate the lowering of the stakes, hence the slimming down of "rents." This scenario will probably never be played out on a real political stage, but that need not stop us from pointing out that it represents a plausible conjecture about the practical effect that the progressive espousal in our social ethics of the "when in doubt" principle would have.

Between "must" and "must not"

A recognition that consequentialism as a guide to political action backed by coercion is unsound, flatulent, and unable to live up to its pretensions would leave only deontological rules potentially standing. The most important rule, overshadowing all others, is undoubtedly the negative one
'mposing on the state the general duty of abstention from using coercive

power for purposes whose consequentialist justification is of the on-balance kind and where the sign of the balance is open to reasonable doubt. Is there anything further to say? Are there, in the shadow of the negative rule, positive ones laying on the state the duty to use coercion in order to accomplish certain things?

If there are no things requiring coercion that the state *may* but *need not* do, i.e., if there is no optional middle ground between what must and what must not be done by coercion, it suffices to define what the state must do. If what it must do can be specified and justified, things it must abstain from are defined by the same token: they are all the things whose achievement involves coercion and that the state has *no duty* to do. Positive deontological rules yield, as a residue, the negative one: "abstain." In a severe political deontology, treating coercion as a very grave matter not to be taken lightly, and for that reason admitting no discretionary, optional areas of the political domain, there is only "must" and "must not," but no middle ground open to doubt, hence no latitude either for deciding whether the doubt is reasonable or not. Putting it differently, if the optional use of state coercion is excluded, so that the only uses of it that are permitted are mandatory ones, the description of the mandatory area adequately describes the prohibited area as well: the latter is whatever is not covered by the former.

Certitude about what must be done would do away with the need to resort to the potentially controversial finding of "reasonable doubt" about the occasions where abstention by the state is its duty. However, this ideal can hardly be attained. The very reason why reasonable doubt has an irreducible element of subjectivity militates also against an uncontroversial, agreed position about the cases where it is certain that the state has a duty not to abstain, but to act. Given all the things that the state could do, any degree of indeterminacy in the subset labeled "must" entails the same indeterminacy in the complementary subset labeled "must not."

The indeterminacy is not resolved by the usual liberal device of enunciating a list of "musts" – the prevention of harm, the protection of rights, the production of public goods – both because each of these purported duties of the state is poorly defined and indeterminate in itself, and because it is by no means proven that these functions are totally and intrinsically political, and could not wholly or partly be fulfilled by nonpolitical, noncoerced, cooperative arrangements. Swallowing them whole and uncritically as the archelypal and irreducible duties of the state is to swallow a hook by which individuals in a civil society find themselves committed to a form of political life that many find overwhelming and unduly intrusive. The three duties of harm prevention, rights protection, and public-goods production between them are sufficiently broad and have sufficient capacity for expansion by reinterpretation, to leave no part of life outside politics and no resource whose use is not subject to nonunanimous coercive collective choice.

Inviting coercion

Recourse to first principles in political ethics suggests a path, albeit a narrow one and poorly signposted, out of this thicket of fuzzy definitions and indeterminacies. The first principle that seems to me the least demanding, hence the easiest to subscribe to though no doubt less easy to put into effect, is that applying coercion is legitimate when it is positively invited by the prospective coercee.

For an isolated individual, the only case when it is not absurd to bring down coercion on his own head is when he thinks he needs help to overcome his own weakness of will. The case is well known and can be taken as read. In every other case he would be silly to ask to be coerced to do what he wanted to do, and sillier still if he asked to be made to do what he did not want to do.

Interactions of two or more persons, however, can create situations ("prisoners' dilemmas") where inviting coercion is the rational thing to do, given certain expectations about the actions of the other persons or, more fundamentally, about their rationality. The object is to transform a noncooperative "game" into a cooperative one by improving the credibility of promises. There is, to be sure, an argument to the effect that this is only half the battle. Making agreements fully credible by enforcing compliance presupposes that agreements are reached in the first place; this is the basis of what Jules Coleman calls "thin contractarianism" (Coleman, 1988, ch. 10). "Thick" contractarianism, by contrast, recognizes that bargaining about the distribution of the prospective surplus to be produced by overcoming a prisoner's dilemma is itself liable to fail, and there may be no agreement to comply with. This type of theory, then, contends that the emergence of market solutions is prevented by "pre-market failure" (ibid., pp. 262–76). To resolve this more "fundamental" (p. 267) failure, an antecedent "political association" is necessary to lay down a "property rights scheme," including rules of property, liability, and tort.

How the scheme allocates property rights in the premarket situation, i.e., under what distributive conditions all participants will agree to a political association that will enforce the scheme, is thought to be a bargaining problem of great complexity. The claim that rational behavior will lead to a universally agreed properly rights scheme is not very plausible (p. 267). The upshot is that the stale exercising coercion without the prior consent of its subjects may be necessary for Pareto-optimal resource allocation.

The problem, it seems to me, arises from the wholly artificial starting position where distribution is, so to speak, up for discussion, and there are no established, preexisting property relations. (It is worth stopping here to note that while in the theory that Jules Coleman calls "thick contractarianism" people bargain *ex nihilo* about distributing unowned wealth among themselves, and likely fail to reach a bargain solution, in the contractarian theory of Buchanan and Tullock, and of David Gauthier, the base line from which bargaining starts is one where wealth is already owned. The solution does not establish a "property rights scheme" *ex nihilo*, but modifies the one that already exists in the state of nature.) A grand bargain to decree who shall own what is then necessary and may well fail to be reached. But there is, of course, no call for such an overall bargain, for patterns of ownership emerge and evolve over time in virtue of unilateral acts (see pp. 173–6) and bilateral contracts, and can be sufficiently determined by them. The "thick theory" with its "pre-market market failure" creates its own difficulty.

"Market failure," or more precisely the possibility that people may not succeed to base schemes of corporation on contracts, but may need coercion, or ties of affection and solidarity, is a vast field of study that occupies the better part of game theory. The most we can do here is to allude to some of its more robust conclusions. The situations where it can be rational for me to invite coercion have at least one common feature. It is that the best outcome of the interaction for each of us is obtained if neither of us seeks the best outcome for himself. Contract is the most important of such situations.[6] The best outcome for me is if the other party performs and I default. Second best both for me and the other party is if we both perform. Mutual commitment to seeking the second best by each will ensure the best possible for all. If each is coerced to respect his commitment, each can have full confidence that none of the others can take advantage of his trust. Let us note, for consideration presently, that coercion, let alone coercion by a single central political authority, is not a necessary condition for commitments to be credible, and that instead of "full" confidence, partial, probabilistic confidence in the other participants may be sufficient for the best outcome for each to be obtained (or at least approximated in a mixed strategy equilibrium).

From the condition that for coercion to be legitimate it must be invited by the prospective coercee, it is only one step to hypothetical invitation, the crucial first step in social contract theory. Its argument refers to a contract situation where, assuming the parties were rational, they *would* invite coercion if it were absent (i.e., if the invitation were not redundant to the citizens of an existing coercive state) and if they were not too numerous to communicate and agree among themselves on a jointly binding invitation, i.e., if "transactions costs" were not too high.

"Transactions costs," default and free rider temptations, and "holdout" temptations that can obstruct the solution of bargaining problems, are the three suboptimal unfruitful situations where it is conceivable that rational persons caught in this type of predicament might rather escape from it under coercion than remain in it and escape coercion.

However, it is not good enough that they conceivably might, or that under certain types of mutual expectations, whose presence inside their heads we cannot verify, it would be rational for them to wish to do so. Hypothetical invitations have no better standing than hypothetical contracts. What is needed for the application of coercion to be above moral suspicion is that the prospective coercees *do* actually invite it. The way to provoke this, hence to test the legitimacy of the state, is for it to stand back and not to proffer political solutions, by legislation, regulation, and taxation, to such tasks as the enforcement of basic social conventions (notably concerning torts, externalities, and the amenities of civilized conduct), of contracts and the provision of public goods. It is only when politically imposed and publicly financed solutions are not readily available that those concerned can tell whether voluntary "grass-roots" solutions would or would not work, and the necessary conventions to stabilize them would or would not emerge soon enough; and only if they really do not is there an ethically defensible case for calling in the state to help. Finally, and here we have come full circle, it is only by first withstanding these tests that certain tasks become duties the state must assume, duties about which there could hardly be reasonable doubt.

THE FEASIBLE IS PRESUMED FREE

The freedom to choose and the things one is free to choose

The question of whether freedom is valuable or a free society is good ought not to enter at all into a properly thought-out political doctrine, liberal or other. It should be resolutely ignored. Whichever way the question were answered would, it seems to me inevitably, steer us in a teleological direction, and undermine the foundations on which the society that we could consider free might stand and survive. What Richard Epstein says of civic virtue and happiness goes almost certainly for freedom too: "to make it the direct end of human conduct is to guarantee that it will not be obtained" (Epstein, 1985, p. 344).

An answer that freedom is *not* valuable is eccentric, nobody (or as good as) is prepared openly to voice it, and though it has intrinsic interest, we will not let it detain our argument. Answers affirming that it *is* valuable are of two sorts.

In one view, freedom is a final value. Arguments to show that it is valuable are neither possible nor necessary. There is nothing else more fundamental than itself, that could commend it and impart value to it.

This, of course, is a view that effectively stops argument, which is perhaps to be welcomed, but at the same time exposes freedom to the most devastating kind of relativism. It may seem valuable, perhaps very valuable to me, but nothing obliges you to agree with me, especially if you grew up in a different culture. On such intellectual foundations, freedom will be safe, if at all, only in a political community where it is already deeply ingrained; but it will not have the force freshly to colonize other, less free, polities.

The other kind of possible answer is that freedom is valuable for what it does for us: it is not a final, but an instrumental value. Having it enables us to choose what we prefer[7] and protects us from being made to choose what we do not prefer. Some call this the absence of coercion (Hayek, 1960), the ability to lead one's life according to one's own lights, nonsubjection to the arbitrary will of another (Hayek, *passim*), an enabling condition to carry out one's life plan (Rawls, 1971), pursuing one's own projects (Lomasky, 1987), or autonomy (Raz, 1986). Probably little attention should be paid to such expressions and little is gained by an exegesis of their more or less significant differences. They all give freedom an instrumental role. However, defending freedom instrumentally by discovering some other, more nearly final, value to which it contributes, merely postpones the relativist devastation. For any instrumental value gets its worth, at one or several removes, from a final one. If no value is noninstrumental, no instrumental one could be valuable either, for an instrument that is merely a means to another instrument is worthless unless the latter is valuable; but the latter is worthless unless it is more than merely a means to yet another instrument, and so on. Value could only be recognized and found at the end of an infinite regress, that is to say nowhere. Consequently, any disability that final values suffer due to their finality and that freedom as a final value would suffer with them, is transmitted back to the corresponding instrumental values, including freedom if the latter *were* an instrumental value.

Furthermore – and this is the major disability – as and when attempts are made to give an account of what freedom is *for*, the concept bursts at its seams, starts to expand and risks absorbing other values that, on the evidence of our ordinary language, are distinct. There is presumably a reason why different words are used in ordinary language to denote them. This reason should be respected and they should be kept distinct.

Since freedom, whatever else it is, is *also* the absence of deliberate man-made obstacles to action, "being free to do something and being able to do it" (Plant, 1992, p. 124) cannot be properly dissociated. Before we know where we are, the freedom of ordinary speech and freedom as the set of the alternatives among which we are free to choose are confounded. We find ourselves saying that richer, more attractive alternatives, as well as greater knowledge and the ability to discern them, mean more freedom. Money, brains, looks, talents, opportunities are all part of freedom, they all pass under the spreading umbrella concept that swallows up much that ordinary language knows by separate words. One depressing end result is that we now call, without the least semantic embarrassment, both the freedom to choose and the set of things available to be chosen by the same name of freedom, distinguishing between them only by the misplaced adjectives "negative" and "positive."

It is not inevitable that discourse about freedom should degenerate into discourse about all good things *and* that the latter should also be called "freedom." But the confusion is difficult to avoid, and current practice, for instance the frequent claim that "welfare rights" are a derivative of freedom, and valuing freedom implies recognizing them, does all it can to make it worse confounded.

A deontological frame

Neither the confusion nor the effort it would take to dissipate the worst of it are really necessary. The awkward, shapeless, and unruly concept of freedom that seems deeply infected by consequentialist thought can be sidestepped altogether. In its place, it is a simple task to fit a frame of familiar deontological rules. Those who wish can call the space framed by the rules "freedom," but nothing is lost if this is not done.

The basic rule is that a person is presumed free to do what is feasible for him to do. This presumption is subject to two compatibility conditions. One relates a person's proposed actions to his own obligations, the other to harm to others. Where these conditions are satisfied, the presumption that feasible actions are admissible has the effect of relieving the defendant of the burden of proof that his action is in fact admissible, and must neither be hindered nor sanctioned. The burden of proof is clearly placed on the plaintiff instead, who challenges the admissibility of the action. This is in harmony with fundamental rules of action in both Roman and common law. A well-known rule is that the accused is presumed innocent until proven guilty; another is that possession gives rise to presumption of title. Remarkably, this harmony ceases in the realm of public law. Citizens are apparently not *as a rule* presumed to need no permission to do what is feasible for them to do. Instead, actions seem to be presumed forbidden unless specifically permitted, and citizens are given civil "rights" under constitutional provisions, and entire "bills of rights" to that effect. Indeed, these "rights" are incoherent unless seen as suspensive conditions of a tacit presumption that everything not covered by them is forbidden by legislative discretion if not by legislative *fiat*. The affirmation of these "rights" grossly ignores the norm at the root of liberal thought, that whoever proposes to stop another from doing what is feasible must show a right to prohibit or obstruct the particular feasible action.

The rule and its two conditions have intuitive appeal but, like the value of freedom that is self-evident to lovers of freedom but not to nonlovers, this appeal too lacks universality. However, two other, less relative arguments support it. One is epistemological. There are two rival presumptions: "everything is admitted that is not specifically excluded," and "everything is excluded that is not specifically admitted." Whichever hypothesis is adopted, either the list of excluded, or the list of admitted actions is sufficient for identifying any action as either admitted or not. Both are not needed for guidance in choosing actions. However, the list of feasible actions is indefinitely long. Compiling the full list of interdictions is, under ordinary circumstances, a less onerous task than compiling a full list of permissions; enumerating what we must not do, and monitoring that we do not do it, are less exacting than listing what we have no right to do, and monitoring that we do not do what we have no right to do. However, if no lists of either kind are readily available, distinguishing between what is admitted and what is excluded becomes a matter of probabilistic inference, and in the extreme case where neither a priori grounds nor indirect, circumstantial evidence favor certain actions over others, putting one's proposed action in one category rather than another becomes a random choice. Discovery of admissible actions, then, is more likely, and the risk of mistaking an excluded action for admissible is less likely if the first presumption prevails than if the second prevails. The worst of both worlds is if there is a list of excluded actions, a list of "rights," and an unspecified zone about which no clear presumption exists, allowing free play to political discretion. Such a configuration is typical of para-totalitarian government.

The other argument is that the presumptions of admissibility and of inadmissibility are not morally equivalent. In a borderline case, the first presumption permits a proposed action to take its course unless a good cause is shown why it should not. Harm and contrary obligation constitute such causes under the suspensive conditions of the "feasible is free" principle. If the action is harmless and breaches no obligation, it is free. Harm or obligation has to be proven to stop it. The second presumption stops the proposed action unless good cause is shown why it should be allowed to take its course. Let us suppose for argument's sake that there is symmetry between the suspensive conditions of the two presumptions. Both presumptions are suspended only with respect to harms and breaches of obligation, and nothing else. For the second presumption, this means that *unless* it can be shown that the proposed action *is* harmless and breaches no obligation, it must *not* take its course. If the universe of harms that the particular action must not cause is not clearly and unambiguously bounded, it is impossible to prove (i.e., verify) that the action would be harmless. The universe of imaginable harms is too vast and ill-defined for every possible harm to be enumerated, examined, and its chance eliminated. Likewise, if the universe of obligations is not strictly circumscribed, it is impossible to prove that there is no obligation that the action would be in breach of, i.e., no right that it would violate. If both universes are properly and narrowly bounded, proof is possible in principle but hard to produce in practice.

There is, in addition, a built-in invitation to object to proposed courses of action simply because the objection costs little and has some chance of succeeding or being bought off. This rewards motives that can be cynically selfish, busybody, or merely frivolous. Extravagant claims of harms and rights by third parties get leverage and bargaining power under this principle that is probably out of proportion to their moral worth. Even if an action is not challenged for ulterior motives or out of sheer busybodiness, the formal requirement to show that it would cause no harm and breach no obligation (i.e., that no one's right could be opposed to it) is sufficient to stop any and all action and freeze everyone in impotent immobility – or would do if it were taken quite seriously. As it is, it merely suffices to render ordinary processes of social cooperation excessively legalistic, litigious, costly, and precariously dependent on judicial, administrative, and regulatory review.

The meaning of coercion

When we say that a person should be presumed free to do what is feasible for him to do, subject to the "harm" and "obligations" conditions, we risk creating a false impression, for "free" could well be understood to mean "costless." Plainly, an action that is both harmless to others and is not in breach of an obligation, can be socially costless in the sense that it need use no resources that others could have used instead, and create no negative externalities for third parties. But individually being free to do something is never costless, for doing it loses the doer the opportunity of doing any of the other mutually exclusive alternatives. His cost of doing one thing is the forgone value to him of not doing the next-best thing. This is of course a recognition of an analytic truth[8] that economics owes to the Vienna School (Wieser), that has done to cost what the recognition that "utility" cannot be added or subtracted across persons has subsequently done to welfare (Leube, 1994, p. 370). Its significance for the present purpose is in clarifying the concept of coercion, often left nebulous both in theorizing about state power as the enforcer of collective choices that individuals might otherwise not abide by, and in discussing relations among individuals or groups of widely differing power.

When we say that A coerces B, we consider that A has given B reason to believe that if B committed a certain act, or omitted another, A would inflict some sanction upon him. This relation between A and B has two properties that must be understood as matters of degree and not of kind, quantitative and not qualitative. The first property of coercion is B's belief in A's ability and determination to inflict the sanction, and in his own inability to escape it; we are dealing with a probability that may of course range from low to high and that A seeks to raise in B's mind by standard strategies that make threats credible. The second property of coercion that is a matter of degree is the sanction itself, assuming that the threat fails and the sanction is administered. From being flogged, through being rapped on the knuckles, to being tapped on the cheek in mock reproof by a lady's fan, sanctions can obviously range from the grave to the merely symbolic. It would be absurd to call being tapped by a fan a coercive threat. Lest the concept of coercion be trivialized, a line must be drawn somewhere. Doing so across a continuum, a range of fine gradations, is going against the grain of things, but it must be done to preserve the serious, indeed grave character of coercion. I will attempt to draw such a line presently.

Loose usage of the words "coercion," "duress," or "being forced" can usually be traced to confused thought about what it is to do harm, to hurt, to inflict a sanction. We hear, for instance, that someone was "forced" to accept an offer or enter into an arrangement because he had "no alternative." What is really being described is a case where the person finds that none of his existing options is anywhere as good as the new one he is being offered. It is not a case of coercion, whereby one or more of his existing options are actually made worse by the credible threat of a sanction, a harmful, hurtful, costly consequence attaching to them. Offering a square meal to a starving man for a day of his labor is not coercing him to work, whatever else it may be: it does not make any of his options worse, though (if he elects to work) it makes it sadly obvious how very bad they are even in comparison with such a stingy offer.

A somewhat analogous source of confusion, liable to arise in consequentialist thinking and particularly in its utilitarian version, is to assess commissions and omissions only in terms of their effect. A's threat to deprive B of his next square meal is not analogous to A's threat not to offer B a square meal. The first is doing him a harm, and may be coercive (depending on where we draw the line between the serious and the trivial). The second is witholding from him a benefit that B may well have expected to receive, and perhaps understandably so in view of his hunger and A's opulence, but which A was under no obligation to extend and was at liberty to deny. Talking of coercion in the context of witheld benefits is to dilute the concept to the point of uselessness.

By committing coercion, A intrudes into B's feasible choice set, and makes some options worse, or at least look worse, without making any option better. A temptingly good offer is perhaps "compelling," but not "coercive," unless accompanied by the threat of a nontrivial sanction.

The success of coercion may be assessed in terms of the cost A must incur to dissuade B from taking certain options or to make him take others. The cost is the sum of maintaining the credibility of the threat of a sanction and of the carrying it out if the threat fails to achieve its object. Obviously, by "investing" in the first kind of cost, the second kind can be reduced: the more credible the threat, and the graver the sanction it threatens, the less likely it is that it has to be put into effect. The more credible and the graver the threat and the more consistently the sanction is applied whenever the threat fails, the better will be the future compliance of the coercee with the coercer's will; hence by incurring higher coercion costs today, the coercer can expect to save such costs in the future.

Perfectly successful coercion, if it existed, would be costless. A protection racket that terrorized restaurants, nightclubs, and dry cleaners with a gang of cruel and implacable enforcers, and has done so long enough, could dismiss the enforcers and even the friendly collectors of protection money. Paying it would have become second nature to the victims. In practice, things are never so perfect, and tax inspectors and the occasional audit are needed to make it nearly so. However, the fact that most states can collect in taxes a large part, often half or more, of their subjects' resources without exercising noticeable violence does not make them any less coercive.

At this juncture, we must meet the argument that compliance with taxation, and indeed with any collective choice, is due not so much to the latent threat of sanctions and the certainty of implacable enforcement, but to awareness by individuals that compliance is to their own benefit, for they are getting more in protection, and public goods of all other kinds, than they give up in taxes and obedience to laws. Saying this is tantamount to making tax-paying and obedience, on the one hand, and the getting of protection and public goods, on the other, look exactly like any ordinary exchange in execution of a voluntary contract. Such a line of reasoning, however, runs head-on into the very justification of the state. If political exchange is voluntary, there is no need for binding collective choice. All who wish to give and take, will do so uncoerced. Society then is a club whose members pay the dues and obey the rules, but those who would rather not, need not join. A society, however, where all or most would rather just take than give and take, cannot function as a club would. Here, coercion is necessary to make some give so that they, and others, should be able to get. Asserting that political exchange is voluntary, while in the same breath justifying coercive collective choice because it enables political exchange to take place, is hardly conducive to clear thinking about either exchange or coercion.

Coercion, involving as it does a credible threat by A to do some harm to B if the latter will not bend to his will, has the prima facie appearance of a wrong. It thus faces a presumption of illegitimacy: failing a sufficient reason that justifies it in a specific instance, it is to be treated as illegitimate, and the burden of showing the existence of a sufficient reason is on those who seek to overcome the presumption against coercion. I do not believe that there is any plausible general statement of what must pass for sufficient reason that would rule out disputes and divergent intersubjective judgments about it and neatly divide all cases of coercion into two clearly recognized classes, the legitimate and the illegitimate. In particular, I do not believe that the two most obvious potential sources of such a general definition, namely legal positivism and natural law doctrine, can generate wide intersubjective agreement on some frontier line between the legitimate and the illegitimate.

The presumption against coercion speaks for abstention or restraint in cases of doubt. Even a modest concern with matters of right and wrong, as distinct from real or putative expediency, should make us uncomfortable about dubious, marginal cases. The sole subclass of cases where there seems to be little possible doubt that coercion is legitimate is that involved in the upholding of conventions against harms to persons and violations of property and contract. The harms and violations in question are of a nontrivial, serious character, their seriousness qualifying them as torts under custom. Like all other conventions, those against serious bodily harms and violations of property and contract have not been designed or decided by anyone. They are best understood as signposts to equilibria in game-like social interactions, i.e., suggestions of what is the best conduct for each, reciprocally compatible with the best conduct of everyone else concerned. They have evolved spontaneously over long periods, the most crucial ones about life and limb, trespass, theft of livestock and valuables probably stretching back into prehistory. As distinct from conventions of civility, conventions against torts tend to involve mandatory sanctions, with the provision of the necessary coercion being the subject of what may be seen as a related secondary convention. A convention to respect property may thus be backed by a convention to come and help catch the thief, to punish him and to force restitution. There may even evolve a tertiary convention to sanction those who do not respect the secondary convention, do not help catch thieves, or do not otherwise contribute to the cost of upholding the primary convention. The primary convention, representing the equilibrium in which each is doing the best for himself consistent with all others doing the best for themselves, has a certain moral value that is historically consecrated and seems less controversial than other rival values requiring other, often more extensive coercive threats for their achievement. If coercion has a legitimate hard core – which it undeniably does – it is constituted by coercive threats and acts that uphold these conventions against torts.

Sanctions, as we have noted earlier, can range from the trifling to the unbearable and unthinkable. Calling the threat of any sanction including trifles, coercive would trivialize the concept and undermine the presumption of its illegitimacy. Where should the line be drawn across the range, beyond which a sanction is to pass for being coercive? There is much to be said for not taking the name in vain, avoiding needless dilution and confining coercion to a narrow range of threatened acts, such as serious bodily harm to person and violation of property, that is acts that would themselves be actionable torts if they were not employed in the service of legitimate coercion. Extortion of protection money and of taxation by the threat of hijacking or otherwise taking property would both be

coercive under this definition, though the enforcement of parking regu-
lations by the threat of small fines would not be. The legitimacy or
otherwise of regulating the parking of cars would not be a question, while
taxation would be, and would have to be answered on the strength of the
reasons offered to justify it. The anarchist who condemns all regulation as
coercive, hence illegitimate, seems to me to be wasting arguments and
weakening the presumption against coercion on which his case at least
partly depends.

This line that I think should be drawn to separate the coercive from
the noncoercive thus has some merit, but it is not indisputably right. It
fails to capture (indeed, it deliberately excludes) cases of moral intimi-
dation, for example conformist bullying by the media of mass persuasion.
It is not altogether clear where it would leave the various cases of the
use of economic power as a threat. The question merits some attention,
for such threats, real or supposed, are perhaps the most frequently cited
reasons for resorting to politics.

... and how not to stretch it

Economic power, acting on the options of others by the (albeit implicit)
threat of its use, is often cited as coercive. No amount of conceptual
clarification will persuade the average wage earner facing his supervisor,
or the small business man anxious to keep the custom of a much bigger
one, that he is not being coerced in certain bargaining situations. It is
nonetheless worth pointing out that with such a usage, coercive acts spill
over, ethically speaking, from the domain of right and wrong to the
domain of the putatively equitable and reasonable. Legally speaking, it
would classify as coercion acts or the threat of acts that "deprived" a
person, the employee or the small businessman, of an option he did not
have in the first place. He may have expected to strike a certain bargain,
or renew it on the old terms. He may have considered that this was a
reasonable expectation, and third parties may have thought his expected
terms equitable.[9] For all that, however, the bargain on the hoped-for terms
was never an available alternative in the feasible set of the "economically
weak" party, and not having it in the first place, he was not deprived of
it when the stronger party presented his unexpectedly tough terms. A
bargain over terms is a contract, and a contract, depending on at least
two parties, is never in the feasible set of only one of them,[10] only an
unexpired offer of one party is in the feasible set of the other.

Stretching the concept of coercion beyond *existing* options, so as to
make it cover *reasonable expectations* as well, is of course not a matter
of the improper use of logic and language. Between stretching and not
stretching a concept, we choose as we see fit. One usage is not true and
the other is not false. Adopting one or the other is a matter of political
and legal judgment. It is quite conceivable that some way down the road

we are travelling, political thought will have evolved to the point, and legislation will have been put on the books to the effect, that the terms of *all* contracts between parties of disparate wealth or "economic strength" are to be subject to court approval, and the threat of nonrenewal of an expiring contract on the same or better terms will become tortious coercion. This is not yet standard practice. It would be stupendously inefficient if it became the standard, though that is perhaps no reason for expecting it not to happen. Nor is it the principal argument against putting the thwarting of expectations on the same footing as the spoiling of actual options. The main argument, it seems to me, remains the rock-bottom distinction between what the first party *is* free to do with his endowments without violating the "harm" and "obligation" conditions, and what he, no matter how reasonably, *hopes* to be able to do, subject to a second party's agreement. If withholding the reasonably hoped-for agreement is deemed coercive in cases where the first party is "economically weaker" than the second, and if coercion has legal consequences, the first party's "freedom" becomes incompatible with that of the second party. Any principle that entails this incompatibility renders the system of justice self-contradictory. It is an unjust principle, both if justice means concordance with "natural right" and if it means the respect of rights resulting from agreements.[11]

If coercion is held to be a grave enough injury to call for redress, extending the scope of its meaning is a grave matter, too. Freedom of contract can no doubt produce harsh terms on occasion, as Hayek's oft-cited parable of the thirsty man in the oasis and the extortionate price of water shows, and as many other situations of monopoly and monopsony tend to produce on a less cruel scale. If such results are to be prevented, the prophylactic remedy is to be sought in the causes of monopoly and monopsony. They are less intractable in our type of economic environment than in the desert oasis. Doing away with the freedom of contract in cases of transactions between "strong" and "weak" parties, on the grounds that a person's reasonable expectations, especially if he is weak, should enjoy the same protection as his effective options, looks like a remedy that is worse, morally more objectionable, than the alleged wrong it would be designed to right. For it is hard to conceive that loading the system of justice with mutually contradictory elements can possibly contribute to more perfect justice.

"Having no alternative"

In ordinary speech, a person is said to "have had no alternative, he was coerced." What is usually meant is that though there was at least one alternative, i.e., to resist the coercion, it was too painful, too unpalatable, too costly for him to accept. It is worth making this point in the face of the barrage of rhetoric about capitalism, industrial society, materialism, racism, sexism, city life, suburban life, alienation, or, more grandly still, "the system," leaving people with "no alternatives."

There is, however, a special form of coercion that literally leaves no meaningful, noncasuistic alternative. If someone puts an armlock on you and calls "say Uncle or I will break your arm," and if you are heroic enough, you can clearly choose not to say Uncle and have your arm broken. But what of the command, by someone much stronger than you who is holding you by the scruff of the neck by the waterside, "jump in or I will throw you in"? Whether you jump or are thrown, you end up in the water; you had no real alternative, though you did have a casuistic one.

This special case is significant, for it is a simulation of the kind of coercion a state, possessing sovereign power, can and does exert in a vast number of everyday cases. The fiscal laws decree that a person in given circumstances must surrender a given part of his income or wealth for public purposes. Short of removing himself, this income and his assets from the legal reach of the state – an option that is not available to most ordinary people – the solvent individual, however ready to envisage costly alternatives, simply has none once he has exhausted all possible legal recourse. It is no use his accepting to be fined or to go to prison, he will be made to pay regardless, if need be by a lien on his income or seizure of his assets, just as the person who would not jump was thrown in regardless. Interestingly, every other coercive threat of the state, designed to ensure obedience to the law, is of the more general kind, which leaves the subject a genuine choice between two unpleasant options, in this case between obeying the law or breaking it and risking punishment. Whether anything ulterior and sinister about the state's differential intent can be read into such differential treatment – whether paying tax is the one duty the state *really* wants its subjects absolutely to fulfill – is something about which more extended speculation would be otiose.

In lieu of freedom-talk

At this point, I will try to wind up what I think needs to be said about the deontological rules of politics in lieu of speaking about the politics of freedom.

Each individual is endowed by circumstances with a set of actions it is materially feasible for him to carry out. Some are inadmissible because they would cause harm to others that would be of a degree and a kind to constitute, by the long-standing conventional norms of society, *torts* and call for remedy. Others are inadmissible because the individual, by contracts he concluded with others, has undertaken not to choose them; they would constitute defaults, *breaches of obligation*. Every other feasible act of his is admissible. Among them, there are some he has undertaken to carry out, *at the option of others*, as his side of a promised exchange.

He does not choose them, others choose them for him. These contracts or para-contractual undertakings to perform as promised if called upon to do so, define his contingent obligations.

The counterpart of his obligations are rights of others, while his *rights* are nothing else but obligations to him accepted by others. The exercise of the right and the fulfillment of the corollorary obligation describe *the same event* in different words, just as "A collected his loan from B" and "B repaid the loan to A" describe the same event. The evidence of an obligation is the contract, and as between obligor who bears a burden and obligee who expects to benefit from it, the burden of proof is on the obligee, the claimant of the right, for it is in his interest, and not in the interest of the burden bearer, to prove the claim. Every genuine right of one person has the agreement of another as its source, cause and evidence. The deontology of rights is their epistemology.[12] We know what they are by the way their existence is revealed, namely by the contract. Without it the consent of the bearer of the burden would be alleged and hypothetical at best, and the deontology of rights would rest on nothing more substantial than unilateral claims to benefits at the expense of others who never declared their willingness to assume them.

A brief digression seems to be called for here. What do we mean by "every genuine right" having agreement as its source? How about the right of the unemployed to unemployment benefit, or of the child to instruction in a state school? In what sense do these rights spring from agreement, and are they "genuine" or not? The commonsense answer is that the monarch or the legislator has agreed that the state should provide these things and place the corresponding burden on the tax-payer. An instance, the state as tax collector and welfare dispenser, has been interposed between obligee and obligor; there is no direct evidence that the obligation of the latter is voluntarily borne. On the contrary, there is a presumption that it is not. Does this deprive the putative right in question of the attributes of a "genuine" right? Although the unemployed can until further notice successfully claim their benefit and the children their instruction, their right is specious for all that, not because the obligation is involuntary, but because it is *ex gratia*, noncontractual, subject to repudiation, hence precarious. The benefit is undoubtedly an entitlement for the time being, but unlike a right, it can be modified or reduced or withdrawn altogether without the rightholder's agreement, and without other cause than a decision of the lawgiver based on a judgment of expediency. Genuine rights, of course, cannot be curtailed or withdrawn without the rightholder's furnishing cause or giving his consent.

With torts and obligations taken care of, the set of admissible actions becomes a residual: an admissible action is the exercise either of a right (entailing the fulfillment of someone else's obligation) or of a *liberty*. A liberty is any feasible action that is neither a tort, nor the breach of an obligation, nor the exercise of a right. In order to be feasible, a person must be able to perform it without another person's being required to perform *onerously*. Some liberties are exercised all by themselves: I can go for a walk on the common without requiring anybody's active cooperation. Others depend on someone else's exercising a matching liberty: I can only contract to buy a house if the owner is willing to sell at my price, and if he is, his action, though required for the accomplishment of mine, is not onerous. On the other hand, my going for a walk and singing loudly as I walk must surely be onerous for the other strollers on the common, but it requires their onerous *forbearance*, not their onerous *action*, hence on my proposed definition it passes for a liberty of mine (if local convention does not decree it to be a nuisance).

Contrast this with one of the senses in which Nozick uses "right" in his *Anarchy, State and Utopia* (1974, p. 92): "rights, that is permissions to do something, and obligations on others not to interfere". Rights, of course, are not permissions but claims for performance by another. Yet liberties are not permissions either; if they were they would be most confusingly misnamed. Who would be competent to grant permissions and on what authority? And assuming an authority to grant or withhold them, why is its or anyone's permission required to do anything whatsoever? The only reason is if there are grounds for objecting to the thing being done, for surely no permission is needed to do it when no objection can stand against doing it. If there are objections, a positive permission might have the function of overriding them as insufficiently strong or unfounded. However, strong and well-founded objections are gathered under the "harm" and "obligation" headings. I propose to take it that the two together exhaust the set of valid objections. Suppose, however, that they do not, and that there are other contingencies where a feasible action that is neither a harm nor the breach of an obligation might yet be objectionable and require permission. Under the presumption that the *feasible is free*, it is for the objector to prove the validity and strength of his objection. If he fails, the proposed action needs no permission, and if he succeeds, it ought not to get it. It is only under the opposite presumption, namely that everything is forbidden unless it is permitted, that this logic is reversed and the permissions that Nozick (and others including, however deplorably, constitutional texts as well) call "rights" make sense and become necessary.

Coercion fits into this scheme in a way that is by now fairly evident from the foregoing. Coercion may be applied either to the inadmissible or to the admissible subset of the set of feasible actions. Applied to the inadmissible subset, it will characteristically function to deter tortious harms and breaches of contract. It may be administered by agreement among some or all of the parties interested in maintaining the security of life and property and the respect of contracts. Social conventions that are not self-enforcing, yet survive, operate in this way by self-administered coercion, and the sort of political doctrine sketched in this chapter, inspired by properly agnostic, hippocratic, and minimalist principles, will consider this legitimate, though space does not permit a fuller explanation of the reasons why. If it is the case that certain social interactions, *as well as* the cooperation needed to enforce Pareto-optimal solutions for them, are single-play prisoners' dilemmas (a contingency which is possible though it looks farfetched), social conventions to overcome them would probably fail to take root and state coercion would be necessary. If it were invited by the parties, it would be legitimate; the conditions and the problem of testing the credibility of such invitation when the status quo is not the state of nature, but some social order that already incorporates coercion by the state, has been touched upon earlier (pp. 156–8).

Coercion applied to the admissible subset of actions is prima facie illegitimate. It deforms the values and hence the opportunity costs of rights and liberties, and does so by threatening or committing torts. Coercion, then, must be deterred in the same way as torts. It is possible that certain public-goods problems cannot be overcome by contract, perhaps because transactions costs in large-number situations would render such contracts unprofitable.[13] Under such circumstances coercive interference by the state, with admissible actions covered by rights and liberties, might be just as legitimate as coercion to deter torts and to ensure the execution of contracts. However, these circumstances are unlikely to be as prevalent as is assumed in the received theory of why society needs the state, and the deontology of politics must on no account be based, as it so often is, on the facile supposition that the circumstances in question do in fact generally prevail.

LET EXCLUSION STAND

Exclusion or fair shares

It is a widely accepted tenet of modern politics that justice demands the benefits of social cooperation to be shared in some fashion agreed to be fair. It is one of the tasks of politics to procure agreement on what is fair. Another is to see to it that benefits are in fact shared in the agreed fair manner.

As it stands and before it is interpreted, this tenet is perfectly general and consistent with any imaginable manner of distributing benefits. For one, it is consistent with the prevailing pattern of ownership of the factors of production and with every owned factor receiving benefits equal to its marginal product. Under this alternative, it is at least implicitly deemed fair that lawful possessions and voluntary exchanges should determine who gets what. The result is what might be called a primary or "natural" distribution (except that "natural" distribution, just like "natural" right, is a persuasive label full of subliminal suggestion, and is best avoided). The role of politics, if there is one, is then confined to upholding the customs and laws of property and contract; and it is not certain that even this limited role is indispensable; for nothing, neither deductive reasoning nor experimental evidence, proves that property and contract cannot be adequately and economically protected by extra-political means.

Under any other of the countless possible conceptions of what is fair, politics is called upon to play a deliberately redistributive role, and fairness is invariably interpreted as a norm requiring politically decided and enforced adjustments in distribution. The propertyless, the weak of will, the short of talent, and the short of luck are deemed to be excluded from the benefits produced by social cooperation, or at any rate to share insufficiently in it. Collective choice backed by the power of the state, must therefore be employed to *break down exclusion*, and make the better endowed give up a part of their property or income in favor of the less well endowed. Let us remind ourselves in passing that giving up part of the income from property is tantamount to giving up part of the property, for it is the capitalized value of the income it yields that provides its exchange value, hence the opportunity cost of replacing the lost income.

"Breaking down exclusion" is a pleasing goal, especially if it is done to bring about fairness, the more so as we are likely to benefit from our particular idea of it. Its pursuit is one of the principal temptations that make people have recourse to politics. Since it creates gainers and losers, it willy-nilly implies a "balancing" between the good of some and the bad of others. As such, it cannot serve as a warrant for the use of coercion. Any attempt to justify it must be undertaken on consequentialist grounds. However, such grounds, as argued on page 49, are insufficiently firm and should not be admitted in any ethically well-founded political doctrine.

The problem of original ownership

There is another, more direct and less general, moral argument in defense of exclusion, or of the categorical nature of property, whose ownership entails no obligation to share it with others and to include nonowners in the benefits it produces.

Once property is owned, its voluntary transfer from one owner to another takes place either in exchange for value received or as a unilateral gift. A new pattern of ownership results from the agreement of the parties (for accepting a gift or a bequest is also a matter of agreement), and as such it is uncontroversial: the transferee's title is no worse than that of the transferor. Each owner owes his title to the agreement of the previous owner, along a chain of valid transfers stretching back into the past. However, the legitimacy of the chain can be called in doubt if a link is defective. The very first link, in fact, has not ceased to excite controversy at least since Pufendorf and Locke – for what is the standing of subsequent transfers if the purported first owner was in fact a usurper and his title was invalid? If original ownership is moot, it is highly contestable that someone can ever become the rightful owner of anything that was previously unowned. If what is unowned cannot be legitimately appropriated, legitimate ownership is forever impossible, since no one can become the rightful owner of something that was previously unowned.

Since every present-day title would be precarious if a fault in any preceding title, no matter how far back along the chain of transfers, could serve as ground for invalidating it, custom, and more lately the law, forestall the chaos that would result by imposing a statute of limitations. But this is strictly a matter of expediency, and the passage of property from unowned to owned status, no matter how far back it is supposed to have been accomplished, can still be open to challenge in moral justice if not in law, for there is no agreed statute of limitations on moral claims. The legitimacy of what is indifferently called "first taking," "first appropriation," "original occupation," or "first possession" does for this reason have a significance for present-day exclusion and for what passes for the theory of private property that is quite out of proportion to the quantitative share, in today's stock of wealth, of the things that can be supposed to have been *first appropriated* rather than subsequently *produced* from owned inputs in accordance with mutually agreed contracts, and remaining *unconsumed*.

The problem of accepting that something unowned and at least contingently accessible to all should, by virtue of some private act, become owned and access to it excluded except by the permission of the owner, has been stated in these terms: "the idea that individuals can, by their own unilateral actions, impose moral duties on others to refrain from using certain resources and that the moral force of these duties can be transmitted by processes like exchange and inheritance, is a very difficult idea to defend in an unqualified form" (Waldron, 1988, p. 253).

Depending on the precise nature of the unilateral action of the prospective owner, and on the access nonowners have previously enjoyed to the resources in question, separate arguments are available according to cases to answer this charge. The basic defense, however, is quite general and straightforward. It is that if a prospective owner *can* in fact perform it, taking first possession of a thing is a feasible act of his that is *admissible* if it is *not a tort* (in this case not trespass) and violates no right; but this is the case by definition, i.e., by the thing being identified as "unowned." Taking exclusive possession of it is, in terms of our classification of possible acts, a liberty, and as such only a contrary right can obstruct or oppose it.[14] The opponent of this simple thesis is trying to have it both ways: he is *both* asserting that the thing has no legitimate first owner from whom a second or *n*th owner could have legitimately obtained it by agreed transfer, *and* that there is nevertheless somebody who has been and still is entitled to use the thing and therefore can validly object to being excluded from it. But an entitlement to use the thing is an at least partial antecedent ownership claim needing an owner, or the permission of an owner, before it can be made; ownership cannot both exist yet not exist. If, on the other hand, the objectors have been using the thing without being entitled to it, because no third party had excluded them by taking first possession, and because they were unable, unwilling, or uninterested to perform the act of taking first possession themselves (whatever that act may consist of), their enjoyment of the thing was precarious, not vested. Its appropriation by a third party may have deprived them of an *uncovenanted advantage*, but it did not violate their rights.[15]

What, then, is the act whose performance constitutes appropriation and vests ownership in the performer? There is in fact not one act but two alternative ones, depending on the type of access nonowners have, prior to the act, enjoyed to the thing. One could be labeled "finding and keeping"; the other, despite its possible misleading historical connotations, "enclosure."

"Finders keepers" and the moral arbitrariness of luck

A thing of value lying unnoticed in a ditch by the wayside could be found by anyone who passes. If it is found by a person who then hides it or takes it home for his own exclusive use, it is appropriated by him and has become his putative property. Maintenance of his ownership is conditional on his successful exclusion of all others who would seek to make use of the newly discovered property in question without the owner's permission. Exclusion involves costs, some once-for-all, some continuing, which can be considered as part of the price of ownership. The thing appropriated by the finder can obviously no longer be found and freely used by anyone else. Anyone who was at all likely to pass that way in the indefinite future has, by the act of the finder, lost some, no matter how small, probability of finding the thing, i.e., some probability of enjoying an advantage. Admittedly, if all accept the rule that the finder is keeper, i.e., that first possession confers ownership, the mathematical expectation that the nonfinder may one day also find a valuable thing becomes worth more to him, for he could then keep the thing, and no one would challenge his control of it. This would reduce the exclusion cost of protecting his ownership. But the bird that has just slipped out of his hand might have been too painful a loss to be offset by the chance of secure possession of the bird in the bush, once he catches it. Nothing ensures that the expected utility of a finders keepers rule will tell him to leave well alone, in the hope that tomorrow it will be his turn to catch a bird, or to find something else.

Is this a ground for challenging the *fait accompli*, disputing the title of the finder in the thing, or for making recognition of his title subject to some bargain? Trading the respect of private property against some redistributive compensation, so that the new owner must in effect purchase the acquiescence of the propertyless in his ownership, is an idea that underlies a large body of modern political thought. It is sometimes alleged, not only that such a bargain is ethically required to justify property, but that it is an empirical fact, and the necessary condition of the social acceptance of capitalism. No evidence has to my knowledge ever been offered for the belief in some implicit bargain of this kind, and in the nature of the case none could be offered. Our present interest, however, is not in the truth of the empirical proposition that respect for property is obtained, or can only be obtained, by compensating the propertyless, but in the ethical proposition that such compensation is due.

If finding useful things were mostly a matter of luck – which in certain basic but not very important cases it clearly is – the ethical proposition could be reduced to requiring that the lucky compensate the unlucky. There is no particular reason to confine the application of this norm to cases of "finding" property; every bit of luck in every case where luck matters in shaping a relevant outcome, would carry a moral liability to compensation.

The force of the claim that the lucky ought to compensate the unlucky reposes on the belief that whatever is "morally arbitrary" ought not to come to pass and calls for redress. However, we may readily concede that the effect of luck on the distribution of good things is morally arbitrary, without being led to draw any conclusion about redress; the step from the one to the other is a moral *non sequitur*. Moral questions are strictly about right and wrong. The random hand that destiny impartially deals to each of us is arbitrary, and it is manifestly lucky for some, unlucky for others, but it is not a matter of right and wrong. It is a matter of the way the world is made. Redress cannot be called for on moral grounds. At best, remedy could be called for on grounds of compassion or love-thy-neighbour.

It is a category mistake to believe that every distribution is either right or wrong; some, perhaps most, may simply be arbitrary, and this characterization need not imply anything about their moral quality. Only certain distributions, arising out of relations of trust and responsibility, are matters of distributive justice.[16] The relations between finders and nonfinders, owners and nonowners are not, a priori, such relations. Hence finders keepers poses no question of justice, and creates no liability to compensation or redress.

Finding by sheer luck is a limiting case. Finding as the pure result of incurring finding costs, where the scale or intensity of the "search" by would-be finders is pushed to the point of equality at the margin between the value of the mathematical expectation of the find and the finding cost, is the opposite limiting case.[17] All cases of finding are presumably situated between these limits, with only a minority sitting on either borderline. The nearer an actual case lies to the search-optimizing ideal where marginal finding cost is equal to the probability-weighted marginal value of the find, the less reason popular opinion would be likely to have to question the legitimacy of the resulting ownership or to ask that, in return for respecting the finder's find, nonfinders be compensated. However, if this is how popular opinion sees the justice of the matter, it is in a muddle, and not for the first time either. Questions of the justice of finding, of chance, exclusion cost, desert, and profit do not really lend themselves very well to resolution by popular opinion. They are, for that very reason, best handled in a well-ordered society as matters of rigid custom or strict law (though not necessarily statute law) rather than of equity. This seems to me necessary, even if barring considerations of equity loses us the capacity flexibly to adapt rules to particular cases.

"Enclosure" and exclusion cost

A useful thing may be there for all to see, with neither chance nor finding cost being necessary to realize its existence; yet it may not have been appropriated, its use may not be reserved to any defined set of persons, and any chance comer may have free access to it. The squatter who takes the thing, or carves out a portion of it, can establish first possession by excluding everyone else's access to it. He puts up a fence, patrols the boundary, has fearsome dogs, manhandles trespassers, and utters more or less credible threats against all who would try to dislodge him. He "encloses" the thing and incurs exclusion costs. By analogy with finding costs in the preceding section, "enclosure" is advantageous up to the point where the marginal exclusion cost is just equal to the use value of the enclosed thing to the encloser;[18] but there may well be opportunities for profitable enclosure where the thing can be appropriated at a marginal exclusion cost falling well short of its marginal use value, leaving an "unearned" surplus; these cases are analogous to the windfalls that accrue when finding a thing is at least partly a matter of good luck, rather than of spending resources by way of finding costs.

The analogy with finding, however, is incomplete. Those who, however casually and sporadically, used to enjoy access to the unenclosed thing, now lose an actual benefit, and not merely the probability of an opportunity. In the preceding section, it was argued that no compensation was due for the latter, since the nonfinders were not *entitled* to a find. It is arguable that the excluded are not entitled either to be included, since they have done nothing to secure their liberty of continuing access to the unenclosed thing against another's liberty of taking exclusive possession of it. The enclosure worsens their situation, but does not violate their rights. But this argument may possibly be faulty, for it ignores the force of such contingent circumstances as precedent and the possible "common pool ownership" character of free access.

Both points are somewhat involved, and full justice cannot be done to them here. However, the following brief considerations should suffice for the present. Prior to its enclosure, some people used the thing merely in passing, on an ad hoc basis. Others, however, used it regularly enough for their access to amount to established precedent. They have no title, but they have some kind of reliance-based claim against the enclosure, and some compensation for their loss of usual access seems to be due in return for their acceptance of the exclusion. It may even be that access was not really free to all comers, but was informally shared by a closed set of people, and all those outside the set were virtually excluded in the sense that had they attempted access to the good, the attempt would have been opposed, or endured only under protest. This situation is perhaps not commonalty or "common pool ownership" properly speaking, and if it had been, the problem of first possession and the passage from unowned to owned status would not have arisen, since the thing would not have been unowned. But an unowned good regularly used by an identifiable closed set of persons is sufficiently close in character to the village common to render compensation in case of enclosure mandatory. It is fairly clear that enclosure of a common, and even of a quasi-common, could only secure voluntary acceptance if compensation came close to offsetting the reliance-based damages suffered by the quasi-owners. Yet their acceptance of the exclusion is necessary for what is, effectively, a transfer of title rather than the appropriation of an unowned thing. Acceptance on their part, in turn, may reduce the necessary exclusion cost. It is an empirical question whether it would reduce it by an amount greater or less than the compensation; in a world where compensation was settled by mutual agreement rather than statutory means, this amount would tend to approximate to the exclusion cost the agreement has saved.

First possession as liberty that has prevailed

The reader must step carefully around here to avoid possible confusion. It was said that to the extent that the taking of first possession by "finding" and "enclosure" was a feasible act, it was also admissible, hence a liberty, since the thing possessed was by definition previously unowned and no one had a prior right to it. Those deprived of its use by exclusion lost an opportunity, or an actually enjoyed advantage, but in so far as the advantage was not vested either by agreement or by customary regular usage (encouraging and justifying reliance on continuing nonexclusion), this was not sufficient ground in justice for denying the passage of the thing from unowned to owned status. The liberty of the finder and encloser not being opposed by a contradictory right, it must be suffered to prevail.

This nutshell argument, however, provokes an obvious counter-argument meant to shatter the nutshell. Let us admit, it might run, that taking first possession is a liberty, since it is both feasible and unopposed by a right. Prior to their exclusion, however, the access of all comers to the unowned good was a liberty, too: it was feasible and unopposed by a right. Rights prevail over liberties, but in this set of relations between persons and acts, no rights figure at all. They are *exhypothesi* altogether absent. This is precisely the problem; we want to defend a particular theory of how and why rights can arise and fill this void. The theory of ownership by first possession expounded in this chapter affirms that the liberty to find and to enclose should prevail. But why should it prevail over a contradictory liberty, that of all comers to have free access to the as yet unowned thing? The clash of the two liberties is at best a draw. At worst it is the liberty of freely using the unowned thing that should prevail, for it represents the status quo, and that should not be changed without a good argument in favor of the change. Consequently, only two possible conclusions subsist. Either unowned things must forever remain unowned, or the loss of those who lose the advantages of free access to them – and they may on a strict reading include society as a whole or even all humanity – must be compensated. But this attack involves a muddle about the nature of liberties as distinct from rights. Rights must all be mutually consistent; it is fraud to assume two obligations whose fulfillments are mutually contradictory, like selling my house with vacant possession to Jack and granting a lease on it to Jill. Indeed, a theory of rights that holds clashes between rights possible is seriously wrong.[19]

Rights cannot, but liberties can and do clash. There is nothing in their logic to prevent that. We are both free to voice our opinion at a public meeting, we both start to shout, and either none of us is heard, or you shout louder than I and prevail.

But not all clashes are tolerated by a given; conventional system of liberties. Some clashes would have results that mature social conventions or law have long declared unacceptable. My shooting at anything that I dimly see moving in the wood would clash unacceptably with your liberty to pick mushrooms in the wood. The liberty to pick mushrooms is, for obvious reasons, accorded priority; hence I am not at liberty to shoot and must not shoot. Shooting you carelessly is a tort, not a liberty. It is feasible but not admissible. However, the clash between free access to an unowned good and exclusion from access to it, is a clash between two liberties, and not between a liberty and a tort. More accurately, the latter is not a tort under the type of social conventions, customs, or laws that are respected in our type of civilization, though of course there is no telling that it will not become one if our civilization goes on changing and our sense of right and wrong changes with it. Pending such changes, however, excluding others from a previously unowned good is no more tortious than was its previous unexcluded, promiscuous use. Whichever of these two liberties prevails de facto, prevails. If exclusion is successful and just claims for compensation on grounds of reliance are satisfied, the thing passes legitimately into the ownership of the finder encloser. The fundamental reason is that there is this case no principle of right or wrong at work to compel the de facto result to be overridden, which perhaps also explains why the dictum "possession is three parts of the law," though emphatically not the whole law, does not generally strike us as an immoral guide used by cynical courts.

The contingent incidence of exclusion costs

In both of the above scenarios, the act of first possession is completed by the excursion of nonowners, and it is the owner who bears the exclusion cost. But this need not be the case. Anyone else can bear it, or be made to bear it, or some of it on the owner's behalf. It is strange that in all mainstream theories of property, as in theories of the state as producer of the public good of law and order, it is invariably "society," the sovereign or the "government" which assumes the exclusion cost or, as the matter is usually but less pertinently put, "protects and enforces property rights." One of two assumptions seems to be made: that only society or its proxy can do it, or that only it can do it efficiently. The first assumption is hardly tenable and I propose to dismiss it. The second is, empirically, an open question; it may or may not generally be the case, and experimental proof seems unobtainable. However, even if it were true and could be *known* to be true, it would still not follow that a randomly chosen owner, or local association of owners, or all owners as a class, could do no better than to entrust the exclusion function wholly to the state.

From an owner's point of view, inasmuch as this property is not protected by the unrequited service of others, the rational choice is to have as much and as good protection of it, and of his associated rights, as to equate the marginal return from better protection to its marginal cost. He does this by buying it, hiring it, or producing it himself in the form of self-help. The appropriate inputs are different for different types of exclusion; the lock, the fence, the safe, the electronic tag on merchandise in the shop provide one kind of barrier to unauthorized access to private property, the anti-racketeering squad, the Serious Fraud Office another, the recourse to peer group help, to arbitration, or to action at law yet another. Every kind of barrier has more or less close substitutes that perform a comparable though seldom identical service. In the real world at least some of them are nearly always performed "in house," by self-help. No matter how efficient the police, the supermarket still makes its own costly arrangements to prevent people from carrying off its wares without paying for them. Other functions are "contracted out" to specialized providers, guard services, credit information bureaux, quality assessors, rating agencies. Yet others may be dispensed with by dint of avoiding the kind of transaction that would call for them: thus, contract enforcement costs can be saved by not dealing with fly-by-night parties, nor with notoriously litigious ones.

Some services, particularly those that involve adjudication of disputes about who owns and who owes what, and with enforcement of the findings, are usually performed by institutions of the state. But this need not be so, and it is difficult to make a plausible case that alternative arrangements would be less efficient and less impartial. The state has, over the centuries, increased its "market share" of these services, but this is not in itself proof that it is the superior provider. The relative efficiency of the state and its potential competitors is obviously "path dependent."[20] The assertion of centralized sovereign power at the end of the Middle Ages enabled states to establish and protect their monopoly of certain lucrative aspects of exclusion, for other potential providers of such services were put at a disadvantage by virtue of their disarmed and subject status. The state, moreover, can become and remain a monopolist without possessing any of the supposed merits of the "monopoly of the legitimate use of force." History, both past and contemporary, is rich in examples where it abuses its sovereign power and gets away with providing a law-enforcing and property-protecting service that is neither efficient nor impartial.

What one needs to retain from this is that the assumption of exclusion cost by society, by owners, or by both in some proportion, is a contingent fact, not a necessary truth arising from the immanent features of social life. This is worth stressing again and again, for the contrary belief, namely that property owes such security as it ever has to the collective effort of society to protect it, is deeply embedded in the postEnlightenment consciousness. Indeed, it is thought by most of those who think about the matter, and *a fortiori* by those who teach it, that society is prior to property and the state is prior to the "market." This belief, and its equally unsupported twin that ownership and voluntary exchange could not exist without a preexisting "institutional infrastructure" that can be characterized as a Hobbesian social contract, are mutually entailed (see p. 156). They have profound consequences for the evolving shape of liberal doctrine and for political practice; for they rationalize the basic disposition of political man to consider the system of private property as an unspoken contract whereby "society" affords security of tenure to property owners, and in return justifiably gains a decisive say in the distribution of property and of its fruits, warranting some "socially chosen" breach of the principle of exclusion.

Contract and the "right to contract"

Property, according to the simple taxonomy of rights and liberties put forward in the third section (pp. 158–71), is properly speaking not a "right" (nor a "bundle of rights") but a liberty to act upon owned objects.

The liberty to act upon them includes the classic triad of use, usufruct (if indeed these two are really distinct, which I am inclined to question), and disposition.

The most important liberty of disposition is of course the freedom of contract, whereby an owner transforms some of his liberties to use the benefit from his property into obligations for himself and rights for others; for example, a lease obliges the owner to renounce the liberty to use his property in certain ways, and vests a right to use it in the lessee, the owner being obliged to cede possession.

Note that while the owner had *liberty* to use, the nonowner needs a *right* to use, which the lease confers upon him. Using "liberty" for the one and "right" for the other, though perhaps pedantic, underlines the fundamentally different nature of these two relations, the second of which depends upon agreement while the first does not. Likewise, an employee who enters into a labor contract exchanges his *liberty* to do as he likes during working hours against an obligation, and his employer gains the *right*, within the limits fixed by contract or custom, to direct him to do as *he* likes during working hours.

This sounds, and is, trite. The sole point of stating it is to drive home the understanding that a liberty is first of all a matter of feasibility, a *fact of life*, while a right is a matter of another party's obligation that he has *agreed* to assume. A reminder to this effect is not altogether redundant, for like property itself, the freedom of contract is also coming to be regarded, in modern social theory, as a privilege the parties enjoy by the grace of society, which gives them "rights" to engage in the practice of contracting, forbears to interfere with it if the terms are "socially acceptable," and enforces compliance. The last of these supposed contributions, as I have argued in connection with the enforcement of exclusion, is merely a contingent fact. It may or may not be the case or it may partly be the case. There are many alternative ways, some more powerful and some more costly than others, ranging from self-help and group convention to bought help, for enforcing compliance. The first two alleged collective contributions to the institution of contract, namely granting the right to contract and refraining from interference with contracts, however, beg a conceptual question. Can one be granted a right to a liberty – and is noninterference with a liberty, e.g. with the freedom of contract, a matter of social forbearance, that could be withheld or extended at society's pleasure? Even the usually crystal-clear Richard Epstein, surely not a legal philosopher one would expect further to confuse an already confused issue, seems to lean towards an interpretation of the concept of contract that requires the parties to be *entitled* to do what they are free to do: "if one asks why C and D are entitled to enter into a contract with each other, the answer presupposes that the rest of the world has a duty not to interfere with the formation of their agreement . . . C's right to enter into a contract with D cannot be acquired by a contract between themselves ... again collective recognition of the entitlement lies at the root of the common law" (Epstein, 1985, p. viii). Much as one must hesitate to disagree with Epstein on the common law, or indeed on all matters of common sense, on the face of it he gives comfort to a curious and curiously illiberal understanding: for it is surely inconsistent with both common sense and liberal doctrine that C must first acquire a right to contract, or the collectivity must first recognize his entitlement to do so, before he *can* contract with D.

It is not clear why the parties need a *right* to enter into an agreement they consider both agreeable and mutually binding and are capable and competent to conclude. The agreed exchange of binding promises, to which the parties need no "right," entitlement, or authorization from anyone, is logically prior, and distinct from the enforcement of perform-ance should one of the parties attempt to default on his promise. Suppose "society" through its agent, the state, offers the parties to enforce the contract in case of need. They have the choice of accepting this offer or resorting to some alternative arrangement, depending on whether the enforcement cost demanded by "society" is higher or lower than the cost of private, peer group, or any other possible provider of enforcement, and also on which is more effective and rapid than the other. Is it the acceptance of society's offer by the parties, or the mere making of it, the assurance of its availability, that renders the making of the contract subject to an entitlement which must be "acquired"? And is it this offer that entails a "collective recognition" without which the rest of the world could interfere with it at will? If it is not the offer, then what is? And what if the offer is declined – or if it is not made at all, as was the case in the Praetorian "formulary" law of republican and early Imperial Rome?

If the contract is an institution under customary or formal law, it is surely anomalous that its very existence should somehow be made depen-dent on what is no more than one of its contingent features, i.e., a particular mode of enforcement. Do men and women have to "acquire a right" to marry, a "right" society has a right to grant (hence also to withhold) by virtue of the legal protection it provides for the institution of marriage, and the legal facilities it offers for dissolving it? Surely, these protections and facilities, such as they are, do not *make* the institution, however much they may *shape* it and enhance its convenience. Legal support does not create the institution. If, on the other hand, the contract is a voluntary agreement before it is an institution, it is difficult to see why the parties should have to acquire a prior "right" or entitlement to conclude it, and what would happen if their "entitlement" were not granted collective recognition. Would reciprocal promises cease to be binding? Isn't this confusing an obligation with one of the several means to which recourse can be had if it is not respected? It is incomprehensible on what grounds the parties' "right" to contract, i.e., to carry out a feasible joint action that is not a tort nor the breach of an obligation, does not go without saying but needs to be questioned, and why such a question requires an answer.

If anything is questionable and requires an answer, it is the collectivity's right to subject the freedom of contract to an "entitlement," to be granted by itself, and to be withheld in certain circumstances. I am far from claiming that there are no such circumstances. In cases of force, fraud and unconscionability, it is perfectly arguable that some formal or informal body or institution which may be, though it need not be, the collectivity, society or the state, should have authority to release a party from a contractual obligation and protect him from the other party's attempt at enforcing performance. For this, however, force, fraud, unconscionability, or some other weighty ground must first be *shown*. The onus of proof is not on the parties to show that their contract provides *no* such grounds. The recognition that there may exist a class of contract-dissolving grounds in no way permits the conclusion that the freedom to contract when some such ground is *not shown* is a social privilege, a "right" granted by society to the contractors, and that society's "duty not to interfere" is a corollary of the right it has granted them.

The mirage of the common pool

"Contract is a social privilege granted to individuals" takes its place alongside "the state is prior to the market" and "property rights are defined and enforced by the political authority," to form the threesome of half-truths and misunderstandings which helps legitimate the politics of redistribution. For redistribution may be the chosen aim of a teleologically inspired political ideal, and consequentialist ethics may provide it with a case for holding that one distribution is recognizably better, more just, or more uplifting than another. But if contract is free, if the source of property is first possession and contract, and if the distribution of benefits and burdens in society at any time is the result of the preceding pattern of ownership and a continuous process of voluntary exchanges that modify it, interference with contracts, imposed exchanges, and forced and unrequited transfers of property, would be prima facie illegitimate intrusions into liberties, and violations of recognized rights. Coercive redistribution could perhaps still be legitimized after a fashion – perhaps after the frank and forthright fashion of Princess Mathilde Bonaparte (cf. p. 143), perhaps by claiming that contracts between unequals are to be classed as made under duress, or perhaps by resorting to more windy, obscure, and pompous formulations – but the ideology concocted from such disparate elements is hardly a heady brew. The troops will not march far on it. How much more liberating is an ideology that leans on a nonexclusive conception of property; for if owners do not *really* own it, but *share* ownership with society, if the terms of contracts are subject to social approval, and if a certain pattern of distribution must obtain before the processes of voluntary exchange become legitimate,[21] no (individual) liberties prevail in the matter of property, no (individual) rights arising from voluntary agreements are violated by involuntary transfers, and redistributive politics, restrained, if at all, only by expediency, can be underpinned by what promises to be a coherent ideology. On a closer look, however, the promise remains sorrowfully unfulfilled.

The foundation stone of this ideology is the inchoate intuition that the accumulated stock of wealth is owed to the entire history of social cooperation since the day our ancestors climbed down from the tree. It is a common pool, and it is absurd that some individuals should be allowed to exclude others from particular parts of it that they claim as their "absolute" private property. They may, to be sure, practice a measure of exclusion, but not on their own terms, and no more than society, the co-owner, will countenance. Why, then, allow owners *any* degree of exclusion – why not go all the way and declare that all property, or all property that matters (productive wealth), is "social," and its use and disposition entirely a matter of "social choice"?

The ideology, it seems to me, reveals an odd fault line here. The whole stock of accumulated wealth is owed to the whole sum of social cooperation over time. It is this debt, owing to prior contributions, that creates social ownership, and supports its primacy over individual claims today; social ownership is a matter of justice, of *suum cuique*, and its ground is apparently deontological. However, like any common pool ownership, "social" ownership loosens the link between the bearing of burdens and the enjoyment of benefits: it permits those who have sown only a little to reap much, leaving little to reap for those who have sown much. It punishes good and rewards bad husbandry. In less biblical language, it is a hotbed of inefficient factor allocation, free riding, and the worst kind of principal–agent problems. The remedy, of course, is not merely exclusion, for a common pool also excludes those left outside it. Social ownership, too, excludes other societies than ours. To be free from the vices of the common pool, it must be exclusion under single or several private ownership. It does not matter whether it has one owner or many, the equity in a property must be clearly divided and each share must separately belong to one natural or legal person. The efficiency gain of private over common pool ownership generates a surplus. The difference between the redistributionist and the socialist ideology is that the former believes in the efficiency gain, does not feel like throwing it out of the window, and therefore accepts, on consequentialist "on balance" grounds, the exclusion implied in private property. In the final reckoning, it ends up with property that is both excluded and shared, both private and public. This is a schizophrenic understanding of property, which is deontological for its "socially owned" and consequentialist for its private *persona*. Such, I submit, is the contemporary liberal conception of property, which underlies the modern liberal redistributionist ideology. Whatever else it is, it is not coherent.

Moreover, the deontologically derived social *persona* is but a figment of a feverish imagination. The stock of wealth at large is said to be owed to society at large, because it is impossible to trace or undesirable to break down society's global contribution into the myriad bits and pieces, past and present, contributed by each cooperating individual. How to tell who made what, who invented, innovated, improved what – and to what extent it was his efforts that produced a given increment of wealth, to what extent those of everybody else, his teachers who taught him, his doctor who cured him when he was ill, the policeman who kept him safe, and the literally countless others whose contributions were all necessary for him to make his contribution? How to trace each contribution to the contributor?

But the answer is relatively simple. The "tracing" has already been done at the time the contribution was made, and has duly left its permanent mark on the ownership structure of the "stock of wealth." It does not have to be done a second time. The producer, the inventor, the teacher, and the policeman all contributed what they did in exchange for value received. This value may or may not have been equal to the marginal product of each, but though the question is intrinsically interesting, and I do not know how to answer it, I do not think I have to. It suffices that each gave and received what he did in the course of voluntary exchanges, which constituted valid transfers of title to the goods and services in question. Some of what each received he consumed. The remaining bit, if any, he added to the "stock of wealth" simply by virtue of the fact that he did not consume it, and it was clearly labeled as *his* contribution of the exchange value thereof, because he held title to it. If he neither sold it nor gave it away, nor bequeathed it to his heirs, it is still clearly labeled as his. Every other bit is likewise labeled with the name of its contributors or his legal successors. No unowned bit is unaccounted for.

Arguably, every bit is interdependent with every other, and none could have been contributed without all others also being contributed at the same time, or earlier. But this no more means that every bit is "owed to society" than that every bit is owed to every other. *Nothing is owed*: everything has been paid for, one way or another, in a manner and to an extent sufficient to call forth the contribution. There is no further common pool-type claim overhanging the lot, for no payment must be claimed twice. They who see an overhanging claim in favor of "society" are seeing a mirage, or the wishful image of one.

NOTES

1 There is a special case that ensures the perfect match, though there is little to recommended it for all that. Under it, liberty, or (in a more cautious formulation) a set of key liberties, is given lexicographic priority over all other values by the just political institutions of society; no tradeoffs are sought or accepted. The lexicographic priority results from the unanimous choice of the parties who contract to be bound by these institutions. The parties are, for this purpose, a single person. His marginal rate of substitution of liberties against other values is infinity.

2 There are two unsophisticated variants of this formula. One states that the policy benefits more people or more voters than it imposes costs upon. This is the democratic variant. The other states that the benefits, in terms of money or "wealth," exceed the costs. This is the cost–benefit approach of the workaday economist, as well as of the judge walled in by the "Law and Economics" perspective.

   I am not suggesting that because they are unsophisticated, these variants should never be used. They seem to me to have some grounding in common sense in some, essentially nonpolitical, morally not acute contexts. But they cannot bear the weight of the heavy guns of sovereign prerogative and lawful coercion – at least morally they cannot.

3 Utilitarians think that the basis for interpersonal comparisons can be found in "how desirable certain things are," in knowing "what makes life enjoyable and how [a person] with his individual differences is placed to exploit his possibilities" (Griffin, 1986, p. 188); "comparisons involve a general profile of prudential values" (ibid., p. 120), i.e., objective entities.

   One of the premier utility theorists, John Harsanyi (1977, pp. 58–9) proceeds by linking each person's preferences objectively to ascertainable general causes or variables and using them as a proxy for everyone's preferences, which then become homogeneous and comparable.

   The avowed nonutilitarian goes much the same way: "workable criteria for . . . the relevant interpersonal comparisons must, I believe, be founded on primary goods or some similar notion" (Rawls, 1982, p. 170).

   The common strategy is to save interpersonal comparability, i.e., aggregation, by replacing heterogeneous, *personal* predicates by homogeneous and *impersonal* ones. But the substitution is exactly that: it replaces something with something different without furnishing any conclusive proof that they are not really, relevantly different. Instead, it slips in an arbitrary value judgment that rules them relevantly the same.

4 There need be no scheming, no stealth, nor any conscious partisan ideological effort involved in these processes. Constitutions are expressed in language and their meaning shifts with the ebb and flow of public opinion and public understanding of the language (cf. Epstein, 1985, p. 20).

5 There is, in fact, a clear distinction between the effects of the "when-in-doubt" principle and the status-quo-protecting Pareto principle. (On the conservatism of the latter, cf. Peacock and Rowley, 1979, pp. 24–5.) The former relates to doubt about the algebraic sign of the difference that the state-enforced institution or policy measure makes to the goodness of an overall state of affairs. There is doubt whether it is positive or negative. The presumption is against the maintenance, and not only against the novel introduction, of some state-enforced feature of the state of affairs, and the burden of proof is on those who advocate its preservation if it already exists or its introduction if it does not. The Pareto principle, by contrast, creates a presumption against any change in the state of affairs and puts the burden of proof on the advocates

of change to show that it would not make anyone feel worse off or that no one would object to it.

6 Every executory contract is of course a single-play game of prisoner's dilemma with "default" as the dominant strategy. The received wisdom is that contracts would be "vain breath without the sword" – at any rate so spoke Hobbes and we can, I think, safely go along with him this far – *and* that the sword must be that of a monopolist of the use of force – which does not follow at all. "Swords" of the contracting parties, and of their neighbours, peers, colleagues, associates, competitors, customers, and suppliers are deterrents to default that are not demonstrably more inefficient than monopolist enforcement by the state. Many historical episodes show that the private enforcement of customary contract law thrived whenever the state for one reason or another was unable forcibly or amicably to displace conventional cooperation.

What default is to contract, tortious acts are to social conventions about respect for life, limb, and property. Their incentive structure is a prisoner's dilemma and trespass, larceny, "conversion" represent the dominant strategy. The received wisdom is that without the strong arm of the protective state, we would make each other's lives unliveable and society would founder in "anarchy." This of course does not follow from anything, except perhaps from the vague feeling that the state must be serving some purpose, and if we could have order without it, it would prove to be a useless creature and would wither away. The reason why the institution of contract does not need the state either for its emergence or for its survival, and why in reasonably healthy communities life and property are broadly respected, and social conventions sanctioning breaches of such respect with ostracism, mutual assistance, "civic policing," etc. are maintained, is basically simple. Default and tort are dominant strategies in single-play prisoners' dilemmas only. But in real life there are very few genuinely single-play games. Most of life's social relations are in reality probabilistic repeated games. Every player who expects to live another day runs some risk of meeting some player again in some game or another.

7 Amartya Sen (1993, p. 39) has pointed out the difference between the availability of alternatives and the availability of the best alternative. He rightly distances himself from the view that removing everything from a feasible set except its best element is not a real loss for the chooser, since he wishes to choose the best element anyway. If freedom is purely instrumental, it does not seem to matter that less preferred alternatives are removed as long as the preferred one subsists. If their removal matters, freedom must have some kind of intrinsic, noninstrumental attraction.

8 That the cost of having (or acquiring) something is the value of the best of the forgone alternatives, is a proposition entailed in the concept of cost, and can be analytically derived from it. In ordinary language, this concept is called "opportunity cost" to distinguish it from historical cost, i.e., the money or goods against which the acquired thing was originally obtained. Only the latter can be "objectively" ascertained, but it is not a significant or very useful concept – except for tax accountants.

9 This is a version of Hayek's case (1960, p. 136) of the oasis in the desert where the owner of the only well charges an unheard-of price for water. Hayek considers that a traveler arriving in the oasis is being coerced by the well-owner. He must think that the traveler had reason to expect that water will be sold at an affordable price. It is this reasonable expectation that the well-owner has destroyed. However, he has not destroyed or worsened any actually existing option of the traveler. The latter's expectation about the price of water in the oasis was simply mistaken.

10 This point has been made to me in a private communication by Dr Hardy

Bouillon. It is made, in somewhat different language, in his *Freiheit, Liberalismus und Wohlfahrtsstaat*, (1995).

11 The principle is unjust in terms of justice as the respect of rights resulting from agreements, even if the agreement were of the dubious hypothetical kind imputed to individuals behind a "veil of ignorance." I do not think the imputation can stand up to critical scrutiny. However, if it were accepted, it would supposedly mean that the parties have agreed to recognize rights to "equal maximum freedom" compatible with the same freedom for others (Rawls, 1971, pp. 60, 250) and to give this principle absolute priority over distributive considerations. How, then, can the freedom of contract be accorded to the poor but denied to the rich? The only way out is to exclude the freedom of contract from the scope of the freedom or freedoms of which each party must have a maximum compatible with the same for every other. Many contemporary liberals, notably Dworkin, do exclude the freedom of contract from the list of freedoms to be maximized or even safeguarded.

12 Charles Taylor, while deploring moral skepticism, correctly observes that one defense against it is "a pervasive feature of modern intellectual culture, which one could call the primacy of the epistemological: the tendency to think out the question of what something *is* in terms of the question of how it is *known*" (Taylor, 1993, p. 208).

13 This statement is certainly not intended to mean, and I trust it does not mean, that high transactions cost is a sufficient condition for public-goods problems to defy voluntary cooperative solutions, nor that low transaction cost is sufficient for public-goods problems to have such solutions.

14 Rousseau is worth quoting here " ... the positive act which establishes a man's claim to any particular item of property limits him to that and excludes him from all others ... in so far as he benefits from this right, he *withholds his claim*, not so much from what is another's, as *from what is not specifically his*" (Rousseau, 1762, pp. 186–7, emphasis added).

15 It will be noted that this position is opposed to the one taken under Lockean inspiration by Robert Nozick. For the latter, "[t]he crucial point is whether appropriation of an unowned object worsens the situation of others. Locke's proviso that there be enough and as good left in common for others is meant to ensure that the situation of others is not worsened" (Nozick, 1974, p. 175). He distinguishes between two kinds of worsening: the loss of opportunity and the loss of actually enjoyed advantage. If the proviso means that neither kind of worsening must take place, it cannot be satisfied in a finite world. If only the second kind of worsening is barred by the proviso. Nozick believes that the institution of private property and the market economy whose proper functioning it permits, are sufficiently beneficial to enable the proviso to be satisfied.

This, of course, will remain a matter of judgment. It is possible that first appropriation improves the situation of most people in the long run, but worsens that of some or perhaps of most in the short run, calling for a balancing judgment. I believe that setting conditions which then require such balancing to be performed is undesirable. The position developed in the text does not require that nobody loses as a result of first possession, as long as the losses were not vested interests.

16 The reader may note this departure from the well-known position of Hayek, for whom the notion of distributive justice is itself a category mistake. Plainly, however, there are questions of distributive justice in the treatment of children by their parents, in the marking of examination papers, in the allocation of scarce underpriced public housing, in sharing out the burdens of a joint undertaking, and so forth. Here the relations of trust and responsibility largely

determine the appropriate distribution, and deviations from it are prima facie unjust. "The concept of distributive justice is applicable within the context of limited associations, with limited and definite aims held in common. Such aims give guidance how the fruits of common activities should be distributed" (Lucas, 1980, p. 220).

17 It is not immediately obvious where, between these two limiting cases, Israel Kirzner's (1978) particular conception of the finders keepers principle fits in. It seems to me that it can best be fitted in by equating the input of the finder's entrepreneurial acumen, his scarce talent for discovering arbitrage opportunities unseen by others, to the incurring of a resource cost. But I am in no way claiming that Professor Kirzner would agree with this interpretation, for it could call into doubt the existence of his "pure" profit.

18 Judge Posner makes a related but somewhat different point: "the pattern by which property rights emerge and grow in a society is related to increases in the ratio of the benefits of property rights to their costs" (Posner, 1992, p. 35).

19 John Gray (1989, p. 148) believes that we lack a theory of acquisition that can help in adjudicating "apparently conflicting property rights," and illustrates the conflict by the following example. The catch from a certain fishing ground falls because of industrial pollution by a coastal plant. The "right" of the fishermen to fish in their traditional fishing grounds conflicts with the "right" of the industrialist to employ a polluting process.

   In fact, no rights are involved, hence none can conflict. The fishermen's liberty to fish is intact, but there are fewer fish. Whether compensation is due to them for the negative externality they suffer is a question of prevailing liability rules. They may favor the fisherman or the industrialist. We may consider a particular liability rule just or unjust. But if the fishermen have had property rights in the grounds, the industrialist would have violated them by killing their fish. There would still be no conflict of rights, apparent or real. The fishermen would win an action for remedy and the industrialist would desist or compensate.

   Consider an amended example. The fishing grounds have an owner; he leases them to the fishermen, and unbeknown to them also sells an easement to the industrialist to pollute it with his effluent. There is a conflict of two putative rights, but only because the conflicting obligations have been fraudulently assumed.

20 Cf. Ellickson (1991, p. 253): "Once an informal control system has been established among neighbours, for example, their marginal cost of referring additional disputes to it may be lower than before. Conversely, *once the state has assumed the major role*, even more state control may be utilitarian" (i.e. efficient) (emphasis added).

21 Onora O'Neill (1982, p. 321) thinks it plausible that in order to guarantee that the process, for instance the process of voluntary exchange, is followed, the outcome of the process must fall within an "acceptable" range. We must ask what happens if the outcome falls outside the range – for instance if voluntary exchanges give rise to a very unequal distribution of wealth. We can only speculate about how O'Neill would answer the question. She might say that under such conditions the poor might consider the share of the rich unfair, and would violently or "democratically" upset the applecart of voluntary exchanges that produced the unfair outcome. Of course they may or may not try to do so, and may or may not succeed. But this has nothing to do with the *legitimacy* or otherwise of exclusive private property and freedom of contract. It concerns its *capacity of survival* under conditions of extreme inequality, which is an interesting empirical question, but not germane here.

   If she does not mean survivability, what does she mean? Could she mean that unless the process of voluntary exchanges produces acceptable outcomes, it is not a voluntary process? Whether the outcomes are acceptable to an outside observer, a philosopher of social justice, is of course quite irrelevant. It is the parties to the exchanges who count. Yes if "acceptable" signifies "acceptable to the parties," the statement is analytic: if I enter into a contract whose terms are unacceptable to me, I entered into it involuntarily (but then why did I?). Acceptability of the outcome to all parties "guarantees" that the process is followed, but guarantees it tautologically, since we have just defined the voluntary process as one that produces acceptable results. Unacceptable results *mean* that the voluntary process was not followed: some other process was.

None of this is helpful. Nor does it bear out O'Neill's suggestion that *both* process *and* outcome may have simultaneously to satisfy certain conditions in a satisfactory theory of just distribution. It is hard to see why we should bother with the process if we know what outcome would be "acceptable." This would be like insisting on having an election, although only the election of the right candidate would be acceptable. Why not bring about the right outcome directly, by giving to each what he ought to have?

REFERENCES

Bainville, J. (1941) *Reflexions sur la politique*, Paris: Plon.
Bouillon, H. (1995) *Freiheit, Liberalismus und Wohlfahrtsstaat*, Tübingen: J. C. B. Mohr (Paul Siebeck).
Buchanan, A. (1985) *Ethics, Efficiency, and the Market*, Oxford: Clarendon Press.
Coleman, J. L. (1988) *Markets, Morals and the Law*, Cambridge: Cambridge University Press.
Ellickson, R. C. (1991) *Order without Law: How Neighbours Settle Disputes*, Cambridge, Mass: Harvard University Press.
Epstein, R. A. (1985) *Takings: Private Property and the Power of Eminent Domain*, Cambridge, Mass: Harvard University Press.
Fried, C. (1978) *Right and Wrong*, Cambridge, Mass: Harvard University Press.
Gray, J. (1989) *Liberalisms: Essays in Political Philosophy*, London: Routledge.
Gray, J. (1992) *The Moral Foundations of Market Institutions*, London: Institute of Economic Affairs, Health and Welfare Unit.
Gray, J. (1993) *Post-Liberalism: Studies in Political Thought*, London: Routledge.
Griffin, J. (1986) *Well-Being, Its Meaning, Measurement and Moral Importance*, Oxford: Clarendon Press.
Harsanyi, J. (1977) *Rational Behaviour and Bargaining Equilibrium in Games and Social Situations*, Cambridge: Cambridge University Press.
Hayek, F. A. (1960) *The Constitution of Liberty*, Chicago: University of Chicago Press.
Kirzner, I. (1978) "Entrepreneurship, Entitlement and Economic Justice," *Eastern Economic Journal*, 4, 1, 9–25.
Leube, K. R. (1994) "Begreifen und Verstehen," in K. W. Noerr, B. Schefold, and F. Tenbruck, *Geisteswissenschaften Zwischen Kaiserreich und Republik*, Stuttgart: F. Steiner Verlag.
Lucas, J. R. (1980) *On Justice*, Oxford: Clarendon Press.
Nozick, R. (1974) *Anarchy, State and Utopia*, New York: Basic Books.
Nussbaum, M. and Sen, A. (eds) (1993) *The Quality of Life*, Oxford: Clarendon Press.
O'Neill, O. (1982) "Nozick's Entitlements," in J. Paul (ed.), *Reading Nozick*, Oxford: Blackwell, 1982.

Peacock, A. and Rowley, C. K. (1979), "Pareto Optimality and the Political Economy of Liberalism," in A. Peacock (1979).

Plant, R. (1992) "Autonomy, Social Rights and Distributive Justice," in J. Gray, *The Moral Foundations of Market Institutions*, London: IEA Health and Welfare Unit.

Posner, R. A. (1992) *Economic Analysis of Law*, 4th edn, Boston: Little, Brown & Co.

Rawls, J. (1971) *A Theory of Justice*, Cambridge, Mass: Harvard University Press.

Rawls, J. (1982) "Social Unity and Primary Goods," in A. Sen and B. Williams (eds), *Utilitarianism and Beyond*, Cambridge: Cambridge University Press.

Raz, J. (1986) *The Morality of Freedom*, Oxford: Clarendon Press.

Rousseau, J.-J. (1762, 1947) *The Social Contract or Principles of Political Right*, in E. Barker, *Social Contract*, London: Oxford University Press.

Schelling, T. C. (1984) *Choice and Consequence*, Cambridge, Mass: Harvard University Press.

Sen, A. (1993) "Capability and Well-Being," in M. Nussbaum and A. Sen (eds), *The Quality of Life*, Oxford: Clarendon Press.

Sen, A. and Williams B. (eds) (1982) *Utilitarianism and Beyond*, Cambridge: Cambridge University Press.

Taylor, C. (1993) "Explanation and Practical Reason," in M. Nussbaum and A. Sen (eds), *The Quality of Life*, Oxford: Clarendon Press.

Waldron, J. (1988) *The Right to Private Property*, New York: Oxford University Press.

9 Conventions

Some thoughts on the economics of ordered anarchy[*]

1

Theft, robbery, and default have robust attractions. Property and contract look fragile by comparison. On the whole and most of the time, they nevertheless prevail. This result borders on the counterintuitive, since it goes against palpable interests. Why is it that these interests nevertheless usually fail? It is far from self-evident that they should. An explanation is needed. The standard one is that property and contract prevail because the state enforces the laws that secure them. But unless cooperative behavior is for some reason first established, how can the state itself prevail? – since it is not obvious why it should. For it must stand up against the same robust, palpable interests as the very institutions it is supposed to protect, and must somewhere find the strength that property and contract need, but apparently cannot find in their own defense. Simply assuming that the state does uphold them, because after all this is what the facts are saying, is to my mind shallow, as well as potentially circular. Exploring the possibility of an endogenous theory may well permit a deeper insight into these institutions – even if the theory is no more than a coherent but counterfactual account of how they might have arisen, rather than a factual one of how they did arise.

It has become a commonplace that the application of such concepts as rational choice, maximization, efficiency, and equilibrium presupposes some institutional framework, within which the rules of property and contract have pride of place. On the specific content of this institutional framework depends the form that social cooperation takes in the division of labor and the allocation of other resources. Doesn't, however, the dependence go the other way, too, so that what we are really facing is interdependence?

Marx, as we may remember, maintained that it was the economic "infrastructure," the "forces of production" (by which he basically meant

* A lecture delivered at the University of Jena in the series Max-Planck-Institute for Research into Economic Systems (ed.): Lectiones Jenenses (Jena Lectures), Jena 1995. Reprinted with permission.

technology) that engendered the institutional "superstructure," the "relations of production" (by which he basically meant property relations). The standard view in contemporary thought is the exact opposite. It stands Marx on his head: legal and political institutions are the "infrastructure" that supports the economic "superstructure," without which some of the principal forms of social cooperation, notably the beneficial interaction of free agents in markets, would not even be possible. Here, the dependence goes from the legal and political to the economic: law and its enforcement are prior to market exchange.

However, even if no causal priority is imputed to institutions, it is standard practice to take them as exogenous data, rather than as part and parcel of a rational-choice explanation of social interaction. For example, in noncooperative game theory (or, as Schelling would have it, the theory of interdependent action), it is assumed that credible commitments do not exist; in cooperative game theory, it is assumed that they do. It is of course perfectly legitimate to make assumptions of this sort. But it does not help us to understand where contracts come from, and why they are credible. If they are "given," who gave them?

Lastly, what if was "given" is suddenly "taken away"? The recent collapse of the set of bizarrely contrived institutions that used to pass for the socialist system, and that looked as if it had been deliberately designed to breed the most monstruous and perverse principal–agent problems, drives home the recognition that such a far-fetched question can confront us in real life. Even if it were just idle speculation, it would behove scholarship to explore it. The recent (late 1980s, 1990s) historical accident that "took away" a set of socialist institutions painfully erected on a gigantic scale over seventy years argues that conducting such thought-experiments is not a wholly idle pursuit.

2

Lest my purpose be misunderstood, before going on I should like to come to terms with a class of theories that I believe are misdirected, seeking as they do to explain institutions endogenously by demonstrating their efficiency. Harold Demsetz, in his justly admired papers on the emergence of property rights (esp. Demsetz, 1964 and 1967), contrary to most economists who tend to take property rights as an initial datum, puts forward a theory of why and how they came into being. For him, they evolved to fulfill a function, namely to let property users internalize externalities when the gains from doing so exceeded the costs. With hunting grounds in seventeenth-century Quebec used by the Indian inhabitants as a common pool, overhunting was the predictable result. This imposed a negative externality on hunters as a whole. The rise in the value of furs with the advent of the organized fur trade has increased the potential benefit from "privatizing" the hunting grounds, with access to a given area reserved to a given family. As the sole owner of this piece of hunting ground, the family could fully internalize the net benefit from stopping the overhunting. The same cause produced the same effect in the late nineteenth century American West (Anderson and Hill, 1975). Open range ranching led to overgrazing. When the value of cattle increased as transport to Eastern markets became cheaper, the gain from preventing overgrazing came to exceed the cost of fencing in portions of the range and reserving its use to a single rancher. In either case, internalizing all the positive and negative effects from hunting or grazing removed the previous difference between maximizing the total net benefit from a given area of land, and maximizing the net benefit accruing to a particular user of that land. Only when there is a single (personal or corporate) user, entitled to all residual benefits after bearing all costs, can he maximize *his* returns by maximizing the "social" return, that is by adopting the most efficient hunting or grazing practice. Multiple users have overriding, "dominant" free-rider incentives to abuse resources at each other's expense.

It also follows that if resource use has become more efficient in private ownership, the people who used to have free access while the resource was in common pool, must now be better *off as a group*. But it does not follow that *some* of them are not worse off, absolutely or at least relatively. The distribution of the benefit remains problematical. This is where functional theories of institutions, destined to evolve toward ever more efficient solutions, must watch their step. For, contrary to central command-obedience systems, an individual incentive-based system is not teleological. It has no identifiable purpose and is not seeking out efficient solutions (Streit, 1992). If it evolves and grows particular institutions, it is not because social benefit is maximized thereby, but because free agents adopt courses of individual action that seem best to them, and never mind whether their action promotes or on the contrary frustrates social efficiency. If it promotes it, it will do so as pure happenstance.

For take Rancher Smith whose cattle is now excluded by Rancher Jones's fence from part of the range. He has lost something. It is true that he will also gain something, and probably more than he has lost, if he follows Jones's example and fences in another part of the range, stopping all strange cattle from grazing there. But it is surely even better for him both to get this gain, and also to stop Jones from inflicting any loss on him? Fairness and reasonableness need have nothing to do with what he thinks is the best outcome for him if he can get it. He may well try to tear down the fence Jones has put up, and the cost to Jones of internalizing the grazing externality of the open range is not the cost of putting up a fence, but also that of permanently guarding it from Smith, *or* of buying off Smith's intrusions. "Normally," Jones and Smith ought to reach a mutually profitable bargain over the division and enclosure of the range they formerly shared. But this might fail to come about or fail to work for a number of reasons. One of them is the possibility that Smith will no sooner shake hands on a bargain with Jones than he will break it, cutting Jones's fence while protecting his own. Jones will have little choice but to adopt symmetrical tactics.

Only if there is literally boundless open range left for the cattle of both, will Smith and Jones have no rational reason to contest each other's attempt to "privatize" any part of it. If there is only a finite area of open range left, however vast, any diminution of it by enclosure increases the probability that some future act of additional enclosure will cause an opportunity loss (a forgone gain) to Smith, Jones, or both. This is just another way of saying that Locke's proviso for legitimate first occupation, i.e., that "enough and as good is left to others," is inconsistent with finite resources.[1]

However, since strictly speaking even the most unreasonable and wild fence-cutting, agreement-refusing, or agreement-breaking tactics to oppose enclosure and exclusive occupation by others can be rational, satisfaction of the Lockean proviso (assuming it could be satisfied) might still not suffice to assure the passage from common to private property. Showing that the passage is beneficial to a group *as a whole* is not the same as showing that the institution of private property will in fact emerge, and will not be effectively opposed by a strong enough subgroup within the group. The more stringent condition of Pareto-superiority, i.e., that the group as a whole would gain from it and no individual within it would lose, looks more promising; but even this condition fails to rule out successful opposition by the envious or the egalitarian who will not stand for some members of the group gaining more than he does. Unless we are prepared to call ends irrational, we cannot simply sweep acts of envy aside as irrational, and it would not help if we did. The fact that it would be collectively beneficial to privatize certain resources does not permit us to predict that they will in fact be privatized. What it does is to alert us to a latent distribution problem: will the collective benefit be shared among the members or will it fail to be realized due to a failure to settle the question of how it is to be distributed? Clearly, the share (if any) each can successfully claim will bear some relation to his bargaining power, which in turn is a matter of his capacity to stop everybody else from getting anything, by spoiling the privatization attempt altogether. It is difficult to say more than this in a first approximation.[2]

For these reasons, social or collective benefit and functional superiority do not prove much. To say, as Demsetz does of private property (1964/ 1988, p. 136) that "its existence is probably due in part to [its capacity to reveal] social values upon which to base solutions to scarcity problems" appears to take a teleological view, assigning high purposes to institutions and explaining their emergence by their capacity to fulfill them. Yet nobody in his story of the common hunting grounds, or in the story of the open range, is concerned one way or the other about the high purpose and valuable signaling function of private property. To listen to Mandeville, this is perhaps just as well.

3

Consider next the problem of stability once some solution has been reached for the distribution of a common pool resource among the "hunters" or "ranchers." For argument's sake, let us take it that a tacit convention to respect private property has been widely adopted. If everybody continues to adhere to it, property is secure. There is no need to incur "enclosure costs" to exclude from it all others whose access is not authorized by the owner. There need be no fences, no locks; houses can be left open with valuables lying about. Armed guards, fingerprint data banks, and criminal courts are superfluous. There is, then, a strong incentive, created by the very confidence in established convention, to deviate from it and steal with both hands. Even if many continue to adhere to it and do not become opportunistic thieves, there is a sense in which the convention has broken down if a large enough fraction of individuals concerned deviates from it and steals when the risk–reward relation tempts it. The convention, in other words, is not self-enforcing, and is liable to break down. A certain expenditure of resources is needed to keep noncompliance (theft, trespass etc.) down to a level at which the convention is still usefully functioning. The optimum level of expenditure (current cost or investment) is one where the marginal cost of enforcement is equal to the marginal benefit from the increased security of property. Somebody, however, must bear this enforcement cost. Paying it generates externalities: it is possible to benefit from the greater safety of property in general without contributing to its general costs. It is perhaps best if my neighbor contributes to the cost and I do not. My neighbor, of course, is symmetrically placed and may take the same view, in which case neither of us will contribute, and the convention will not be enforced.

Beneficial conventions that are not self-enforcing are logically equivalent to noncooperative games whose equilibrium solutions are Pareto-inferior; technically, they work as prisoners' dilemmas. The players are condemned to a suboptimal outcome, failing to maximize the available game sum – unless they transform the game, or it is transformed for them, into one where their reciprocal commitments not to adopt the "dominant" noncooperative strategy can be made credible to each other. Under most standard rationality assumptions, the commitment will be credible if it is "common knowledge" (all players know, and each knows that the other knows that he knows that the other knows, and so on) that the dominant strategy will bring down adverse extra-game consequences on the player's head that outweigh its intra-game advantage. This is typically the case if the dominant noncooperative strategy is likely to be severely punished after the game, i.e., if the nonself-enforcing convention is enforced.

There may be a secondary convention, as it were a satellite of the primary one, whose sole function is to enforce the latter. The classic example of such a combination is the convention of queueing: the primary convention is to wait one's turn in the queue, and the secondary or satellite convention among the more civic-minded queuers is to shout at, menace, and push and pull back into line, any queue jumpers, always provided there are not too many of those. Enforcement and the level of noncompliance are in an equilibrium which may be unstable over some ranges, stable over others.

In the queueing example, nothing enforces the enforcing convention; no tertiary norm stands behind the secondary one. Hence, if it functions, it must be self-enforcing. However, there is no prima facie reason to believe that all or most other nonself-enforcing conventions will be backed up by a satellite convention among civic-minded adherents that will be self-enforcing. In fact, there is a prima facie reason for holding the contrary.

Punishment of noncompliance is in general costly, as are other measures of enforcement. Punishment and some, perhaps most, measures of enforcement create strong externalities: anybody can benefit from the enforcement of a useful convention whether or not he bears any part of the cost. If and to the extent that this is so enforcement is not self-enforcing, but is itself enforcement dependent. For all we know, we may be facing a series of successively higher-degree enforcing conventions, each depending on the next-higher one. No matter how high one goes, there is never a highest convention that is no longer enforcement dependent. The normal way of dealing with this kind of logical mischief is to lose patience and postulate an arbitrary stopping point, beyond which we simply refuse to carry on the argument. In the present case, the stopping point is the state.

Conceived as an entity of an altogether different kind from the individuals and organizations that are subordinated to it, the state does not maximize its own utility, profit, or wealth; it does not respond to incentives, but seeks to carry out society's mandate, or rather its own reading of the variety of signs and noises emitted by society that must be interpreted by politicians, judges, and high officials in order to know what society's mandate really is. The state, then, is society's agent. Some even view it as an agent that is in some metaphysical way exempt from the principal–agent problem that in every other case we regard as intrinsic, logically inseparable from the agency relation. On reflexion, this is a strange view to take, but it is necessary to support the assignment to the state of the role of stopping point, of ultimate enforcer. For only then can we say that its contract with society, under which it acts as its enforcing agency, is not itself in need of enforcement, lest it should breed parasitism, extortion, sloth, bureaucracy, partiality, and other familiar vices.

This stopping point, then, acts as a *deus ex machina* postulate: for if it is impossible to deduce, by way of individual rational choice theory, a cooperative solution to the ordinary first-degree enforcement problem, then how is it possible, with the aid of the same premises, to deduce the state as the cooperative solution to any *n*th degree enforcement problem? It can, of course, always be introduced as an exogenous datum. But that, so to speak, is where we came in.

4

James Buchanan (1979, p. 282), in implicitly making the very existence of crucial institutions depend on the state as last-resort enforcer, claims support by both Hobbes and history: "Institutions matter. The libertarian anarchists who dream of markets without states are romantic fools who have read neither Hobbes nor history." Reading history, however conducive to wisdom and understanding, is a notoriously inconclusive way of reaching specific conclusions about such vast, amorphous and diffuse features of the past as markets, states, and their interdependence. Buchanan reads one lesson from history; I for one would read a rather different one, and the chances are that neither of our readings is very near the mark.[3]

Let us, however, read Hobbes by all means. In *Leviathan*, he marks off two alternative "models" of the conflict over property, one producing stalemate at the status quo, the other permanent trespass and the continuous overturning of any status quo. The first model applies when, or perhaps because, force is just matched by equal force; the second and contrary model when, or because, attack gathers more force than defense.

To establish the first alternative, Hobbes lays down that "the difference between man, and man, is not considerable ... the weakest has strength enough to kill the strongest, either by secret machination, or by confederacy with others" (Hobbes 1651/1968, p. 113) and "the fear of coercive power ... where all men are equal ... cannot possibly be supposed" (ibid., p. 196). In such a configuration of equal opposing forces, unless technology is biased in favor of attack, a given distribution of property can, and among rational men will, always be successfully defended by the incumbent. If one individual seeks to change the property status quo by excluding from it another, the other has just enough force to resist (kill) him; in case of unequal forces, the weaker can have recourse to a "confederacy" strong enough to resist. The important point is that in this model, coalition forming has the object of equalizing the opposing forces. Consequently, whether the property status quo is efficient or inefficient, it cannot be altered by way of a stronger coalition forming on the side of the efficient change (or indeed of *any* change, whether efficient or not), and imposing it on the weaker one.

The second alternative, by contrast, stipulates that the role of "confederacy" is to create force inequality in favor of the attacker: " . . . if one plant, sow, build, or possesse a convenient Seat, others may probably be expected to come *with forces united* to *dispossesse*, and deprive him . . ." (ibid., p. 184, my italics). Since the attacker, being "probably" a coalition of united forces "hath no more to feare, than another man's *single power*" (ibid., my italics), the attack is generally successful. A new status quo is created, and by the logic of the model becomes the new target of attack by a new coalition. It is this second model that Hobbes and all his intellectual descendants implicitly invoke when they argue the impossibility of contract and order in anarchy, and the imperative necessity of "a common power set over them both, with right and force sufficient" (Hobbes, ibid., p. 196).

Nobody has, to my knowledge, bothered to ask the obvious question: why in a Hobbesian world should coalitions form only for attack and never for defense? What happens if, in any conflict over property, both the attacker and the defender are free to attract allies? Why can't we make the commonsense assumption that the force of the coalition gathered to back a given side in the conflict will be proportional to the "payoff" (gain or avoided loss) the side would get if it won the conflict? To meet the objection that this would amount to a doubtfully rational "maximax" strategy guided only by the best possible outcome and taking no account of intermediate or worst-possible alternatives, the assumption could be recast in terms of the mathematical expectation of utility payoffs. However, the essential point would, as far as I can see, remain intact: incentives work both ways, they may attract coalitions on both sides of a conflict, and the tacit supposition of an asymmetry, giving a natural advantage to the attacking coalition, must be justified. Failing that, it must be rejected.

5

How to justify the supposed asymmetry? If a given population is free to form coalitions, prior to the emergence of institutions (such as a convention to respect property, contract, or both, since the two will almost certainly come or go together), the resulting interaction will in effect be an *n*-person "distribution game," whose game sum is the aggregate property of the *n* players. Let there be, for simplicity, only three players, each equally "strong." Their "strength" (muscle, arms, economic power, political influence) can be employed with equal effectiveness to defend the property status quo, or to change it to one's advantage; technology is neutral between attack and defense, and there are constant returns to scale. Defense, then, wins against attack of equal or lesser strength.

Attack, to win, must have greater strength. (A special case of this distribution game is democracy, where "strength," instead of having a quite general significance, is reduced to "number of votes," and a simple or qualified majority wins.) Whatever the status quo before the game, the solution of the game is a distribution of property decided by the winner, and the stronger coalition necessarily wins.

Evidently, since players are equally strong, in a three-person game, if any two players can agree on how to divide all property between them, that division will be the solution of the game and the third player will be left propertyless.[4] If he tried to obstruct this outcome, he would incur some cost, only to be defeated; therefore if he is rational, he will not try. The winning coalition knows this; therefore it will not negotiate with the loser. (However, if they believed the loser was irrational, or precommitted to a costly defense unless bought off, the winners might be prepared to buy him off.)

Of the two members of the winning coalition, one, the "poorer," now has less property than the other, the "richer" (in the limiting case, they will have equal property; but the reasoning below holds in the limiting case as well). The "poorer" and the propertyless "poorest" can now improve their joint payoff by forming a new coalition that, being stronger than the solitary "richer," can dispossess him. One of the new winners will now be the "richer," the other the "poorer." The latter can again improve his payoff at the new "richer's" expense by forming a coalition with the new "poorest" and dispossessing the "richer." The solution, in other words, will always remain unstable. It will rotate round and round, always superseded by another of the same form and the same instability. Only the members of the winning and losing coalitions will be changing places cyclically. The mechanism by which strength (including, in a democracy, voting strength) is attracted by prospective payoffs and produces a certain distribution of the game sum (i.e., in the present example, of property) is analogous to other well-known social-choice cycles (Arrow, Sen). There is no distribution of property to which at least one other is not "preferred" by a stronger coalition, leading to a perpetual cycle of redistribution.

This, I think, goes some way to justify the strange asymmetry in what I called (in section 4) Hobbes's second "model," where coalition always produces an imbalance of force in favor of attacking the status quo and dispossessing the possessor. But it only goes some way, and not a very long way either. For it is clear that while the unstable solution of each round of the distribution game is the direct consequence of each player acting rationally, a perpetual cycle of dispossession and redistribution is *not* going to be the solution of indefinitely repeated rounds of the same game. The players will soon see new costs and new incentives appearing, which will alter their view of expected payoffs and of the rational strategy they must choose to maximize them.

6

Over any three rounds of this game, each player takes turns to be once "richer," once "poorer," and once "poorest." The statistical average return to each is one-third of the property available for redistribution. Two players can improve their joint return from the game by forming a coalition, and having taken all property, refusing to desert the alliance despite the availability of an even higher payoff to the deserter in the next round. This refusal to quit a coalition in order to join a new one imposes a stable solution on the game, i.e., it "stops" it from rotating. However, is it rational for the "poorer" player not to desert his richer partner?

By deserting, he can only hope to improve his position from "poorer" to "richer" for a single round. In the round after that, he must expect his partner to desert him, causing him to fall all the way from "richer" to propertyless "poorest." Therefore standing fast, respecting his richer coalition partner's property, and accepting that his position is permanently poorer, would be his best strategy provided the poorer position represents, in the worst case, not much less than a one-third share of the property to be divided. This is so because, if the game is not stabilized and redistribution continues indefinitely, he can statistically expect to average out with a share of one-third, *less* the cost and disutility of periodic dispossession. He will want to do no worse than this (settling for less would be irrational), but anything better is a bonus.

Note that the decision to "stop the game," stand fast, and not desert, is the poorer partner's alone: if he is prepared to accept his roughly one-third share, the richer partner cannot permanently improve his own position, and will be happy to stabilize his share at around two-thirds, rather than revert to the cyclical average of one-third. The propertyless has no choice if the coalition of the propertied holds.

Note also that while a three-person game under the very abstract conditions stipulated here produces a stable distribution of about two-thirds or less to the first player, about one-third or more to the second, and nothing or next to nothing to the third, an *n*-person game under less neat and artificial conditions would probably produce a solution that was messier, less structured, and more like real-life distributions of wealth, the more so as real-life distributions are influenced by many more elements in addition to coalition forming to produce concentrations of force, influence, or voting strength.

What I have just attempted to demonstrate was that on full reflexion it is reasonable to expect private property to emerge, and to prevail over the temptations that threaten it, as a product of the same robust incentives that we would, perhaps a little hastily, expect to provoke, not respect for property, but theft, robbery, dispossession, and default instead. This result, let me add, owes nothing to decency, sympathy, a sense of fairness, and a desire for mutual accomodation. Such motives, residing in our better nature, are almost certainly important in human conduct, but it seems to me gratifying that we can find an explanation that is at least coherent whether or not it is right, for a crucial institution of the social order, property, from the most elementary assumptions of rationality, without having recourse to any special motivation springing, not from human nature *tout court*, but from our *better* nature.

The logic of the "distribution game" rests, not on any collective quest for efficient solutions for a whole group, but on individual maximizing behavior. The resulting game solution implies an escape from the costly, futile, and sterile "churning" of repeated redistribution; it stabilizes a set of property relations. If this is socially efficient, it is so as an almost accidental by-product of each individual doing the best he can for himself. Any regard he has for the interests of others serves only to help foresee their likely reactions to his alternative strategies, in order to let him choose the best one given that others will also choose their best ones. This, in other words, is still a Hobbesian world of every man for himself, except that it produces property relations that are stable and orderly, instead of being precarious and chaotic.

How is this world, where property relations are merely facts of life upheld by forces that are mightier than the forces that would overthrow them, transformed into one where they are respected as parts of the legitimate interests of others? How does the convention of respect for property – not for one's own, but for yours, his, and hers – arise and take root?

How does *any* convention arise and take root whose operation favors some more than others? There is little doubt that Hume is right: The passage of time lends legitimacy to almost any stable state of affairs that is not downright vicious or stupidly inefficient. Original occupation, exclusion, the forcible enclosure of previously accessible common resources, and their taking into private property, gradually recede into the distant past; passage of title from the original occupiers and "finders" to new owners by sale, gift, or bequest comes into the foreground and promotes a sense of legitimacy.

This is not to suggest that the passage of time alone can bring into being a convention of property that is self-enforcing because everybody's best policy is to respect and never to violate it. Property no doubt needs a secondary convention for its enforcement, protection, and deterrence of violations. Such a secondary convention may be self-enforcing (a sufficiently large and strong body of property-owners supporting it in spontaneous cooperation) or not; in the latter case, it needs the support of binding contractual arrangements for the provision of resources devoted to enforcement. It is to contracts, and their enforceability, the pivotal problem in the social order, that we must finally turn.

7

While property is best understood as an *n*-person, and in its most elementary form a three-person, game, the essence of contract, i.e., a promised exchange, is a two-person game where the two available pure strategies consist of performance of the promise or default. The contract is optimally efficient if the value of the two performances is equal at the margin to each party. If it were unequal for one party, it would pay him to increase or reduce the contract sum, and if this were not consistent with equal marginal value of performances for the other party, they could both improve their expected gain from the contract by changing the relative price of the performances to be exchanged until marginal equality was established. This maximization condition is naturally subject to the budget constraints of the parties, and to any indivisibilities.

Like the property distribution game, the key to the solution of the contract game is coalition forming to create an inequality between the forces favoring rival solutions: the larger payoff attracts the stronger coalition that can impose its payoff-maximizing strategy on the weaker one. In the property game, the stronger coalition secures the larger payoff by overriding the status quo. Once secured, it preserves its larger payoff by stabilizing the new status quo. Where, however, is the larger payoff in the contract game; how does one get it; and how can stronger and weaker coalitions be formed in a game that has only two players?

Assuming the gains from trade promised in the contract are maximized, the value of the two performances is equal at the margin. Let performances be nonsimultaneous. The player who is meant to move first can choose to perform or not to perform as promised. In the former case, the second player will default, because he can make no further gain from the contract by performing what he promised. In the latter case, he will try to force the first player to perform. In each of these possible configurations, each party would gain a payoff equal to the contract sum if he succeeded to make the defaulting party perform; and each defaulting party would save the contract sum if he successfully resisted the attempt. A rational player would be willing to employ his strength, or otherwise spend resources up to, but not exceeding, the contract sum to force the other party to perform.[5] Neither side can gain more than this by frustrating or subduing the other side; hence no side would be willing to spend more than this to enforce the other side's performance. Whether the players act alone, or find extra-game allies to form coalitions, they have (at least in the ideal contract) strictly offsetting incentives, and would lose even from successful enforcement if they incurred enforcement costs in excess of the contract sum. The solution of the game, then, is stalemate: whatever the status quo (whether neither side performs or one side performs), it can be effectively protected and will not be overturned by enforcement. The plaintiff will never subdue the defendant.

This conclusion, reached after telling the first and most Hobbesian half of the contract story, is preliminary. It seems strongly to support the standard belief that contracts, to be binding, require a third-party enforcer who stands outside the particular contract, and whose capacity and willingness to incur enforcement expenditure is not limited by the incentives the contract offers. But what incentives motivate the third-party enforcer?

We have seen that the standard belief runs into nasty obstactles. Third-party enforcement is to let the genie out of the bottle without knowing how ever to put it back. It has every chance to breed a dangerous principal–agent problem, whose putative solution is either an infinite regress of ever higher-order enforcers, or a *deus ex machina* final power, exogenous and unexplained. However, all this is perhaps no great matter, for the preliminary conclusion, namely that contracts are per se unenforceable, is wrong.

8

To get it right, the story of the contract must be told to the end. First, let us recall that the problem of enforceability impinges primarily, if not exclusively, on contracts with nonsimultaneous performances, such as credit transactions. It is a fair guess that such contracts are found indispensable as social cooperation becomes complex and sophisticated,[6] but they are nonetheless only one kind of contract among two. Second, and more important, the apparently dominant strategy in such contracts, to "take the money and run," is seldom really dominant in real life among contracting parties who can calculate.

Running off with the money nearly always involves heavy costs in terms of rebuilding a life elsewhere, replacing lost goodwill and regaining the status of an acceptable contract party. It will pay if the runaway leaves little of value behind, and if the contract sum was big enough; but for understandable reasons these two conditions tend to be mutually exclusive. He who has no valuable life to regret, little reputation and goodwill to lose, seldom gets to make contracts that leave him with big money to run away with. For default to be definitely a dominant strategy. it is best if the defaulter is anonymous and transient; yet who will willingly perform first, face to an anonymous and transient second performer? The usual game theory assumption of anonymous (interchangeable) players, for all its helpful effect to clarify the logic of a given game, must not be allowed to confuse a situation where it is plainly not applicable. Anonymity predictably produces default, but anonymity deprives the party to a contract of the opportunity to lay his hands on the money that would make defaulting worthwhile. This point has obvious relevance to the so-called "large group problem," which I hope to address later (section 9).

Take a two-person contract game witnessed with a minimum of attention by a nonplaying group of indeterminate size. Members of this "kibitzer" group, however, have been, are now, and expect in the future to be playing in other contract games. The first player performs his obligation under the contract, the second defaults, and the fact comes to be known by some "kibitzers" in the surrounding group, who in turn can pass this knowledge along if they deem it worth doing so. The first player as plaintiff now recruits a coalition to help him enforce the contract,[7] offering it a reward up to but not exceeding the contract sum in case of success, nothing in case of failure. This coalition, however, may find that it would pay it to incur enforcement expenditure in excess of the contract sum. The reason for this apparent extravagance is that the maximum payoff it can expect is not simply the contract sum, but also the value of some positive externality or "spillover" upon those other contracts to which members of the coalition are or can expect to be parties. There is a degree of payoff interdependence: first performers to certain contracts benefit from the enforcement of the claims of other first performers in other contracts. Such spillover effects enhance the reputation of the enforcers who came to the aid of the plaintiff, teach a lesson to the defendant and other would-be defaulters, and discourage their potential coalition partners. As such, they reduce enforcement costs throughout the group. This gain, a positive externality, is probably more perceptible in the close "neighborhood" (the same locality, the same line of business, the same peer group) than at distant points near the edges of the group: hence it is more likely to be internalized.

The defendant, for reasons symmetrical to the plaintiff's, will also recruit a coalition to oppose enforcement, holding out as reward some sum up to, but not exceeding, the contract sum he would save if he could get away with default. His coalition, however, assuming it is formed, can only hope for a best-case payoff equal to the reward offered by the defendant *less* negative spillover effects on future contracts the coalition members expect to wish to conclude. The most important negative spillover effect is likely to be the reduced willingness of third parties to enter into contracts with a defaulter's coalition partners. Members of both coalitions, if they calculate (however crudely and with however large a margin of error, as long as the error is not systematically biased), will internalize the positive and negative spillovers created by coalition action, which would help determine their willingness to enter, or abstain from, a given coalition.

Internalizing the neighbourhood spillover effects increases the coalition payoff from enforcement, and decreases that from default, relative to their common benchmark, the contract sum. The asymmetry between the two, reflected in an asymmetry between the resources either side could rationally spend in order to win, obviously improves the odds that the enforcing coalition will win. Consequently, in the limit it will not pay at all, but merely entail useless expenditure, to oppose such a coalition; and the consequence of *that*, in turn, is that where potential enforcement is powerful, actual enforcement cost under moderately favorable conditions may be reduced to vanishing point: if the defendant's coalition will not form, it is hardly necessary for the plaintiff's coalition to form as long as it is common knowledge that the incentives are present for it to form as occasion demands.

At this stage we are, it seems to me, fairly entitled to two deductions: (a) default will normally fail to find coalition support, and (b) enforcing coalitions will form readily, and will tend to be sufficiently powerful.

In sections 5 and 6, I have advanced a reason why, among rationally maximizing individuals, "common pool" resources would pass into private property, and why a certain, no doubt unequal distribution of property would be finally stabilized, ultimately giving rise to a convention of respect for property. I have not tried to prove that the convention would be self-enforcing. Lack of space forbids the marshalling of arguments for or against, but on the whole I think they are inconclusive: whether a group or an entire society can make its property convention into a complex self-enforcing one depends on contingencies, including its history, and there can be no certitude about the matter on a priori grounds. It is this uncertainty that makes a self-enforcing contract convention particularly critical for the orderly functioning of society: if contracts can be relied on, any other convention can be made enforceable, for compliance can be contracted for, and if not, protection from noncompliance and for its punishment can be.

9

My argument that successful enforcement generates positive, default negative externalities; that prospective coalition partners internalize them; and that consequently enforcement will attract the support of the stronger coalition, is for all its simplicity not decisive. Challengers of the theory of ordered anarchy have a last-resort objection to it, the Large Group problem. This objection enjoys more generous credit than its intellectual content deserves; but in the present context it cannot be bypassed. It must be dealt with, if only to show why the credit it is accorded is excessive.

In the large group, individuals are alleged to lack the incentives that would lead them to choose cooperative solutions in the same kind of repeated, game-like interactions that take place in small groups. This belief is based on a putative analogy between social groups with many members and n-person indefinitely repeated prisoners' dilemmas where n is a large number, or the players are anonymous, or both. This analogy is almost totally false, and based on elementary mistakes. The subject is large and cannot be done full justice here, but a few pointers should suffice.

Unlike the abstract large-number supergame where all players are alike, homogeneous for the purposes of the game, and all play only in the same game and in no other, the large group in society is always eterogeneous. It is the sum of small groups, which, in turn, are only homogeneous for some purposes and heterogeneous for most others; their heterogeneity is often relevant for the game. All players do not play in one and the same game. The characteristic configuration is that small groups, their subgroups, and in the vast majority of cases (i.e., in the most frequent form of social cooperation, the contract of exchange) pairs of players, each play in a different game, or in other words are parties to a different contract. Some, probably many, of the same players take part in different games, running parallel or with a time lead or time lag; and most of these games are repeated with the participation of some previous players and some new ones. Hence there is a complex and dense web of communication in which it is both easy to send[8] and profitable to receive information about prospective players (contract partners). Consequently, the play of a player is rapidly translated into a reputation that influences his chances of being invited or admitted to other games, and the terms he can hope to get. In all these respects, far from an analogy, there is an almost total contrast between the real-life large group and the *n*-person game where *n* is large. Lastly, there is some, albeit weak, analogy between the real-life *large* group with its numerous small subgroups (down to the two-person group made up of the two parties to one contract) and the *n*-person game where *n* is *small* rather than large. This weak analogy concerns the vulnerability of cooperative small-group solutions to the probability that the next game in a repeated series is going to be the last, beyond which by definition nothing matters, hence the noncooperative strategy becomes dominant. A contract between two parties who will never deal again with one another is in this sense a "last game." But unless neither will ever deal with *anybody else* either, the consequences of the noncooperative strategy in *their* last contract carry over into contracts with *others*, where they continue to matter. Contracting continues in the same and connected localities, trades, and communities as long as society keeps functioning.

In transposing the "large group" objection from game theory to transactions cost economics, the objectors claim that economies of scale impose mass markets, hence a great multitude of "impersonal transactions" between unknown parties:[9] thus they bring the faceless, nameless player back into play. It is no doubt true that there are proportionately more "impersonal" transactions in a modern economy than in earlier times. Many supermarket customers are unknown to the checkout girl. But they pay before rolling out their trolley. If not, they produce a credit card; and the credit card company is not unknown. It is equally true that where performances are not simultaneous or are incompletely defined in the contract (cf. Hart, 1991), serious precautions are generally taken to ensure that the second performer, far from being impersonal, is thoroughly known, vouched for, and has a reputation to lose.[10] It is this that raises entry costs in industries where quality and service are important, difficult to define and to litigate.

Under these conditions, the invocation of "impersonal exchanges" is hardly intelligible, as is the claim that third-party enforcement makes such exchanges possible, – for there *are* no such exchanges, with or without third-party enforcement. They are imaginary constructs, except in the world of cash-and-carry – a world to which enforcement of any kind is irrelevant.

10

One object of the present paper was to prove that, contrary to James Buchanan's verdict, it is possible for romantic fools *both* to see coherence and good sense in a theory of ordered anarchy *and* to read Hobbes. In fact, I find Hobbes a positive help to drawing the outlines of such a theory.

Why, then, is it that states are ubiquitous? The inference is universally drawn that just as a mammal must have a lung or a brain, a normal developed society must have a state as a requirement of organic completeness, without which it cannot function properly; the state as a superior form of social organization is imposed by the processes of cultural selection no less inexorably than the lung is by natural selection.

The answer to this type of wide-eyed social determinism had, once again, best be a Humean one. As he remarks with some asperity in the *Treatise* (1739/1978), governments "arise from quarrels, not among men of the same society, but among those of different societies" (p. 540). An anarchic society may not be well equipped to resist military conquest by a command-directed one. But this is a less general claim, less decisive and different from the one underlying practically all received theory of political and economic institutions, namely that the state is a necessary prior condition of social order in general, of property and contract in particular, so that it would be needed and wanted even in the absence of any threat of foreign attack. To listen to Hume again, "the stability of possession, its translation by consent, and the performance of promises ... are ... antecedent to government" (p. 541).

The weight of arguments seems to me decisive that whatever causes states to be everywhere and ordered anarchy nowhere, it is not some kind of utility-maximizing logic, some putative economic necessity due to which property and contract cannot exist without being enforced by the state. The reasoning, leading from the *prevalence* of centralized, sovereign third-party enforcement to its *necessity* is manifestly a mistake of inference, a *non sequitur*.

A more modest claim holds that while ordered anarchy, based on conventions, with their enforcement "made or bought" by the directly interested parties themselves, may well be feasible, it would be inefficient. Among its tools, violence must figure: and violence is an industry that operates under increasing returns to scale.[11] It is, for this and perhaps other reasons, a "natural" monopoly.[12] A corollary of the increasing returns thesis is that the state, using the threat of violence, reduces transactions costs below what they would be under private contract enforcement. Both these proposition run into intrinsic difficulties. How will monopoly enforcement affect the distribution of income between the monopolist and its customers? Will transaction costs really be lower if they must provide monopoly rent to the enforcer? – and so on.[13] Such difficulties, however, are as nothing next to a blunter and more powerful objection. It is that we have not the faintest idea whether the state is or is not an efficient enforcer, whether statute laws are efficient substitutes for the conventions of property and contract, and whether the existence of a state over a territory, or of several states across territories, raises or lowers transactions costs. Any assertion that it does one or the other is almost entirely a matter of guesswork based on practically no evidence. In fact, valid, *ceteris paribus* evidence is impossible to produce, since comparisons of public and private enforcement regimes that cannot coexist are impossible. No one can pretend to know what a place at a time would be like if the omnipresent state with its monopolistic claims were absent, and had been absent from Day One, rather than present one day, crumbling the next, and leaving its moral footprints and material debris on the ground. The anxious conviction that anarchy is chaos and mayhem, exemplified by postcolonial Africa, Lebanon in the 1980s, or the ex-Soviet Union in the 1990s, springs from a misunderstood and misplaced empiricism that confuses historical experience with experiment.

NOTES

1 Nozick (1974, p. 176) uses a different route to demonstrate the same result, i.e., the internal inconsistency of the Lockean proviso in a world of finite resources.

2 Libecap (1989), suggests that the higher the ratio of benefit to cost, the more likely it is that a solution will be found.

3 Douglass North, reading with the eyes of the professional historian, wonders whether "voluntary cooperation can exist without . . . a coercive state to create cooperative solutions?" He thinks the answer is contingent on circumstances, and "the jury is still out" (North, 1990, p. 14, citing North, 1981). He adds (1990, p. 58): "If we cannot do without the state, we cannot do with it either." The truth of the matter is no doubt the obverse: we can live with it if we must, *and* also without it if we must. Neither is always comfortable, and both must be learnt by practice.

4 In an even more extreme solution, two players might actually enslave the third. For this to be an equilibrium solution, the economics of slavery have to be more favorable than the economics of wage labor. A similar consideration may influence the choice between leaving the third player wholly propertyless, or letting him have some property.

5 There is a parallel between this somewhat absurd situation, where the two parties taken together spend twice as much as their greatest possible gain which only one of the two can gain, and the economics of thieving as depicted by Gary Becker (1992, p. 8). In his Nobel lecture, he relates that in his earlier work (1968, n.3), looking for a way to impute social cost to crime against property, which, at first sight, looks like a pure transfer from owners to thieves, he has put the social costs of thieving at approximately equal to the aggregate dollar value stolen, since "rational criminals would be willing to spend up to that amount on their crimes." He then remembers that potential victims would also be willing to spend resources to protect their property against crime, therefore one should add this expenditure to the resource cost the thieves incur, to get total social cost. He does not say whether protective expenditure is equal, greater or less than thieving expenditure, but the two together are implicitly estimated to exceed, perhaps by a great deal, the aggregate sum stolen.

6 In fact, such contracts have apparently *always* been an integral part of exchange. Primitive tribes bartered with other, strange tribes by leaving their surplus goods at some conspicuous midway spot. The foreign tribesmen came, picked them up and left their own surplus goods on the spot. It must be added that although the parties did not personally know each other, both sides knew perfectly well whom they were dealing with – which is why the deal, where one party performed first, despite the risk that the other party might default and just walk off with the goods, became a reasonable proposition.

7 An enforcing coalition may use a range of costly self-help measures, from threats of discrimination and actual ostracism, to violence to compel performance and to punish. But it may just as well provide money to hire enforcement services. A trade association may have a budget for such purposes, just as long-distance traders in antiquity, medieval, and even more recent times used to hire (subsidize) foreign potentates to protect their interests against brigands, debtors, and interlopers. The choice between enforcing and hiring enforcement is basically the same as the classic "make-or-buy" choice, well known from the theory of the firm.

8 In a given line of business, the spread of information about the quality and reputation of a person or firm spreads like wildfire, and knows no frontiers. Information is "cheap" to send and "cheap," to obtain, for the less than respectable reason that businessmen are like idle old women in one respect: in their delight to spread and to listen to gossip.

9 To quote Douglass North (1990, pp. 55–8) again, third-party enforcement (by the state) is hard to do without, because self-enforcing solutions require that the game be played indefinitely between the same parties who must have "perfect information," but "[i]n a world of *impersonal* exchange, we are exchanging with multiple individuals and can acquire very little information about them" (p. 58, my italics). To a practicing business man, the idea of dealing with nameless unknowns must be nigh incomprehensible. Whatever the economies of scale he wished to realize, he would simply see no possible occasion to deal with unknown parties otherwise than in self-enforcing contracts; least of all would he deal on credit. He would always place identified parties, banks, brokers, bondsmen, wholesalers, quality inspectors, and so on, between himself and the "nameless" credit customer. Cash customers, of course, need no enforcement and may even remain nameless for all the difference it makes.

10 William Niskanen, one-time chief economist of the Ford Motor Company, relates that in his day the company had hundreds of component suppliers who

had no written contract whatsoever, which did not hurt either Ford or the suppliers.

11 If this argument were taken really seriously, it would be hard to explain why there are many states instead of one world state (perhaps returns do not go on increasing on *that* scale?); why the number of states, instead of steadily diminishing, waxes and wanes unpredictably, with some large states breaking up, some small ones trying to unite. The easy answer, of course, is that when states are getting larger, returns to scale must be increasing, when states are getting smaller, they are diminishing. This defence effectively empties the thesis of all possible empirical content.

12 A summary and lucid critique of the family of explanations of the state's monopoly, advanced by Engels, Kropotkin, Max Weber, Norbert Elias, and Robert Nozick, is found in Green (1988, pp. 78–82).

13 An intriguing public-choice type problem in this respect concerns the incidence of a given aggregate burden of transactions costs. Borne by parties having interests in contracts, they are internalized. Borne by the general public via direct and indirect taxation, as is the case for the part of enforcement costs assumed by the state, they are externalized, and no longer impinge on contract parties. This is inefficient, as is all divorce between the incidence of a benefit and of the cost incurred to secure it. However, this would not stop the business community cheering as enforcement costs were shifted to the state and transaction costs were seemingly lowered. However, their real social cost might have been actually increased by the shift to the state, for reasons the public-choice literature can liberally provide.

REFERENCES

Anderson, Terry L. and Hill, P. J. (1975) "The Evolution of Property Rights: A Study of the American West," *Journal of Law and Economics*, vol. XVIII, 1.

Becker, Gary S. (1968) "Crime and Punishment: An Economic Approach," *Journal of Political Economy*, 76.

—— (1992) "The Economic Way of Looking at Life," Stockholm, The Nobel Foundation.

Buchanan, James M. (1979) *What Should Economists Do?* Indianapolis: Liberty Press.

Cowen, Tyler, (ed.) (1988) *The Theory of Market Failure*, Fairfax, Va: George Mason University Press.

Demsetz, Harold (1964) "The Exchange and Enforcement of Property Rights," *Journal of Law and Economics*, 7, repr. in Cowen, 1988.

—— (1967) "Toward a Theory of Property Rights," *American Economic Review*, Proceedings Issue.

Green, Leslie (1988) *The Authority of the State*, Oxford: Clarendon Press.

Hart, Oliver D. (1991) "Incomplete Contracts and the Theory of the Firm," in Williamson and Winter, 1991.

Hobbes, Thomas (1651, 1968) *Leviathan*, ed. by C. B. Macpherson, Harmondsworth: Penguin.

Hume, David (1739/1978) *A Treatise of Human Nature*, 2nd edn by P. H. Nidditch, Oxford: Clarendon Press.

Libecap, Gary D. (1989) *Contracting for Property Rights*, Cambridge: Cambridge University Press.

North, Douglass C. (1981) *Structure and Change in Economic History*, New York: Norton.

—— (1990) *Institutions, Institutional Change and Economic Performance*, Cambridge: Cambridge University Press.

Nozick, Robert (1974) *Anarchy, State, and Utopia*, Oxford: Blackwell.

Streit, Manfred E. (1992) "Economic Order, Private Law and Public Policy: The Freiburg School of Law and Economics in Perspective," *Journal of Institutional and Theoretical Economics*, vol. 148, 4.

Williamson, Oliver E. and Stanley G. Winter (eds) (1991) *The Nature of the Firm*, New York: Oxford University Press.

10 The glass is half-full[*]

Half of this book, and most of its analytical meat, seeks to show that too many critical social interactions, notably those involving the respect for property and the provision of public goods for large groups, are genuine prisoners' dilemmas and do not have efficient equilibria. Since their invisible-hand solutions are "spontaneous disorders" rather than orders, anarchy is severely sub-optimal, and the state is a Pareto-improving institution. It is good to have some of it, *ma non troppo*: too much state turns out to be, well, too much.

The second half of the book, a summary of familiar Hayekian ("conceit") and public choice ("opportunism") theories, explains how the same kind of unintended processes, which issue in spontaneous disorders and render the state necessary in the first place, will cause it to expand beyond its putative optimum role, undermine some of the surviving spontaneous orders in civil society, and let loose a flood of perverse effects. In the last, and what is for this reviewer the least substantial, part of his work, Nils Karlson proposes the double thesis that the growth of the Western welfare state tends to level off in an inferior equilibrium he quaintly calls "the state of state" – a thesis that is not implausible but that he supports rather thinly – and that measures of "constitutional social engineering," assuming they could be carried out over the opposition of vested interests, could confine the state to its benign role and optimal size.

What deserves a closer look is Karlson's basic thesis, common in one guise or another in every last-resort argument for the state that aspires to both logical and moral rigor, to wit, that far too many of life's ostensible prisoners? dilemmas are really what they look like, namely social interactions with a suboptimal dominant strategy equilibrium. Reaching the optimal solution would require the players to make credible mutual commitments to the cooperative strategy. This is widely believed to suppose a nonplaying agent acting jointly for the players, and enforcing their

* This chapter first appeared in *Constitutional Political Economy*, 1994, vol. 5, no. 3. It is a review of Nils Karlson (1993), *The State of State*, Acta Universitatis Upsaliensis, Stockholm: Almqvist & Wiksell International. Reprinted with permission.

commitment, i.e., a state. The players would be contradicting their own preference rankings of outcomes if they did not agree to the state having the powers that it takes, (though perhaps no more than it takes) to secure the best outcome. (What it takes, and whether there is always a common ordering of all feasible outcomes, are moot points, and various types of contractarian theory treat them variously. Ultimately, however, all have the logic of noncooperative game theory at their base.) The coercion involved in "solving" prisoners' dilemmas is legitimate, morally unobjectionable in that, if it did not exist, all rational men would agree upon it.

Just as these ultimate arguments for the state hinge on one thing, that prisoners' dilemmas are prisoners' dilemmas, the ultimate arguments for what James Buchanan has called ordered anarchy hinge on another thing, namely that quite often they are not. The central thesis of ordered anarchy relies on the serial, connected nature of social interactions. The last game of a series of prisoners' dilemmas is, unambiguously, a game of prisoner's dilemma with the characteristic payoff structure that induces all rational people to default on commitments. However, the players may well not know which game is the last game, nor that there is a last one at all. What if the world never ends?[1] In such situations a supergame is typically a coordination game. It is rarely a prisoner's dilemma, unless the probability that a given game is the last game, or the discount on future payoffs, or of course both, are sufficiently high. Obviously, the higher they are, the closer a supergame comes to resemble a one-shot game unconnected to other games, and the less reason one has to expect it to produce a spontaneous order. The converse – a low probability of the game being the last game, or a low time discount being conductive to a spontaneous order – has the same broad-brush, intuitive appeal.

This is one way of suggesting that the glass is at least half-full, and the prospect for spontaneous orders is promising. Karlson, however, is categorical that the glass is at least half-empty, and in key situations holds no water at all. His reasoning is that, first, it is no use for the game to be serially repeated *unless* the "shadow of the future" is large, and it will not be large *unless* "restrictive conditions ... are satisfied for all the actors" (p. 56). This is persuasive description of the first water. An alternative description of the situation would say that restrictive conditions are needed for the shadow of the future to be *short enough*, and hence for the supergame to shrink to a one-shot game. In stable, everyday life such conditions are unlikely to obtain, though they may well do in times of war and revolution. (They will also tend to be satisfied for the player I should call the Transient Tourist. However, ubiquitous as he has become, the Transient Tourist can hardly demolish a peace-time order that would prevail but for his passing through.) In the second place, Karlson holds that the chances of spontaneous orders emerging from apparent prisoners' dilemmas are "even slimmer" in many-person than in two-person interactions, because of the large-number problem (pp. 52–6). Two objections arise. The less important one is that certain mixed-strategy equilibria could actually be more easily attained in large-number games. In a large group, it may be *ex ante* rational for one part of the membership to contribute to providing a public good for the group as a whole, and for the rest of the group to ride free, along the lines of Chicken or Hawk-and-Dove games; it is a fair conjecture that two persons would find it harder to settle on the respective roles to be assumed, unless Nature allowed one of them to move first and obliged the other to take the leftover role. Karlson admits the possibility of large-group mixed-strategy equilibria, but thinks that they are only "somewhat" more efficient (p. 56) than universal noncooperation. Why, however, should efficiency require pure strategies? The distribution of payoffs (including burdens) in mixed-strategy equilibria can of course be blatantly unequal, and may be thought unfair. But this does not in itself reduce the game sum, and tells nothing about efficiency. A public good may be provided for a large group with all members "fairly" contributing to its cost, or only a proportion of them doing so. Efficiency criteria cannot be read into this proposition.

The more important objection arises against the conventional wisdom itself about the large number problem, a wisdom Karlson accepts. Whether a social game of apparent prisoners' dilemmas is in effect tantamount, for a particular player, to a coordination supergame depends, among other things, on how well his moves are monitored, and on how credible are the other players' implicit offers of reward for nice, and threats of punishment for nasty, strategies. It is tempting to jump to the conclusion that the larger the group of players, the greater is the probability of any one getting away with it, unobserved and unpunished. However, any large group that deserves to be called thus, meaning that it is homogeneous in one relevant respect, is heterogeneous in indefinitely many other respects, some of them relevant, and contains indefinitely many other overlapping homogeneous groups of all sizes. The members of some of these are bound to interact in a variety of parallel games, as do some of the groups *qua* groups with each other. In a differentiated, complex society, any number of parallel games, both present and future, will share some of the same players with the large-number game under consideration. The payoffs of some of the parallel games may be as big, or bigger. Players in a small-number game have incentives to monitor each other's strategies both in the game in question and in other games, including large-number games. Subject to the proviso about the game being unlikely to be the last one,[2] they also have incentives to punish nasty strategies by exclusion or otherwise, and may find it rational to do so in any or all of the (not-last) games where they meet the nasty player.

The large-group problem looks like a problem owing to the tacit supposition that the players' incentives and opportunities to monitor, reward, and punish are somehow confined to one isolated large-number game, and do not probabilistically extend over all games where a nasty player runs the risk of meeting players he has met before, or players who have been made aware of the reputation he has acquired. Players with bad reputations are of course handicapped in current and future parallel games, and may not even get to play. By the same token, players who have built a reputation of carrying out their threats, may deter others from nasty strategies by their mere presence in a game. (Only the Transient Tourist can afford not to reckon with these spillover effects.) All this is well known. It all becomes acutely relevant the instant it is understood that, in living society, any large group tends to be a crazy quilt of innumerable, partly overlapping large and small groups; no game is the only or last game; and any player in a game faces a significant probability of being a player in some other game where his payoff depends on his reputation. The conditions for this *not* to be the case are outlandish and forbidding. Karlson asserts that cooperative behavior in apparent repeated prisoners' dilemmas will not arise even in bilateral, let alone large-number plays "unless certain quite harsh conditions are fulfilled" (p. 91). This is persuasive description all over again: quite the contrary is true; it is precisely the necessary conditions for large-number supergames to have a dominant noncooperative equilibrium that are "quite harsh," and they are unlikely to be met in a society of purely voluntary interactions, i.e., in the absence of a state.

Karlson advances the even more despondent diagnosis that not only prisoners' dilemmas, but even unambiguous coordination games run a high risk of producing spontaneous disorders. He believes that where several alternative conventions of comparable efficiency are available for choice, "the most we can expect" is that different pairs of fully rational players coordinate on different conventions (p. 81) rather than all adopting the same one. He assets that "the informational problems connected with the strategic uncertainty are prohibitive" (ibid.) It is not obvious that they are. The conclusion looks wrong, and seems to be based on mistaken reasoning.[3]

Believing all he does about the intractability of prisoners' dilemmas and the prenatal threats to conventions, it is not surprising that Karlson declares it to be "a theoretical . . . *fact* that the state is needed" (p. 124, my italics) to protect property and solve other public goods problems. His demonstration of the worth of markets, competition, prices, and the proposition that once it starts functioning, the state will turn against them, is as uncontroversial as it is unoriginal. His claim about the "constitutional social engineering" that would become possible, and would put matters nearly right, if only people could be separated by a veil from their "vested" interests, prompts no pertinent comment except that it would indeed be jolly if they could, and it did. He rightly disclaims all illusion that they could, and that it would.

His book about "invisible hands in politics and civil society" suffers beyond its deserts from the all too visible lack of an English copy editor's hand. Less methodology, fewer "boundedly rational adaptational satisficers" and their ilk, and putting right easily remedied linguistic inadequacies, would have secured it a more attentive reading.

NOTES

1 If it is common knowledge that a given game in a supergame *is* the last one, *and* it is a prisoner's dilemma, by "subgame perfectness" every preceding game is also a prisoner's dilemma: backward induction ensures this. Conversely, if the supergame is not a prisoner's dilemma, though universal defection is a possible equilibrium, it is never dominant, and occasional defection, owing to irrational conduct or a random cause, need not prevent the Pareto-superior cooperative-strategy equilibrium from being attained and maintained.

2 If punishing is not costless to the punisher, it is irrational to punish in the last game, and consequently also in all *preceding* games. The incentive to punish in a given subgame depends on the *succeeding* subgames probably not including a last one that ends the supergame. It is only a mild exaggeration to say that since all current and future parallel games count for something, the probability of a game being the last one for the purposes of choosing a strategy is the same as that of all relevant parallel games ceasing, which in turn is the same as all payoffs from social interactions ceasing. I suppose we all trust that this latter probability is very small. If it is not, nothing matters much anyway.

3 Several arguments can be used in rebuttal. Perhaps the most convincing one is that if several equally efficient conventions compete for adherents, the one that is randomly adopted by one more player than the others becomes, *ipso facto*, more efficient, and gains a cumulative advantage, crowding out its competitors.

11 Liberties, rights, and the standing of groups*

There has been, especially in recent decades, a copious flow of demands for ascribing rights to collective entities that, unlike states, cities, or corporations, have no formally constituted legal personality and in some cases could hardly have one. Groups that can be distinguished from neighboring, or surrounding, populations by shared religious, racial, linguistic, gender, or age characteristics, and by "cultural" practices in an ever widening sense of the word, encompassing anything from nomadic grazing to homosexual marriage, are asserted to have a variety of rights designed to preserve and perhaps to accentuate their separate identity. The rights would accomplish this by protecting and fostering their key distinguishing features. If such groups lack these rights, it is being urged that the lack be remedied. In this type of discourse, it is seldom specified how and by whom the rights should, and could, be accorded and how, once accorded, they should or could be enforced. Implicit in the demand, however, is that political arrangements ought to be adjusted, or new ones made, to accommodate the rights and their enforcement.

Many of these arguments, though not all, have a good deal of moral and aesthetic appeal. To that extent, they deserve serious attention. At the same time, they typically lack logical rigor, are put forward with a cavalier disregard for mutually inconsistent claims, and all too often lose themselves in vacuous verbiage. This creates impatience and unease even about the substance of these claims, let alone their form, – an unease I have come fully to share. It seems to me that before the whole set of open questions pertaining to group rights can be judged on their merits, a clearing of the conceptual ground is needed. Section 1 of this chapter, then, is an attempt at clarification. In section 2, I propose to look at the advocacy of group rights through the prism of political philosophy; this part is a critical discussion of some ideological justifications of collective rights. Section 3 deals with certain aspects of their justice, and of their expediency.

* This chapter first appeared in *Economic Approaches to Organizations and Institutions*, Pål Foss (ed.) (1995), Aldershot: Aldershot Dartmouth. Reprinted with permission.

1 LIBERTIES TO PERFORM, AND RIGHTS TO PERFORMANCE

It is hard to credit, but perfectly true, that the social sciences nearly always use the same word "right" to denote two radically different types of relations between agents, objects, and actions.[1] Political philosophy and economics, where rights-talk has very much become the favorite mode of discourse, are particularly remiss in paying attention to which of two animals they are talking about; they are, in addition, probably guilty of spreading this sloppy usage into everyday speech. The confusion caused by saying "right" both when we mean a right and when we mean a liberty is at the root of much that is ambiguous or downright false in so-called "rights-based" political theories. While many rights-assertions are apt to be confused, group rights are, for reasons that should emerge presently, on a particularly shaky foundation.

Perhaps the great down-to-earth divide between liberties and rights is *burden*: both in the sense of *cost* and of the burden of *proof*. A right confers a benefit on its holder. In order for him to enjoy it, an obligor must fulfill the corollary obligation – which is generally onerous to some degree. Only in the limit is bearing and fulfilling it a matter of indifference. The rightholder can require the obligor to perform as foreseen. A liberty, on the other hand, is exercised without calling for specific performance by any other party; apart from negative externalities that may be generated by my using it, my liberty is costless to everybody else. Only I incur opportunity cost if I avail myself of it, and consequently cannot put it to some alternative use. "Costly to others" and "costless to others" are no more alike than black and white. It is all the more incomprehensible that even in learned language they are given the same name.

Let me set out the rights–liberties distinction, not by reference to the situation of some maltreated minority, nor to some point of international or constitutional law, but by considering the pressing problem of getting this chapter typed. Counter-factually, I will pretend both that I can type, and that I have a secretary who can type, too. My two most obvious options are:

1 I will/will not type this paper.
2 I will/will not have my secretary type this paper.

Option 2 conveys the existence of a relation between my secretary, myself, and the work of typing my papers, such that if I instruct her to type the present one, she is under an obligation to carry out my instruction. Her obligation, in fact, extends to a whole class of (albeit imprecisely defined) actions. (It is not in her interest, nor in mine, to be too fussy and legalistic about what she may and may not be instructed to do.) Should she default on her obligation, she must reckon with some likelihood of sanctions on my part, including blame, withdrawal of privileges, or even dismissal. In this relation, I am the right-holder, she is the obligor, and the *source of my right is her agreement* to assume secretarial obligations. That is her side of the contract between us; my side is the consideration, including the salary, that buys her agreement.

The exercise of my right (I get her to type what I want) and the execution of her obligation (she types what I ask her to) are mutually entailed. Neither takes place without the other.[2] But it is not only exercise and execution that are so linked. The right itself, and the obligation itself, are also mutually entailed. No one can have a right without somebody being under the corresponding obligation.[3] Otherwise, the right could not be exercised and it would be nonsensical to describe it as a right. (That what is nonsensical is nevertheless done does not make it less nonsensical.) However, there is no logical vice in calling a relation a "right" when the corollary obligation is borne by a class of liable obligors, without it being fully specified in advance which member(s) of the class will actually be called upon to fulfill it. Thus, if instead of bossing one secretary, I am lording it over a whole typing pool, I have the right to give a typing job to any of the employees in the pool, and they all have the contingent obligation to take it on if asked. Moreover, it may be more convenient for all to have an office-head to whom I can hand over what I want done and who allocates the work among the typists in the pool. The head *transmits* the burden.

In a slightly less transparent case, let us take it that I have a right to be treated at public expense when I am ill. My call for treatment ultimately entails, albeit in a more roundabout way than the mutual entailment between my getting my paper typed and a typist typing it, that the state, much like the office-head in the typing pool example, allocates the cost of my treatment to some or all members of the class of taxpayers, who pay it as directed, perhaps according to a predetermined key laid down in fiscal legislation. From this example of a "right against the state" – a name insinuating that no one is burdened by virtue of the right – we shall draw, as a general lesson, the Principle of Transmission presently. Pending that, let us note that while my right to health care is duly matched by somebody's requisite obligation that is just as real as secretarial work in the previous example, its *source* is different. My secretary chose to be employed by me. She had other alternatives, though they must have been vastly less delectable. Her obligation in any event is clearly traceable to her agreement – a de jure or at least de facto contract. Taxpayers, however, once they have done what they found appropriate to do to avoid such tax liabilities as are in practice avoidable, have no alternative to being taxed (barring outlandish solutions like emigrating to the Virgin Islands). Their obligation to pay tax in general, and to pay my hospital bill in particular, is not traceable to their agreement in any straightforward way. Some strands of political theory attribute to them a kind of agreement, a "social" contract they would have entered into had the occasion for it actually arisen. But the epistemic status of this putative agreement, not to speak of the moral one, is at best dubious, and in any case not comparable in firmness to the actual agreements, backed by evidence, from which spring our rights and obligations in customary, common, and civil law.

Option 1 is totally unlike option 2, above all in one respect: it can be exercised without the necessity of specific performance by any other person. In option 1, my secretary does not have to type my paper. I do it; I have a manuscript, I can type, I have free access to a typewriter, I have paper, I can find the time. In doing it myself, I am exercising a liberty which, like every other liberty I have, depends (a) on my faculties, possessions, and environment (the "feasible set" or "opportunity set" of choice theory), (b) on my being under no incompatible obligation (i.e., on no one having a right opposed to my liberty), and (c) on the compatibility of my exercise of this liberty with the exercise by others of their liberties.

Condition (a) states, crudely speaking, that I can legally and morally do what I can physically do, subject to the remaining two conditions (b) and (c). Condition (c) is not very sharp-edged and is difficult to state in a noncircular manner: for it is all very well to say that my liberties must be compatible with yours and vice versa (the "equal liberty" or "equal maximum liberty" clause that is so confidently advanced in much contemporary political philosophy), but this helps not at all to find the limits of *mine* unless the limits of *yours* have already been drawn (and vice versa again). In a first approximation, we may locate the area of the liberties of others by appealing to the principle of torts. Any feasible action of mine that is harmful to you (over and above a *de minimis* kind of subthreshold harm neither custom nor law will bother about) – say, breaking your leg by negligence or on purpose, trespassing in your garden, stealing your property, undermining your good name by spreading false rumours – for which redress is as a rule provided by convention or law, is a tort incompatible with your liberty. Beyond this core area, there is a less well defined belt of negative externalities, where the exercise of a liberty of mine – to smoke in public, to litter in the park, to drive a little too aggressively – interferes with the liberties of others without providing a solid enough ground for remedy. My conduct in this twilight area, while clearly annoying to others, is not grave enough to call for redress. The arbiter of what is a tort (to be redressed) and what an externality (to be borne, even if with bad grace) is best taken to be social convention; what convention reproves but does not sanction is deplorable but not incompatible with the liberties of others. It may of course provoke protest and retaliation; in suitable cases it may give rise to agreement to desist or to compensate; most of the time, it is simply recognized as a discomfort of life in a particular civilization. It is not a violation of the liberty of others, nor an occasion for legislation.

Condition (b) that makes my liberty subject to my being under no incompatible obligation is equivalent, in the language of Hohfeldian relations, to no right-holder having a right to stop me from exercising the liberty in question, nor to sanction me if I do exercise it. Let the supposed liberty in question be sleeping late on Monday morning. Anyone who wants to stop me as of right assumes the burden of proof of his right. In common and civil law, discharging the burden is not intrinsically hard. I am not at liberty to stay in bed on Monday morning if I ought to be at work instead. It is up to my employer to prove that he is entitled to my best efforts during working hours. If he has proved that, he could also prove that on Monday morning I was in breach of contract. My agreement to the terms of employment serves both as the source of his right, and as its evidence.

In public law, however, the matter is less plain. When has some political authority, the city council or the government of the country, the right to stop me from doing what is both feasible for me to do and not a tort done to others? Its right, *if* it has one, is not a corollary of my voluntary assumption of the corresponding obligation. As I have argued above, the citizen's putative agreement to obey the state under a virtual contract has a debatable status. Even if it were a legitimate hypothesis (though it is difficult to imagine how, for example, it could be tested), it would hardly imply a blanket consent to every right the state or "society" might ever claim, but at best only selective agreement to some. With Hobbes, I agreed to obey Leviathan in everything it takes to impose civil peace – a large and wide undertaking in all conscience. I took this to entail that I had to lay down such arms as I had, and I agreed to that, too. The result is that now, having no arms, I cannot resist Leviathan if he stops me from doing things that would not endanger civil peace; but I have not *agreed* to its stopping me.

The fallback position that steers clear of all speculation about hypothetical agreement or the lack of it is that the state has all the rights against me that the law declares it to have. In a merely formal, procedural sense, the rule of law is satisfied if you and I are not stopped from doing whatever it is lawful to do. (Substantively, of course, the rule of law means far more than this.) What, however, *may* the law declare to be unlawful? – given that its declaration may extinguish a liberty some of us would otherwise have had; and if it does not, what possible point could it have? This kind of question takes us into the high regions of the meta-law. On a level closer to earth, it also raises the problem of judicial review, of constitutions, their effectiveness, and their unforeseen consequences. On an even less lofty level, it takes us up to the often faint line where the law ends and administrative practice begins. Plainly, the irreducible dose of judicial discretion in constitutional law is more than matched by an inevitable dose of administrative discretion in government.

For these reasons, the easy positivist fallback position – the state has such rights to interfere with individual liberties as the law confers upon it – is both too narrow and too wide. I do not believe that in this area purely conceptual analysis can take us very much further. The rights of states and the obligations of citizens – and more generally the autonomy and standing of individuals in the face of some collective entity – are probably destined to remain controversial.

There are, however, two mutually exclusive rules that direct us to take one side or the other of the controversy. One of the two possible rules to follow is that "everything is forbidden that is not permitted." It establishes a presumption in favor of collective bodies as sources of prohibitions, and places the burden of proof on the actor who must show some undisputed moral or legal title (constitutional right, "human right," "natural right") to do what is feasible. The other possible rule is symmetrically opposite to the first: "everything is permitted that is not prohibited." The implicit presumption favors feasible action: if it is *not* a liberty or the fulfillment of an obligation derived from agreement, it must be either a tort or the breach of an obligation, and the burden of proof is on the holder of the right, the prospective plaintiff, the would-be objector to the liberty to show that this is so.

The affinity with the presumption of innocence is quite plain. "Innocent until proven guilty," however, has a near-universal appeal, while the presumption of liberty strikes one strand of opinion as dangerous for social cohesion, hiding a propensity to instability if not downright chaos, and encouraging egoism. Note, however, that the two rules jointly exhaust the methods by which to judge the liberty of an action. They leave us no neutral manner to proceed, no middle ground, no "third way."[4] Logically, rejection of one compels, on pain of incoherence, acceptance of the other. Wriggling through the excluded middle is an exercise in self-delusion.

When we say that the burden of proof may be placed either on the actor to show that he *is* free to act in a certain way, or on his challenger to show that he is not, we do not imply that the actor is always the lone individual and the challenger is always the collectivity that claims him as a member. Every combination of individual and collective actors must be held open for consideration. Some may be found meaningless. Individuals decide their course of action. That they do so under a multitude of constraints, facing poor alternatives, and may well suffer from weakness of will and ignorance, as the "anti-choicist" literature insists, is no doubt very true, but it is immaterial for the present purpose; they may decide neither wisely, joyfully, nor equitably towards others, but they do decide in the commonsense meaning of "decide."

The same, however, may not be true of sets of more than one individual: this is the root problem that bedevils holism. A collective entity chooses a course of action, exercises a right, assumes and fulfills an obligation only in a metaphoric sense. Anthropomorphism is the standard metaphor. In some cases, such loose usage is harmless, in others it is positively useful in reducing needless complexity, and in others it is an unavoidable lesser evil. When, however, the stakes are high, it will seldom do. For what does it mean that a group, such as blacks, women, nomadic herdsmen, Hungarians in Transylvania, or the handicapped, decides, does, claims, or exercises a right? For doing any of these acts, a recognizable "unit of agency" is needed (Dworkin, 1989, pp. 211–12), with sufficient power, functional ability, and legitimacy to stand for, commit, "represent" the collective entity in question. Is the National Association for the Advancement of Colored People a proper unit of agency for American blacks, some national women's league for the women of a country, or the Hungarian Democratic Union of Rumania for the Hungarians of Transylvania? – and what of the countless groups for which no legally incorporated body could even pretend to be the unit of agency? Suppose "an agent has an obligation to assist a certain category of parties in a general way, without specification of beneficiaries among them" (Makinson, 1988, p. 78). "Since those bearing the obligation do not have a duty to assist any particular party, there is no particular party that has a claim on the bearers of the obligation" (ibid.). If the right-holder or the obligor group is unincorporated, lacks a minimum of structure and cohesion, and could not act as a credible unit responsible for its supposed actions, holistic talk about its rights is as good as meaningless, committing nobody.

Even in the presence of a perhaps informal collective decision-making capacity, such as under inherited authority or in a plutocracy, and quite obviously under majority rule, there are deep ambiguities surrounding the unit of agency for any group that is nonunanimous for any reason. "[C]ollectivity x may be a minority within grouping u, whose majority may in turn be a minority within a larger grouping v, and so on through indefinitely many steps" (Makinson, 1988, p. 73). There are "groups, lying uncomfortably between entire peoples and single persons" (ibid., p. 72). The general problem of group identity is what we might call a Russian Doll problem: as we unscrew the doll, we find a smaller one inside it that can in turn be unscrewed to reveal a yet smaller doll inside the smaller one, and so on. As the successive dolls get smaller, they may (or may not) show a tendency to be less heterogeneous, to contain fewer smaller dolls. In assigning group rights or imposing group obligations, we have to choose a stopping point at which we no longer unscrew the doll in search of smaller, more unanimous ones inside it. But the sole just, morally unassailable stopping point is the very last doll, the un-unscrewable individual who (unless he is schizophrenic) unanimously agrees with himself about what he wants and what he would give up to get it. "Multiculturalism" and "minority rights" that enable certain group uniformities to be imposed on all its members have, no less than do "majority rights," a clear potential for suppressing liberties that, *but for these* "*rights*," would 've had a chance to be preserved intact.[5]

Being represented by a unit of agency does not in itself do anything to resolve the "who gets what, who pays what" problem that is inherent in group rights. A group right confers benefits, a group obligation places burdens on some or all of its members, often in indeterminate proportions. Burdens cannot be borne by a collective entity as such. (The same is true of benefits, but for some reason this appears to be not as self-evident.) They are willy-nilly *transmitted* in capitalist orders by such mechanisms as property rights, taxation, and collective expenditures, and in socialist ones by rationing, allocation, requisitioning, or the curtailment of common services. Once all individual burdens and benefits so transmitted have been accounted for, no residue is left.

The Principle of Transmission deals with benefits and burdens; where these matter, as they do in rights (though not or hardly in liberties), holism is more than just a harmlessly slipshod manner of speaking. It is apt to be misleading, often seriously so, though where the benefits and burdens are genuinely indivisible, their imputation to particular individuals is not a straightforward matter, and holistic references to "collective" benefits or costs may have to be admitted. Imputation to individuals is in any case difficult in practice, for "transmission without residue" is seldom a transparent, fully visible process. Its very lack of transparency – especially the circumstance that individuals are often unaware that they are paying for some benefit that accrues to others and that they, in ignorance of its cost to themselves, do not begrudge – is what makes the notion of group rights slippery, and holistic language about them dangerous. Richard Epstein, writing on a key clause of the US constitution, is very properly asking for the moon, as we all ought to, when he lays down: "Statements about groups of individuals must be translated into statements about individuals... No independent rights and duties attach to the corporate form... [A]t all points the rights of groups depend on the rights of their members. No group has a right which is more than a summation of its parts" (Epstein, 1985, pp. ix, 13).

2 IDEOLOGIES OF GROUP RIGHTS

More than one ideology can be pressed into the service of justifying claims of group rights. The task differs according to whether it is genuine rights – bilateral relations involving benefits to one side, burdens to the other – or liberties, or pseudo-rights that are in effect liberties, or (most confusingly) claims that are neither one thing nor the other, but just empty rhetoric – that must be justified.

Justifying liberties as such is straightforward. They rest on three rough-and-ready normative propositions: that doing harm ought to be barred;[6] that promises ought to be kept; and that subject only to these two propositions about torts and obligations, no one is entitled to prevent a person from doing what he chooses to do. (Note that the third proposition avoids referring to preference, value, utility, or rationality. It does not specify why people choose to do what they do, hence it declines any inquiry into whether their ends are good ones and whether their actions merit forbearance). It would be absurd to pretend that these norms of conduct are incontestable. Indeed, they have been ceaselessly contested on both arguable and specious grounds. Yet they still stand and preserve some of their appeal to common sense and to the liberal disposition. I do not propose to defend them here. However, *group* liberties are not "liberties as such." If they were, they could be exercised by separate individual members of the group, each at his discretion. Instead, they are exercised indiscriminately on behalf of every member by some decision-making organ, often self-appointed and self-perpetuating, which lends the group the character or at least the outward appearance of a "unit of agency." Its decision commits to a uniform course of action. Some may like it, others not. They are nonetheless forced to go along with it. This, of course, is in contradiction to the ordinary meaning of a "liberty." Unanimity within the group is the sole escape route from this dilemma. Yet it is questionable whether, *if* the group is unanimous, a group liberty brings anything that individuals' liberties would not accomplish. Such reflections ultimately raise a suspicion: it begins to look likely that group liberties have, as their specific *raison d'être*, the overriding of the liberties of dissenters and the idly indifferent anti-activists within the group, and it is frequently with this unavowed reason in mind that they are advocated.

Justifying pseudo-rights that are logically liberties rather than rights is, of course, a pseudo-task. That it is undertaken at all is due, I believe, mainly to the unwitting and unconscious surrender of many modern liberals to the master rule that everything is forbidden that is not expressly permitted. Only so can I explain the steady background noise about "human rights" that accompanies contemporary politics, encouraged by such gesticulations as the Universal Declaration of Human Rights and the International Covenant on Economic, Social, and Cultural Rights under United Nations auspices, as well as the similar rights utterances of other, even more implausible, international organizations. Human rights talk reaches particular stridency when it is to direct attention to how other countries than one's own maltreat some of their subjects. My "human right," where it is not a name for bounty it would be nice for all humans to have, is reducible to a "right" to be spared from what others have no right to do to me, namely to violate my liberties or rights. If this reduction is just, the concept is a redundant product of the confusion between rights and liberties. In the exquisitely deadpan phrase of the Chichele Professor of International Public Law, "[t]he more traditional term for human rights would be the Rule of Law" (Brownlie, 1988, p. 1).

Half-way between liberties and genuine rights there is a list of hybrid claims that has been rapidly lengthening of late. Their probable ancestor is the "right" to the pursuit of happiness. They now include the right to work, to be educated, to have sufficient material resources or (puzzlingly) to have "equal access" to them; there must also be a right to "a continuing improvement in living standards" and to "development." For all their cloud-cuckoo-land character, these have a form that partly imitates genuine rights in the sense that they cannot be exercised by the claimant group or a random member of it without somebody else either agreeing, or being forced, to perform a matching service (offering a job, teaching), or provide the matching resources (money for an improving standard of living, development aid). Evidently, however, the resemblance to genuine rights is hollow, for no one has accepted, and no one is being put under, the obligation to perform and provide accordingly. Consequently, the claims are empty. They are sometimes euphemistically called "diffuse" claims, in vain and disorientated search of an elusive obligor. Even more aptly, they have been described as "manifesto rights" (Feinberg, 1980, pp. 130–43). Some, such as the "right to develop a culture"[7] and the "right to the equal enjoyment of the common heritage of mankind"[8] look, if anything, more like liberties than rights: clearly, it would be doing it harm to stop a group from developing a culture and from enjoying the heritage of mankind. But it is not evident what, if anything, others must do to help it do these things. Claims of this degree of vacuity, having no substance, neither need nor bear justification.

Left to consider is the more problematic task of justifying genuine collective rights and liberties. The former, as we have seen, involve a claim by, or on behalf of, a collective entity, a nation or a particular group within it such as an ethnic minority, to resources or to special treatment, and the obverse of this claim, namely that particular individuals directly, or by transmission via a collective entity, are obliged to provide the resources or concede the privileged treatment. The grant of the right to some entails the imposition of the obligation upon others. Collective liberties, in turn, *entail* that the analogous individual liberties are pre-tempted and dominated by them, for a collective decision to exercise or to waive a particular liberty, if it is binding, removes its individual counterpart from the realm of individual decisions: once it has been chosen for me and everybody else, I can no longer choose my course of action.

Communitarianism is the natural, though not the sole, ideology of group rights and liberties, if only because it invests the group with the anthropomorphic attributes which, if they were real, would enable it to act and choose, agree and provide, as individuals do, and much ambiguity and many logical faults would be removed. Above all, the virtual personification of the community at one stroke liberates the concepts of group rights and liberties from their major vice, the agency problem that must be ignored or circumnavigated in the passage from individuals, their minds and wishes, to the group mind and the group wish. It does so, of course, at the cost of a goodly dose of holism, some of it harmless, much of it false and illegitimate. The upshot is that the communitarian defense of group rights and liberties is, albeit indirectly, exposed to all the criticism that holism justly provokes.

In increasing order of coherence and intelligibility, the principal grounds upholding the communitarian position seem to me to be these:

1 The true community (and of course not every collective entity deserves the name) "exists in itself," over and beyond its individual members, whom it forms and sustains. It embodies intrinsic values that may but need not be good *for* anyone in particular; it has purposes of its own that are neither aggregations of individual ends nor instrumental to such ends. The real community is prior to its members. They do not constitute it: it constitutes them.

2 The isolated, maximizing individual of abstract choice theory and of the liberal ideology, is incomplete, unformed, incapable of developing his own preferences or choosing autonomously (Taylor, 1979). In fact, he does not exist; there is no "unencumbered self" free to choose his own ends, for some of our ends and values are unchosen. They *are* our selves (Sandel, 1984). In the procedurally regulated politics of the modern liberal state, the person comes to be "disempowered, entangled in a network of obligations and involvements ... umediated by those common identifications ... that would make them tolerable" (ibid., p. 28). " ... the free individual of the West is only what he is by virtue of the whole society and civilization which brought him to be" (Taylor, 1979, p. 45).

These two, closely related theses are sufficiently elusive to resist all criticism: how could they possibly be denied, let alone disproved? Their truth, as far as it goes, is trite. Of course the abstract individual does not exist, only real ones do. Of course preferences are formed under outside influences, of course the individual would be a different man if he lived in a different society. These unsurprising observations, when laid end to end, begin to add up to a mythology that has much nostalgic appeal. As such, it predisposes to a way of thinking about society that finds it only fitting that certain groups, elevated by their history, their virtues and cohesion to the rank of communities, should be endowed with "rights" both against their individual members and against the outside world.

3 Individualist ("atomist") political doctrine ascribes rights to individuals.[9] If they have an obligation to the community (i.e., if the community has rights against them) it is only because they have irrevocably consented to it, or do so now, or would do so if they were rational (Taylor, 1979, pp. 29–30). Communitarianism does not concede any such priority to individual rights. On the contrary, it maintains, a little cryptically, that "the good" ranks before "the right" (e.g., Sandel, 1982, 1984a).

The "good," however, whatever it is supposed to be, cannot be intended to mean some kind of total of the several "goods" of the community's members, because that would be a logical stumble. It is not possible to add the good of one person to that of another and get a total; the entities involved may not be quantifiable and in any case could not be added to each other, being heterogeneous. One social state of affairs cannot objectively be found better than another except when the differences between the two are severely circumscribed, permitting Pareto-comparability.[10] This restriction, if accepted, would reduce a "politics of the good" to impotence and incoherence. (Strictly, it would rather reduce its scope very drastically indeed, until it fit harmlessly within the bounds of a "politics" of inviolable individual rights. In such politics, only those social changes would be admissible that were consistent with all individuals either exercising, or voluntarily refraining from using, or voluntarily exchanging, their rights; no choice could be imposed on them. Such a political world would be presumably unacceptable to communitarians, as well as to most modern-day liberals, despite the latter's catchphrase about rights being "trumps.") The communitarian way out is to postulate, with Aristotle, that there exists a "common good" of the community that can neither be broken down to, nor derived from, an account of the interests and preferences of each of its members.

For a methodological individualist, statements about the common good are metaphysical and do not square with a proper understanding of what society is. They blatantly deny, or at least conceal, intragroup differences and conflicts. Conflict is not resolved even if the reason for a common good being "common" is that it is indivisible and cannot be obtained in small increments by each individual acting for himself – a condition that is firmly stated by sophisticated communitarians (Taylor, 1992, p. 59). Nevertheless, the idea of the common good, to which the members of the community are obliged to contribute, exerts a potent attraction upon the public mind and will no doubt continue to find its way into political discourse.

Which group rights, liberties, or both come to be justified by appeal to the common good depends on which group is entitled to *its* common good; is it all humanity, or the state, the nation, the region, the majority, or the ethnic and "cultural" minorities outside it? Nothing supports the supposition that their respective common goods must be compatible and can fit together without conflict and loss. One is strongly reminded of Rousseau's distinction between the General Will and the "particular general will" it must supersede. The "will" of any kind of minority relative to the corresponding majority is a "particular general will"; but each minority is a majority relative to *its* own minorities, and its will is the General Will relative to the particular general wills of these minorities, and so on in a regress that need have no end until we decide that it should stop. (An ethnic minority may have no other ethnic minorities within it; but nevertheless will have subgroups of other kinds, differing in class, wealth, education, and so forth, giving rise to divergences of interest.) There is no natural stopping point short of the individual, who is indivisible, hence has no minority.

We are back at the Russian Doll problem. How far do we go in unscrewing one doll after another, discovering smaller ones inside each? The common good can be ascribed to one community, or to another within it, or to yet another that partly overlaps with the first – but in the ordinary course of events we cannot ascribe it to each and every one of them at the same time. Scarcity, and the incompatibility of rival values and tempers, prevents it. Communitarianism badly needs to, but cannot, resolve this problem. It is intrinsic in the plurality and nonhomogeneity of human societies and in the partly overlapping nature of most human groupings. The communitarian argument of the common good, such as it is, can only apply to one community at a time, selected in some fashion from the (larger) communities that contain it and the (smaller) ones contained in it. It cannot be generalized. The attempt to do so, if it were made, would lose itself in indeterminacy. Unfortunately for group rights and group liberties, this means that by selecting one level, or one subset in the set of eligible groups, and ascribing the common good to it, we commit ourselves to a moral and political relativism, which is a game two can play: our common good is defined by and rests on our say-so, theirs on their say-so, and there is no possible adjudicator to say, nor any principle for adjudicating by, whose say-so is to prevail.

With no more than a cautious nod to communitarianism, marshaling a more rigorous and basically Kantian argument, Onora O'Neill (1993) uses justice, rather than the common good, to justify group rights. Her defense, it seems to me, no more escapes moral relativism than do the communitarian ones, and peters out in the same indeterminacy as theirs.

She takes for her springboard the precept "treat like cases alike." Its application hinges on abstracting from some differences between cases in order to leave those (relevant) differences which properly define a class of cases as being alike, and unlike other cases that are relegated to other classes. Obviously, she subscribes to the operation of abstracting from selected particularities. It is needed for forming classes of "like cases" and then applying some applicable rule of justice impartially within the class. However, she claims that liberal individualism not only abstracts from cases the predicates that are putatively irrelevant to applying a rule of justice, but in addition surreptitiously *imputes* to them predicates, such as full comprehension by people of their situation, capacity for rational decision, independence, etc., which not only backward or deficient agents do not possess, but "no human agent does" (p. 309). She can affirm this with impunity, since the objection that at least some human beings are bright, can calculate, and have some independence can always be rebutted by pointing out that they are not bright and independent enough, and do not calculate well enough, for what they would need; "enough," of course, is intersubjectively not determinate. This "idealization" of agents produces, according to O'Neill, not abstract, but idealized justice that is blind, not to irrelevant predicates, but to the very group characteristics of poverty, underdevelopment, ignorance, subjection to family ties – which call for their being treated not alike, but differently. Blind justice is blind to "privilege" (p. 304). Clearly, what goes for poverty or ignorance on one ground (inequality) can go for "cultural identity" on another (the need for self-identification). Indeed, it goes for any other possible defining characteristic that can be construed as a vital need, want, lack, or disadvantage. All that is needed is to concede the ground: inequality is only one among many possible ones. The problem of equal treatment, as O'Neill puts it, is "to secure differentiated treatment for *all*" (p. 307, my italics). A mischievous translation would be: treat no two cases alike.

In the limit, O'Neill's argument tends to this result, though she stops well short of the limit by introducing a variant of the Kantian generalization of cases. The same justice can apply to different cases (to a plurality of diverse agents) if it has universalizable principles "that *could* be adopted by all" (p. 313, italics in text) and, though she does not say so, that are of central importance. For they must be broad and basic enough to define a sufficiency of uniform group rights and obligations for "socially guaranteed convergence and coordination" (ibid.). O'Neill appears to have, among other things, obligations of aid to underdeveloped countries (p. 312) and "reverse discrimination and affirmative action" on behalf of women in mind, and it is easy to think of other requirements for "convergence" (although they should perhaps not be thought of as principles, but rather as derivatives of principles). Be that as it may, there is no doubt a good deal that "could be adopted by all"; it is hard to prove of any principle that it *could not* be. This variant of universalizability is impossibly loose, for what possible principle can it possibly exclude? Anything could be adopted by everybody if their circumstances and dispositions were just right for it, and could not be if they were not.

The Kantian test, of course, does not hinge on what could, with a bit of luck, be agreed by all, but on what principle (including any principle of distributive justice) any random person would want to apply to all if he wanted it to apply to himself. By this test, group rights that redistributed benefits in favor of the disadvantaged as a matter of principle would fail resoundingly, for the "privileged" would have good reason to oppose them, since they would have to bear the obligation derived from the principle. If the privileged were not "idealized genderless theorists" (p. 314), nor blinded to their endowments and capacities by a contrived "veil of ignorance," they would be aware of the fate that awaited them once the disadvantaged were given "group rights" to redistribute the advantages of others. O'Neill's argument (ibid.) that the privileged must expect to "interact" with the disadvantaged and must not "deny them agency" (sic) does not change this one little bit. When she goes on to ask whether, in this light, "there are any principles that *must* be adopted by all members of a plurality of interacting agents" (ibid., my italics), the concise answer is no, if by principles she means ones going beyond those of classical commutative justice (do no harm, to each his own, *pacta sunt servanda*). Any sane person wants commutative justice to apply to all; even professional criminals would rationally prefer to be protected from crime, fraud, and breach of contract, and exercise their profession by breaking some laws that others keep rather than try their luck in a society where none keeps them. Beyond commutative justice, the logic of universalizability points the other way. No principle whose application will *predictably* and *systematically* favor identifiable classes of cases (persons or groups) at the expense of similarly identifiable classes, can be universalizable. Hence ascriptions of redistributive rights cannot be derived from universalizable principles. No pleas for "nonvictimization" can help this. Rigorous Kantian reasoning from principles of justice no more justifies the type of rights O'Neill seeks to affirm than does the woollier communitarian argument from the common good.

For an interpretation of liberal individualism that is primarily a search for support to be found within it for collective, especially collective "cultural" rights and liberties, I propose briefly to consider the work of Will Kymlicka (1989). Where this text offends against the very liberal doctrine it seeks to vindicate, apply, and adapt to its enterprise, is in what seems to me an unconscious falling in with the position, odious to the classical liberal disposition but increasingly adopted by contemporary claimants to the title "liberal," that actions must be expressly permitted in order not to be taken for forbidden. At its simplest, this leads Kymlicka to construct arguments to show why people ought to "have rights" (meaning: to be permitted) to do certain things that are important to them, instead of requiring that sufficient cause be shown why they should be stopped from doing them. As he puts it, "if abstract individualism . . . were the fundamental premiss, there'd be no *reason to let people* revise their beliefs," etc. (p. 18, my italics). But no *reason* is needed to *let* people do something they are capable of doing and that is not prima facie a tort: what needs a reason is *not letting* them do it. Awarding them "rights" to various acts and practices no one has proved to have a *right* to stop, is misplaced solicitude, to put it no higher, and is doing them a long-term disservice. We need not forswear "abstract" or "atomistic" individualism in order to *ask* that people be *allowed* to have beliefs, to change them, and to do even more momentous things. We ought never to ask it, whatever kind of individualism we profess. Asking is gratuitously to concede precious ground. It is to adopt, without due resistance, the logic and language of an upside-down world.

Under any recognizable form of individualism, if indeed it has more than one, all we need do is to place the burden of proof where, at least under individualism, it belongs. What needs proving is the reason why anyone, including "society," should have the "right" not to let some act or practice take its course. There are, no doubt, such reasons. They must then be advanced and held up to critical scrutiny. Mixing up rights with liberties exposes liberties to uncalled-for trials instead.

Passing from pseudo-rights to genuine ones, Kymlicka rightly questions rights-claims on behalf of communities by pointing at the woolliness of the notion: "[g]roups have no moral claim to well-being independently of their members – groups just aren't the right sort of beings to have moral status" (p. 242). Consequently, he constrains his own argument to a deduction of *group* rights from premises about *individuals* only. This is not the place for an extended review of his whole undertaking, much of which is solid, but only for a summary assessment of his justification of group rights, which I do not think succeeds. With what is quite excessive deference to Ronald Dworkin, he takes it as read that individuals have a right to "equal respect and concern," *and* that where an inequality of resources or of status is the result, not of their choices but of their circumstances (p. 38),[11] "equal concern" for some reason implies that the disadvantaged have rights to oblige the more advantaged to make good their disadvantage. A truly liberal society would therefore probably resemble "market socialism" rather than "welfare capitalism" (p. 91). This reasoning runs in terms of the popular Rawlsian jargon that talks of "primary goods," of which each must have a "fair share." "Fair shares," of course, is an invincible expression, for it would be absurd to object that not everybody must have them, and that instead of fair shares, at least some people ought to have unfair ones. "Fair," of course, must be interpreted if it is to mean more than approval. If "fair" means something like a qualified "equal," which it seems to do in much of the modern liberal literature including, here and there, in Kymlicka, then it is qualified equal shares that each must have. Those who have "too much" are under an obligation to give up their unfair surplus, for this is what exercise of the right to fair shares entails. However, it happens to be the case that one of the primary goods is to be part of a "cultural community," to have a "cultural context" for one's choices (pp. 167–72, p. 178), and to enjoy "cultural membership" (pp. 135–6). These goods cannot be secured by "a color-blind egalitarian distribution of resources and liberties" (p. 182), for under such a distribution cultural communities must compete for survival, and the weaker ones may be "outbid for important resources" and "outvoted on crucial policy decisions" (p. 183). They must have special rights to a "fair share" of resources and of political authority, where the fairness of the share is treated as if it meant a kind of qualified equality, including equal security of cultural survival. The latter may require positive discrimination and inequality of material resources favoring the weaker community. Equality must, in some cases, prevail *between* communities, rather than between individuals *across* communities.

The entire deduction from premises about individuals to the rights and liberties communities are entitled to, rides piggyback on a somewhat complicated set of egalitarian precepts. "Equal concern" begets a norm of "equal circumstances" which, in turn, generates a right to equal or perhaps just "fair" shares in the primary good "cultural context." (It seems to me that directly postulating this result would not have been more arbitrary than deducing it in a roundabout way from arbitrary antecedents.) If the initial egalitarian principles pertaining to individuals are not conceded, there is nothing to ride piggyback on.

Appeal to one's need for a "cultural context" can lead to startling conclusions. Amy Gutmann (1992) would seem tentatively to adopt it in advancing this syllogism: "If ... a secure cultural context also ranks among the primary goods, ... liberal democratic *states are obligated* to help disadvantaged groups preserve their culture against intrusions by majoritarian or 'mass' cultures" (p. 5, my italics). Now the "cultural context" may or may not be a "primary good," and the latter expression may or may not have a sensible meaning. But admitting both, it is a perfect *non sequitur* to deduce an obligation of states to supply protection for "cultural contexts." This would only follow if we had already agreed to a second term she left unstated, namely that states must supply primary goods to the disadvantaged. Supplying protection for endangered cultural contexts would then follow from the latter being a primary good. Once again, the argument for a collective right rides piggyback on a qualified-egalitarian principle which has no greater compelling force than the claim for the collective right itself; while enlisting its support might be helpful for the argument, making it a decisive step in an attempted deduction is fatal for the intended result.

There is, in addition, a second and lesser *non sequitur* involved in Gutmann's phrase quoted above. It consists in taking it as an empirical fact that the cultural context cannot be chosen, exchanged, assimilated. People in Gutmann's argument either have the one they were born into, or none if it withers away under the weight of another "majoritarian" one. Choosing the intruding majoritarian culture as one's preferred "context" is not allowed as an alternative. Yet, as the metaphor of the American melting pot and other interludes in history suggest, people often eagerly shed one "cultural context" to assimilate another without being coerced in any proper sense of the word. We may regret it that they do, that ignoble material incentives push and pull them in that direction. What, however, are the obligations of the "liberal democratic state" in the matter? Here again, the confusion of rights with liberties obscures the situation. Where two "cultural contexts" are both accessible to a person – which is the typical source of the threat to ethnic and religious minorities, though not to racial ones – by choosing one, or straddling both (as some immigrants do for several generations), he exercises one of his liberties. One choice may be less convenient or favorable in terms of prosperity, status, the education of children, or the quality of human relations. Opting for one of the "contexts," then, has higher opportunity costs than opting for another. As long, however, as the cost of one is not deliberately augmented by the coercive measures the political authority can so easily deploy, nor by wrongful discrimination[12] in social practices, i.e., as long as the substantive rule of law prevails, it is hard to see what a person poised between two cultures and considering his course of action has to complain of. As in every other choice, he must balance his preference for a course of action against its opportunity cost. The claim that for one particular choice, the choice of "cultural context," we have a right to oblige someone else, via the agency of the "liberal democratic state," to make good some of the cost is little short of peculiar. So is the alternative claim that it is entire "cultural communities" that have a right to have their "cost disadvantages," if we may put it so, compensated by nonmembers of their community.

3 THE PRECARIOUS STANDING OF GROUPS

The substantive rule of law may of course *not* prevail; often it does not. Throughout history, tribal chiefs, lords, monarchs, and elected majorities alike have shown a propensity to abuse power both by making inequitable laws and by applying both equitable and inequitable ones inequitably. Doing the former offends against the substantive, doing the latter against both the substantive and the procedural rule of law. The offense, however, is committed for a reason, and it is not declarations and manifestos that are likely to outweigh it. If the offending administration is highly sensitive to the pressure of opinion, well and good, but rights-talk is not the sole nor the most expedient means of alerting opinion that the rule of law is being breached and power is being abused.

Asking for certain collective liberties on behalf of groups which suffer from the use, by more powerful encompassing groups (such as "majorities") of *their* collective liberties, is to lose two battles before fighting a third. The first, and perhaps lesser one is lost by adopting the platform of collective liberties at all. Suppose the majority of a nation exercises its collective liberty to choose, for consenters and dissenters alike, the language in which all are to be taught in school. *If* there are collective liberties, why not *this* one? Dissenters will dissent from it, but it is arguable that nothing actually obliges the majority to offer them education in the language of their choice. Imposing on them the majority view is not wrongful, as would be the decision to exclude them from state-financed schooling altogether. This is, so the argument may run, just one of those numberless cases where a stronger group overrules a weaker subgroup within it. Overruling, and being overruled, is inherent in non-individual choice, i.e., in politics in the deepest sense of the word. If it is wrong to impose the majority language in state schools, what is collective choice for? The sole really logical alternative, to continue the argument, is to leave the choice of school language to the individual parent. Yet in that case it would be anomalous to continue the financing of all schools by the collectivity, out of general taxation, for collective financing ought to carry collective liberties, i.e., decision-making powers, with it. Justice would demand instead that parents should individually pay for having their children taught in the school of their choice, and have their taxes reduced. Carried to its conclusion, this chain of argument leads, in one direction, to the dismantling of the state and the shrinking of politics, and in the other to expanded collective rights and liberties, and enhanced politics.

French history is an object lesson in enhanced politics. First to "define" and "affirm," then to "protect" its identity, the Frankish kingdom relentlessly expanded its "rights" over territory, one by one absorbing the duchies and kingdoms on its perimeter; the monarchy in the thirteenth, sixteenth, and seventeenth centuries attempted, with partial success, to commit the whole country to a single religion and eradicate schism; the Second Empire and especially the Third Republic used the state schools, compulsory military service, and a centralized public administration to extinguish the country's countless local *patois* and to impose a single, "collectively chosen" language. Perhaps rightly, provincial autonomy, religious dissent, and local languages were all seen as risks and threats, against which Frenchness had to be protected. Creating a proper "cultural community," safe from dilution and confident of survival, required politics, the imposition of a "common will" on minorities of various kinds. France, of course, is not the worst offender. "Nations" which are now where France was a thousand years ago, peoples which are still frantically trying to invent themselves as nations (Rumania may be one example, Kenya, Nigeria, or Burundi others), are doing as much and more. Nationalists everywhere offend, and the acknowledgement of collective liberties on the grounds of "cultural identity" unwittingly panders to the very nationalisms we seek to tame by talking "rights" at them. Serbs, cheering on the extermination of Moslem Bosniaks, find justification for their loathsomeness in the imperatives of securing the survival of their Serb identity, a very relative value to others but infinitely great to Serbs, admitting no tradeoffs. The result is a moral *impasse*, which can never be resolved at the level of group rights. How, if we assert them, do we know that they will be successfully exercised *by* the minority outside opinion considers threatened, rather than *against* it because it is felt by some majority to be threatening? There is no realistic remedy that I can see to this fundamental indeterminacy, inherent in the Russian Doll configuration of groups, short of going all the way down to the individual. He is the proper, and least dangerous, "unit of agency" for the exercise of liberties and the holding of rights.

Another way of saying the same thing is that the wider is the scope of politics and the greater its influence upon civil society, the higher are the *stakes* to be won by some and lost by others in successful claims of group rights and liberties. Conversely, the lower the political stakes that can be won, the more nearly will collective decisions approach the nirvana of irrelevance, and the closer rights will get to the status of innocent pleonasms.

The second battle we lose before the fight ever begins is, I believe, a greater one. I have kept insisting on it throughout this chapter, and I apologise for reverting to it one more time; it is the last. Making a case for "minority rights" puts a leaden boot on the wrong foot. It weighs down and handicaps the proper course of reasoning about these matters. It encourages the cast of mind for which permissions are needed, and the "right" to such permissions must be reaffirmed, in the face of the basic presumption that the corresponding acts are deemed to be forbidden, or at least of uncertain status. In both the petitionee for rights and the petitioner, this fosters and legitimizes the very political culture in which such petitions become painfully necessary.

Under the rule of law, minorities do not have to *ask* for liberties. In the worst case, they ask for the grounds on which officials in authority claim the right to stop them from doing whatever is feasible. The presumption, then, is that *the feasible is free*; it is for the authorities to show cause why it should *not* be. It may well be that in the short run an oppressed group is no more likely to obtain justice if the prohibition is challenged than if the permission is demanded. In the longer run, however, the rule of law has more chance to take root if people, both inside and outside the realm where it holds sway, consistently forswear asking for liberties, and challenge prohibitions instead. It is one of the tasks of political philosophy to explain why they should pay stringent attention to the difference.

While in the matter of liberties the onus of proof is on those who propose to obstruct or curtail them, in the matter of rights the onus is on those who claim a benefit from others, for he has to show why the putative obligors should have to contribute to it. In section 1, allusions are made to the reason why accomplishing this is difficult in the field of group rights and why the standing of groups is more precarious than that of individuals. Individual rights are essentially contractual, the source of the matching obligations is agreement, and its prima facie proof is the explicit or implicit contract. However, unless it has legal personality, the group cannot contract. Its rights have no agreed source and no objective proof. Wherever a collectivity has putative rights against, or obligations toward, individuals or other collectivities, a dose of skepticism is in order, for the justice of the claim is basically contestable. If the right in question is not a fresh claim, but has been exercised for some time, the relation between beneficiaries and obligors has the sanction of precedent and custom. Even this, however, cannot extinguish the spark of its moral contestability. May he hear it ever so patiently, the question still remains: why should the obligor carry the burden of his obligation?

If the full circumstances of an involuntary transfer of tangible and intangible scarce resources, including status and privilege, from one individual to another are such that we judge it unjust,[13] an involuntary transfer from a similarly placed individual, or vice versa, or between such groups, must be judged no less unjust. *Injustice does not turn into justice because the beneficiaries, the contributors, or both are numerous,* and form a definable group, a "community." Nor – and this is the more important practical point – does an involuntary transfer lose its unjust character if the contributors are hidden from view by the screen of some institution, such as a government, a municipality, or a corporation. It is all too tempting to grant a right to a benefit to a visible beneficiary, especially when he is in a disadvantaged category or embodies a worthy cause, provided the contributor is a faceless and gigantic institution like a country's treasury, or a solid insurance company. By the Principle of Transmission, it is of course not the Treasury that pays but present and future taxpayers, or (if neither taxes nor the budget deficit are upwardly mobile) the people who would have benefitted from the government expenditures that must be cut. Likewise, it is not the insurance company that pays, but future policyholders. Yet we are usually ready to call for collective rights to benefits to be met by collective contributions, although we would think twice before calling for the same rights if they entailed extracting contributions from identifiable, visible individuals. Just as collective liberties endanger liberties, collective rights must pose risks for justice that individual rights need not do. It may not be possible to prove causality, and I see no way of doing it even if it could be done, but failing proof, intuition strongly suggests that the inexpediency and the propensity to jeopardize liberties and justice, which we find associated with group liberties and group rights, are the shoddy product of the conceptual flaws and ambiguities from which they suffer.

NOTES

1 These are logical relations describing normative or positive moral or legal "configurations." My reasoning in the text is inspired, in an obvious manner that cannot be obscured by my departures from it, by Hohfeld's classic typology of fundamental legal relations (Hohfeld, 1919). He sets up a fourfold classification. For reasons mainly of simplicity, I substitute a twofold one, where Hohfeld's "powers" are subsumed under his "claim-rights" to yield the single category of "rights," and his "privileges" and "immunities" are merged into the category of "liberties." This is by way of being a poor man's Hohfeld,

where some of the original's nuance is lost. But I think more is gained than lost thanks to the parsimony and greater suggestive capacity of this simplified schema.

2 Admittedly, she may type my manuscript without my asking her to do so. Her effort, then, is supererogatory; she is not fulfilling an obligation. She may deem it her duty to fill in idle time in this way, rather than by filing her nails. I may have cunningly anticipated that she would do the decent thing and work unasked, but in doing so I would have employed a game strategy, rather than exercising my right.

3 For instance, my right to vote is a right by virtue of the obligation of political officials to take account of votes, including mine.

4 Setting the two rules on a par may look like moral relativism, for it seems to give the same rank or value to the rule that upholds liberties as to the one that fosters interference with them. It is not my intention to insinuate moral parity between the two; there is, however, parity in functioning, and this is what the text is meant to bring out.

5 In Catalonia, neither Catalan nor Spanish children are taught in Spanish, though some of both would presumably choose to if they could. In Quebec, the liberty to go to an English-speaking school is severely restricted. Neither French-speakers nor immigrants have it. Such measures are deemed necessary to preserve a minority's "cultural identity," and never mind the minority inside the minority who aspire to a different "cultural identity." "Multiculturalism," in some ways a misnomer, is concerned with preserving a tribe. To do so, it must fight against multiculturalism within the tribe.

6 It is a necessary digression to consider how harmful actions are barred. One method is deterrence of future harmful actions by retribution for past ones. What, however, is the just (and adequately dissuasive) retribution for a given tort? If I stole a camel in the Middle East, the authorities might well have my hand (or worse) cutoff. This would seem a little excessive, and a less stern retribution would look adequate to most of my fellow Europeans. But how can the question possibly be *decided*? – since it is a matter of setting against one another the standards, customs and needs of two civilizations that are distant in more than one sense. It seems to me impossible to avoid relativizing the justness of retribution, even without first conceding anything to a communitarian ideology.

The matter stands very differently if torts are dealt with, not by retribution, but by *restitution*. Restitution does not directly aim at preventing harm to others (though it may have that effect, too), but at repairing the harm. If I stole the camel, I must give it back as good as new, or pay its full replacement value if I am solvent, or bond myself to labor if I am not. In addition, I must make whole all the damage I have caused (this is not a call for punitive damages) and the cost of inducing me to make restitution. What passes for just retribution is essentially relative to time and place and it is hard to quarrel with even the wildest-looking views about it. Restitution, however, has a rock-like solidity that depends little on time and place: a camel is a camel every-where, whatever the local "culture."

It is only in personal injury cases that relativism can come back in by the back door, though it is perhaps not a fatal necessity that it should. When it is lay juries, goaded by trial lawyers working for percentages of the award, who assess damages for asbestosis, a botched operation, or the psychic stress suf-fered after a product has proved defective, and when the payor is a malpractice or product liability underwriter with supposedly inexhaustible pockets, resti-tution can take on surprising dimensions. The modern US tort process is a fearful example of how far this can go without being checked by revulsion at the hypocrisy of lawyers, and by plain good sense. However, no other common law country, and no civil law country, displays a comparable tendency to runaway excess.

Communitarianism has, as one of its consequences, an inclination to relativism. The community's norms, customs, and policies can only be judged for internal consistency, including their *Zweckrationalität*. They cannot be criticized from the outside, by reference to other norms, even if the latter have some pretention to universality. This, as we have seen, can be awkward for foreign camel thieves. The dangers, however, are smaller under restitution-based legal systems. Significantly, customary law is overwhelmingly restitution-based, while legal systems where justice is provided by the state tend to veer towards retribution.

7 UNESCO Declaration of the Principles of International Cooperation, 1966.

8 Organization of African Unity Charter on Human and People's Rights, 1981.

9 This is Taylor's (1979) formulation. It is a true representation of doctrines based on natural right theories, Aristotelian, Lockean, and Kantian. (Nearer home, Nozick for instance also *ascribes* rights, along lines that are in part Lockean.) It is not true as regards positive theories, where rights are not *ascribed*, but *acquired* in voluntary exchanges, i.e., where the source of right is the obligation assumed by another, and where liberties repose upon the *absence* of an opposing right.

10 Meaning, roughly, that *if all relevant differences have the same sign*, all positive or all negative, the two states of affairs can be compared in terms of better or worse. If today one person is better off and no one is worse off than yesterday, then today is better than yesterday.

11 Kymlicka is perfectly aware of the thinness of the wall that separates choice from circumstance. Responsibility for one's acts must resist the ready excuses of ill luck and adverse circumstance; the distinction between excuses and genuine handicaps is evidently controversial. Admitting circumstance at all as a factor that attenuates responsibility opens a "slippery slope" type of argument, and nothing assures the existence of a logical or moral stopping point on the slippery slope.

12 Adding the adjective "wrongful" is meant to underline that not all discrimination on ethnic, religious, racial, etc. grounds is wrongful. The Edict of Nantes did not stop people discriminating in favor of their coreligionists when marrying their daughters, and this was not wrongful. The revocation of the Edict and the ensuing discrimination against the practice of Protestantism was wrongful.

13 Many moral maximalists would probably object to this formulation, and it would make classical liberals at least uncomfortable. They would feel that there are virtually *no* circumstances that could save an involuntary transfer from being unjust. It would always be theft if the transferor did not notice it, and robbery or blackmail, backed by the threat of violence, if he did. I do not wish, at this juncture, to debate the issue. The argument in the text does not hinge on the set of transfers that are *both* involuntary *and* just, not being empty. It hinges on the set of unjust ones not being empty. In fact, we know that it is full enough for most involuntary transferors' tastes and sense of justice.

REFERENCES

Avineri, S. and de-Shalit, A. (eds) (1992) *Communitarianism and Individualism*, Oxford: Oxford University Press.

Brownlie, I. (1988), "The Rights of Peoples in Modern International Law," in Crawford, 1988.

Crawford, J. (ed) (1988) *The Rights of Peoples*, Oxford: The Clarendon Press.

Dworkin, R. (1989) "Liberal Community," in Avineri and de-Shalit, 1992.

Epstein, R. A. (1985) *Takings: Private Property and the Power of Eminent Domain*, Cambridge, Mass.: Harvard University Press.

Feinberg, J. (1980), *Rights, Justice and the Bounds of Liberty*, Princeton, NJ: Princeton University Press.

Gutmann, A. (1992) "Introduction" to Taylor, 1992.

Hohfeld, W. N. (1919) *Fundamental Legal Conceptions*, New Haven, CT: Yale University Press.

Kymlicka, W. (1989) *Liberalism, Community and Culture*, Oxford: The Clarendon Press.

Makinson, D. (1988) "Rights of Peoples: Point of View of a Logician," in Crawford, 1988.

Nussbaum, M. and Sen, A. (eds) (1993) *The Quality of Life*, Oxford: The Clarendon Press.

O'Neill, O. (1993) "Justice, Gender, and International Boundaries," in Nussbaum and Sen 1993.

Sandel, M. (1982) *Liberalism and the Limits of Justice*, New York.

—— (1984) "The Procedural Republic and the Unencumbered Self," in Avineri and de-Shalit, 1992.

—— (1984a), "Morality and the Liberal Ideal," *The New Republic*, May, 1984.

Taylor, C. (1979) "Atomism," in Avineri and de-Shalit, 1992.

—— (1992) *Multiculturalism and "The Politics of Recognition,"* Princeton, NJ: Princeton University Press.

Index